A New Star Rating System & Other New Features from Frommer's!

In our continuing effort to publish the savviest, most up-to-date, and most appealing travel guides available, we've added some great new features.

Frommer's guides now include a new **star-rating system**. Every hotel, restaurant, and attraction is rated from 0 to 3 stars to help you set priorities and organize your time.

We've also added **seven brand-new features** that point you to the great deals, in-the-know advice, and unique experiences that separate travelers from tourists. Throughout the guide look for:

Finds   Special finds—those places only insiders know about

Fun Fact   Fun facts—details that make travelers more informed and their trips more fun

Kids   Best bets for kids—advice for the whole family

Moments   Special moments—those experiences that memories are made of

Overrated Places or experiences not worth your time or money

Tips   Insider tips—some great ways to save time and money

Value   Great values—where to get the best deals

Here's what the critics say about Frommer's:

"Amazingly easy to use. Very portable, very complete."

—*Booklist*

"The only mainstream guide to list specific prices. The Walter Cronkite of guidebooks—with all that implies."

—*Travel & Leisure*

"Complete, concise, and filled with useful information."

—*New York Daily News*

"Hotel information is close to encyclopedic."

—*Des Moines Sunday Register*

"Detailed, accurate, and easy-to-read information for all price ranges."

—*Glamour Magazine*

PORTABLE

Algonquin Provincial Park

2nd Edition

by Michelle N. Jones
&
Jeff Warren

WILEY

John Wiley & Sons Canada, Ltd.

Published by:

JOHN WILEY & SONS CANADA, LTD.

22 Worcester Road
Etobicoke, ON M9W 1L1

FROMMER'S is a registered trademark of Arthur Frommer.
Used under license.

National Library of Canada Cataloguing in Publication
Jones, Michelle, 1977–

   Frommer's Algonquin Provincial Park / Michelle Jones.—2nd ed.

First ed. written by Jeff Warren.
Includes index.
ISBN 0-470-83364-5

1. Algonquin Provincial Park (Ont.)—Guidebooks. 2. Natural History—
Ontario—Algonquin Provincial Park—Guidebooks. 3. Outdoor life—
Ontario—Algonquin Provincial Park—Guidebooks. I. Title. II. Title:
Algonquin Provincial Park.

FC3065.A65J64 2004   917.13'147   C2003-906730-0

General Manager: Robert Harris
Editor: Michelle Marchetti
Publishing Services Director: Karen Bryan
Cartographer: Mapping Specialists, Ltd.
Illustrations: Frommer's US and Bart Vallecoccia Illustration
Text layout: IBEX Graphic Communications Inc.
Cover design: Kyle Gell
Front cover photo: Chris Boettger

SPECIAL SALES

Fer reseller information, including discounts and premium sales, please call
our sales department: Tel.: 416-646-4584. For press review copies, author
interviews, or other publicity information, please contact our marketing
department: Tel.: 416-646-4584; Fax.: 416-646-4448.

2 3 4 5 6 7 8 9 10

Manufactured in Canada

Contents

4 Outdoor Pursuits in Algonquin Park — 65

5 Camping in the Interior — 93

6 Lodging & Dining Inside the Park — 112

List of Maps

Welcome to Algonquin Provincial Park

From the air, Algonquin Provincial Park appears to be a scribble of shoreline—rounded blue shapes pressed into the raised forest green. More than 2,000 lakes twist and undulate here, following contours set in billion-year-old stone. From the ground, the molded rock appears as a narrow border between dense evergreens and clear waters. In certain places, there is only this stone against the sky, and the sound of gently lapping waves. More than half a million visitors a year are drawn to the spare beauty of Algonquin Park, their numbers diluted by 7,725 square kilometers (3,013 square miles) of land—an area larger than the entire province of Prince Edward Island. They are drawn, too, by the promise of wildlife. The park lies in a transition zone between northern boreal forest and southern deciduous forest, a condition that has resulted in teeming ecological diversity. More than 1,000 plant and 200 animal species live in the park, and many of them—the moose, the beaver, the loon—are conspicuous as they go about their seasonal routines.

Algonquin Park occupies an irregular wedge of land in south-central Ontario between Georgian Bay to the west and the Ottawa River to the east, just a few hours from both Toronto and Ottawa. The west side of the park is on a dome of Canadian Shield rock; it is a high maple, birch, and beech forest with temperatures approximating those of a more northerly wilderness. The sandy soil composition on the drier east side of the park supports a mostly conifer forest—big pines, spruce, and aspen. Through it all is water, pooled in the old valleys, rushing in countless streams and rivers. The headwaters of seven major rivers—the Oxtongue, South, Magnetawan, Petawawa, Amable du Fond, Bonnechere, and Madawaska—all begin in Algonquin Park. An abundance of water is one of the things that makes the park unique, for it opens the interior to exploration by canoe. There are more than 2,100 kilometers (1,302 miles) of canoe routes in the park; a huge network of lakes, rivers, streams, and bogs connected by overland portages and dotted with shoreline campsites. Hikers are also well served, with more than 140 kilometers (87 miles) of marked backcountry trails. There are no public roads crossing the interior, only scattered access points far out on the periphery. Deep in the interior is where many lasting memories are formed—alone at the edge of a long lake, the heart of nature beating softly in the underbrush.

Paired with this vast interior is another side of the park: the Parkway Corridor. This span of Highway 60 through Algonquin Park is open to visitors who arrive with or without canoes and hiking shoes. Lodges, car campgrounds, galleries, museums, interpretive hiking trails, and other tourist facilities add comforting amenities and educational tools to the wilderness experience. Many of the park's historical sites are located along this corridor. Ontario's oldest provincial park has seen many waves of human history, from its original native inhabitants to the loggers to the old-school park rangers. Though it feels immutably wild, humans have changed the park landscape over the generations. Peeling back these layers is one of the most intriguing things about visiting Algonquin Park. And visitors should remember: these changes continue even today.

1 Algonquin Park Today

Algonquin Park has seen more than a century of change. Initially created to serve the interests of the logging industry back in the 1800s, over the years the focus has morphed toward park and forestry management and finally settled on a thriving tourism industry featuring a massive outdoor education centre. In today's Algonquin Park—which marked its 110th birthday in 2003—you'll see the sheer beauty of the results of decades of immaculate forestry management, unspoiled even by the numerous busloads of tourists from all corners of the world who come to experience the great Canadian wilderness up close and in person. In Algonquin Park you'll encounter an individuality not seen in any other park in the world. Its uniqueness lies in the history of the geographical area, the many stories it has sparked, and the fact that the same flora and fauna that existed a hundred years ago continue to thrive in their natural habitat.

When Alexander Kirkwood suggested in 1885 that the area that was to become Algonquin Park be protected "for the preservation and maintenance of the natural forest," he had in mind protection from settlers and the inroads of infrastructure, but not protection from loggers. Logging-industry support helped guarantee the park's creation, and in return the area was set aside for recreation and timber harvesting instead of settlement. Establishing a park further ensured the protection of the big log-driving rivers (whose headwaters lie within park boundaries), with the added bonus that the government would now fight potentially stock-depleting forest fires. It was a good deal.

The park is divided into zones—three parts protected historical, nature, and wilderness (19%), one part development (3%), and one part—the vast remainder—"recreation/utilization" (78%). Most visitors never see the logging that still goes on within the park, since there is a 30- to 40-meter (98- to 131-ft.) screen of uncut forest around all lakes and portage routes, and during the summer loggers wield their muffled saws far enough from the canoe routes that they cannot be heard. What's more, only 5% of the trees logged in the park are clear-cut. By far the majority of Algonquin Park's stock of trees are harvested using more sophisticated selection techniques that try to safeguard wildlife habitats and stagger the farming of a particular section of forest over 15 to 20 years.

In place is a 20-year management plan that reviews forestry procedures within the park every five years. Renewing in 2005 and running through to 2025, the plan will outline the long-term strategic direction and the details of harvest, renewal, tending operations, and access-road locations for the first five-year term to 2010. The management group works alongside many other groups in regard to the park, including representatives of the Algonquin First Nations, local citizens, biologists, and park officials. Through the government-run management process many voices are heard and valued, and the park's future can truly be said to be in the hands of the Ontario population—who pay the taxes that ultimately run the park itself.

2 The Best of Algonquin Park

There are many Algonquin Parks—the park of the interior, the peripheral park, the Parkway Corridor, and the many campgrounds, museums, historical sites, hiking trails, and interior lakes. This range of options can make planning a trip to the park a bit intimidating. The following rundown of the very best of the park will give you a logistical jump start and help guarantee that you make the most of your trip.

Remember that nowhere in Algonquin Park will you see caged wildlife, nor will you find preservation centers full of stuffed animals (of the taxidermic variety, that is). There are, however, some establishments outside of the park that house some extremely bizarre and illegitimately-obtained stuffed taxidermy. Best to drive right by— the park is where you'll experience Canadian wilderness in the raw, and there, it's completely up to you to experience it, however you choose. Of course, the park and its gateway towns are rife with numerous guides claiming they can show it all to you! Quite frankly, no matter what level of camping/hiking/canoeing expertise you possess, the park is almost certainly better explored on your own.

BEST PICNIC SPOTS

- **Tea Lake Dam Picnic Ground:** Located 8 kilometers (5 miles) from the West Gate on the Oxtongue River, this quiet, sheltered picnic area has sturdy stone barbecue pits and pretty views of the river below. Post-lunch swimming is also an option. See chapter 4.

- **Ragged Falls Park:** Not actually located in the park but 8 kilometers (5 miles) west, Ragged Falls doesn't have any picnic benches. But it does have a big tumbling waterfall, and there are many flat stones and boulders below the falls to lay out a lunch spread if you want to take in the dramatic scenery. Just don't get too close when the water is up. See chapter 4.

BEST KIDS' CAMPS

- **Camp Northway-Wendigo for Girls and Camp Pathfinder for Boys:** Camp Northway-Wendigo was founded in 1906 to teach girls how to live simply in the outdoors without the modern amenities of everyday life. The camp runs on a strict no-electricity rule and all meals are cooked by wood fire. On the opposite side of Cache Lake, Camp Pathfinder is a small canoeing outpost for boys that was founded in 1965. It offers masterful canoe handling and wilderness training at a practical level. Both camps have limited enrollment, and waiting lists generally fill up a year in advance. See chapter 4.

BEST PLACES TO SWIM

- **Lake of Two Rivers Picnic Ground:** Although located right off the highway at K 34, this picnic ground has one of the largest beaches in the park and gets plenty of sun during the day.

The water-level views across Lake of Two Rivers are worth submerging for. See chapter 4.

- **Peck Lake:** Peck Lake is the centerpiece of the Peck Lake Trail, an easy 2-kilometer (1.2-mile) circular ramble. The waters of Peck Lake are cool and clear, and there are many sloping stone shoulders on which to plant yourself in the sun. You get a park-interior swimming experience without actually having to venture very far into the interior itself. See chapter 4.

BEST DAY CANOE ROUTES

- **Barron River:** This may be the park's most famous paddle, a 3-hour journey under the 100-meter (328-ft.) stone walls of the Barron Canyon. The only difficulty with this route is its distance from the Parkway Corridor—about a 3-hour drive. But if you're visiting Achray and the east side of the park, then the Barron Canyon is a must. See chapter 4.
- **Costello Creek:** Located off gigantic Lake Opeongo, this meditative paddle is at the south end of the lake and is easily accessed from the Corridor. Great for animal spotting—expect to see great blue heron and sundry bog life against a distant cliff backdrop. See chapter 4.
- **Hailstorm Creek:** Located off the far-north arm of Lake Opeongo, Hailstorm Creek winds its languorous way through a big bog and nature reserve. It is an excellent place to spot wildlife and an easy paddle, though you will have to take an Opeongo Store water-taxi there if you plan on doing it in a single day. See chapter 4.

BEST INTERIOR LAKES WORTH THE DETOUR

There are more than 2,000 lakes in Algonquin, and all of them have something to recommend them. I have been to only a fraction of the park's lakes, but of those I have visited these two are my favorites.

- **Manitou Lake:** Manitou Lake is huge, rugged, and, because it is located in the little-visited northwest corner of the park, relatively uncrowded even in the height of summer. The campsites on Manitou are excellent, especially the ones on the east-side beaches. See chapter 5.
- **Grand Lake:** Well, it is grand—and long and narrow, with wind-swept shores. Paddling to the far-north end of the lake and back from Achray takes a full day, but it is a day well spent.

Tom Thomson caught some of the dramatic scenery in his famous *Jack Pine* (the tree stood by the mouth of Carcajou Bay until 1977). The cattail marsh at the top of the lake teems with wildlife—moose, herons, and the elusive Virginia rail with its weird trills and songs. See chapter 5.

BEST DAY HIKES

- **Barron Canyon Trail:** The Barron Canyon comes up a lot in this book because it's kind of hard to forget. This short trail (1.5 kilometers [1 mile]) skirts the steepest section and is the definitive way to view the 100-meter (330-ft.) canyon walls from above. See chapter 4.
- **Centennial Ridges:** Most of this hike is along high rocky ridges—really it's a 10-kilometer (6.2-mile) walk across the ceiling of Algonquin Park. The views of lakes and sweeping deciduous forest are stunning, especially when the fall colors are up. See chapter 4.
- **Spruce Bog Boardwalk:** More than any other trail in the park, this is a tour through a truly exotic and *Lord of the Rings*-esque landscape. It's a 1.5-kilometer (1-mile) jaunt through a weird and wonderful bog, complete with a boardwalk tunneling through the shadowy spruce. Children and adults of all ages are mesmerized by the spindly spruce trees, with their moss-laden branches and resemblance to Tolkien characters. See chapter 4.

BEST OVERNIGHT HIKE

- **Eastern Pines Backpacking Trail:** This easy 15-kilometer (9.3-mile) trail takes no more than 2 days to walk. It's an invigorating hike; the air is fragrant with the smell of pine forest, and there are many lakeside views. Highlights include osprey nests, a heronry, big glacial boulders, good campsites on Stratton Lake, and the fine rock pools of High Falls. See chapter 5.

BEST WILDLIFE-SPOTTING TRAIL

- **Mizzy Lake Trail:** If you start on this 11-kilometer (6.8-mile) trail early in the day, you are almost guaranteed a close encounter of the wildlife kind. It was designed specifically with animal viewing in mind and intersects a very large number of habitats: moose, beaver, deer, otters, turtles, herons, hawks, and sparrows. The lingering evidence of bears and wolves spices things up. See chapter 4.

BEST SUMMER PARK ACTIVITIES

- **Conducted Walks:** Every day during the peak summer months, park naturalists lead visitors on rambling hikes through the forest. Each of the walks covers a different subject, from mushrooms to insects to park history. The walks are an excellent way of learning about park ecology, with the added benefit of a bit of exercise. See chapter 4.

- **Public Wolf Howl:** If you're in Algonquin Park in August then you should try to attend the popular Public Wolf Howls. On select evenings, a large group of park visitors listens to a talk about wolves and then follows park naturalists to a spot along the Parkway Corridor. There, the naturalists expertly begin to howl—and, in most cases, their calls are returned by the park's wildest canine occupants. Spine-tingling. See chapter 4.

- **Opeongo Expedition Research Adventure Program:** The Harkness Laboratory of Fisheries Research offers a fantastic tour of Opeongo Lake that is notable for its unique integration of pure outdoor entertainment with a good measure of fish education. Enjoy being whisked by Zodiak to the middle of the lake, where you'll be given the opportunity to actually assist in the lab's aquatic research and preservation work. See chapter 4.

BEST PARK ACTIVITY FOR KIDS

- **East Beach Outdoor Theatre:** Kids love the naturalist-led evenings at the East Beach Outdoor Theatre. The free hour-and-a-half program starts just after sundown, and usually explores some member of Algonquin Park's animal family—wolves, bears, otters, and so on. The evenings consist of a short film, a slide show, and a discussion with the audience. See chapter 4.

BEST WINTER PARK ACTIVITIES

- **Cross-Country Skiing:** Algonquin Park is a very different world in the winter: black trees, white snow, silence. Skiing on one of the many maintained park trails is exhilarating. Leaf Lake Ski Trail on the park's east side has the most extensive network, with some excellent views over the spindly forest. See chapter 4.

- **Dog Sledding:** Several local operators offer guided dog-sledding trips through the park interior. A team of huskies pulls you on your own sled across frozen lakes and through drifts of powdery snow. Adventurers stay in heated tents and eat big, hearty meals. For many repeat clients dog sledding is the experience of a lifetime. See chapter 4.

BEST ACTIVITY OUTSIDE THE PARK

- **Echo Valley Observatory** (outside Huntsville; contact through **Grandview Resort** ⓒ **705/789-4417**): Take advantage of the unpolluted Muskoka sky by seeing it up close—*way* up close. The telescope at the Echo Valley Observatory amplifies celestial objects by 10,000 times. Sky-gazers meet in the evenings at Grandview Resort and are driven to the observatory in a snaking caravan. See chapter 7.

BEST VIEWS

- **Lookout Trail:** The view from this long, rocky ledge is one of the best in the park, encompassing 100 square kilometers (39 square miles) or more of Algonquin heartland. It takes on a whole other dimension in the autumn, since the bulk of the trees below are deciduous and are transformed when the chlorophyll drains from the leaves. See chapter 4.
- **Track and Tower Trail:** The amazing view over Cache Lake is one of the highlights of this moderately demanding 7.7-kilometer (4.8-mile) hike. Hikers cluster on a high, bald rock and look down over an expanse of green and blue. Scattered historical remains give the walk some context. See chapter 4.
- **The Visitor Centre:** Probably the best bird's-eye view of a bog and surrounding area in the whole of the park. The Visitor Centre is perched on a high ridge south of the Parkway Corridor. Tourists gather on the large balcony out back and watch for distant wilderness activity. See chapter 3.

BEST HISTORIC SPOT

- **The Logging Museum:** This is a fascinating walk through Algonquin Park's logging history. A dozen or so relics from that bygone era are arranged along an easy 1.3-kilometer (0.8-mile) trail. Highlights include an old steam-powered "alligator" and a full reproduction of a log dam and chute. A small theater in the reception building plays archival film footage of the manic sawing and loading. See chapter 3.

BEST PARKWAY CORRIDOR CAMPGROUNDS

- **Canisbay Lake Campground:** This is one of the park's quieter campgrounds. It occupies the south end of Canisbay Lake and extends to 16 paddle-in campsites around the lake perimeter. This gives die-hard privacy seekers an effortless flavor of interior camping. See chapter 6.
- **Lake of Two Rivers Campground:** Sprawling and social, this is the campground to target if you want to meet your neighbors. It is an excellent ground for RVs, with ample electrical hookups and big campsites. As with many of the other campgrounds, the majority of the sites are in open pine forest with distant views of Lake of Two Rivers. See chapter 6.
- **Rock Lake Campground:** A pleasing campground at the end of Rock Lake Road, far from the highway but close to many outdoor amenities. These include the Booth Rock Hiking Trail, the Old Railway Bike Trail, and an excellent swimming beach on Rock Lake itself. Most of the campsites are in a breezy pine forest. See chapter 6.

BEST LODGING INSIDE THE PARK

- **Arowhon Pines** (Algonquin Park; ℂ 705/633-5661): This high-end resort is in a class by itself. It features an amazing six-sided dining room with a wraparound porch looking out onto Little Joe Lake. The grounds are heavily wooded and so far from the highway that moose and other wildlife make regular appearances next to the comfortable shared cabins. See chapter 6.

BEST LODGING OUTSIDE THE PARK

- **Dwight Village Motel** (Dwight; ℂ 705/635-2400): A friendly, good-value place to stay for the night if you're heading in or out of the park. The rooms are clean and tidy—nicer than almost everything else along the Highway 60 strip, and priced competitively. See chapter 7.
- **Woodland Springs** (Huntsville; ℂ 877/427-1112): Another excellent-value bed and breakfast, Woodland Springs was a family cottage before it became a lodging. This cottage vibe remains; guests feel instantly cozy anywhere they go, from their cute rooms to the deep couches in front of the fireplace to the gently swaying hammock outside. The gourmet breakfasts alone are worth the price of a night's accommodation. See chapter 7.

BEST RESORT

- **Deerhurst Resort** (Huntsville; ✆ 800/461-4393): This sprawling, 800-acre resort located on Peninsula Lake offers it all to a clientele that comes from all over the world. Voted best resort in Canada and the recent recipient of a $30-million facelift, Deerhurst truly is spectacular. Boasting a PGA–rated golf course and world-renowned executive chef Rory Golden, the resort is equipped with the most amenities anywhere in Muskoka (kayaking, hiking, cross-country skiing, and mountain biking, to name but a few). Perhaps best of all, Deerhurst is able to cater to a wide range of guests by virtue of its numerous room styles and accessible pricing—there's not much more you could ask for in a true Muskoka experience. See chapter 7.

BEST DINING IN THE PARK

- **Arowhon Pines** (Algonquin Park; ✆ 705/633-5661): The grandeur of the great outdoors is reproduced in the whole Arowhon dining experience. Dramatic dining room, high ceilings, dark lake, and excellent food. Expensive but worth it. See chapter 6.
- **Bartlett Lodge** (Algonquin Park; ✆ 705/633-5543): Bartlett is where you'll find the best dining in the park. Part of the charm is logistics: a boat takes you across the bay to the host lodge. The other part is simply the good food: delicious grilled salmon, duck confit—a rotating selection of gourmet specialties always cooked to perfection. See chapter 6.

BEST DINING OUTSIDE THE PARK

- **3 Guys and a Stove** (Huntsville; ✆ 705/789-1815): Some of the most sophisticated cuisine in the area happens here at 3 Guys—lots of grilled meat and fish with a healthy-lifestyle spin. Housed in a big, barn-like structure by the side of the highway and fronting Fairy Lake, the restaurant is always very busy and the staff correspondingly harried. See chapter 7.
- **Riverbend Restaurant** (Huntsville; ✆ 705/788-9484): Expect variety, generous portions, and creative ingredients at Riverbend. The talented kitchen staff try to use all-domestic produce and seafood—meat, fish, and pasta Canadian-style, and the entertaining wait staff top off what invariably proves to be a satisfying experience. See chapter 7.

BEST EVENING ENTERTAINMENT FOR ADULTS

- **C.W.'s** (outside Huntsville; © **705/789-6411**): The most popular Friday and Saturday night drinking hole is located right on the water on the grounds of the Deerhurst resort. It's one of the few places to dance in the area, a big club full of cavorting locals. Open 9pm to 2am. See chapter 7.

Planning Your Trip

Every July and August, more than 300,000 people flock to Algonquin Provincial Park, and many more visit the surrounding area's premium cottage lands. Though the park is massive and it's possible to disappear from civilization, it is not possible to just show up at any campsite or lodging with the expectation that there will be vacancies. Reservations must be made at campgrounds and wherever you intend to find accommodation—otherwise, you could find yourself sleeping in a gas-station parking lot, dodging camper vans and surviving on a grueling diet of beef jerky, Sun Chips, and Coke.

Algonquin Park's size and variety of things to do means there are many ways of experiencing the park, so planning ahead is essential. Camping in one of the campgrounds along the Parkway Corridor is very different from going to one of the peripheral campgrounds at Achray or Brent. Days can be spent on interpretive park hikes with a ranger, or canoeing far from any roads deep in the park's interior. Sleeping accommodations range from historical ranger cabins to swanky lodges to roomy six-sided yurts to your own drafty little tent. In short, the park can satisfy everyone from the hardened adventurer through to the family camper and the luxury-loving porch-lounger. You just need to know what you want, and a little advance planning will help you figure that out.

1 Getting Started: Information & Useful Publications

To obtain basic preliminary information about **Algonquin Provincial Park,** contact the park directly at Superintendent, Algonquin Provincial Park, P.O. Box 219, Whitney, ON K0J 2M0 (© **705/ 633-5572**). They'll send you an information brochure (available in English, French, Spanish, German, Chinese, and Japanese), a current list of park fees, and information on specific park activities as requested. The park information line is open daily from 8am to 4:30pm, and is actually staffed by human beings and not a series of

recorded messages (though the constant busy signal during peak times can be just as frustrating). Alternatively, you can call the **Visitor Centre** at © **613/637-2828.** The staff there don't have access to the full range of information that's available through the park information line, but they are still helpful and it's usually possible to reach a staff member on the first attempt. The excellent official park website, www.algonquinpark.on.ca, contains information on everything from park flora and fauna to updates on special events, and is definitely worth checking out if you're planning a visit to the park. Further information about other provincial parks around Algonquin can be found at www.ontarioparks.com. **Ontario Parks** (© **888/ 668-7275**) can also answer any question you may have directly.

The Friends of Algonquin Park, P.O. Box 248, Whitney, ON K0J 2M0 (© **613/637-2828;** fax 613/637-2138) is a registered charity that supports the park. Members get a 15% discount at the two park bookstores and receive 12 free issues of the park newsletter *The Raven.* Membership costs C\$12 (US\$8.90) for individuals and C\$17 (US\$12.60) for the whole family, and is good for one year from the time you join.

For information on lodging and attractions **west of the park** in Muskoka, contact the **Huntsville and Lake of Bays Chamber of Commerce,** 8 West Street North, Unit 1, Huntsville, ON P1H 2B6 (© **705/789-4771;** fax 705/789-6191) for a free information package, or consult their website at www.huntsvillelakeofbays.on.ca. A popular tourist destination, the Muskoka area is also covered by several websites, the best of which is www.traveltomuskoka.com. The **Bancroft and District Chamber of Commerce,** P.O. Box 539, Bancroft, ON K0L 1C0 (© **613/332-1513;** fax 613/332-2119; www.commerce.bancroft.on.ca), provides the same service **east of the park,** while the rolling hills and pristine lakes south of Algonquin are covered by the **Haliburton Highlands Chamber of Commerce,** P.O. Box 147, Minden, ON K0M 2K0 (© **800/461-7677** or 705/286-1760; fax 705/286-6016; www.county.haliburton.on.ca).

The area around Algonquin Park is extremely popular for summer holiday makers, and many of the area's lodges and inns offer last-minute deals to attract the tourist dollar. A selection of these seasonal specials, as well as a large directory of Ontario cottages, inns, lodges, and resorts, can be found at www.cottage-resort.com.

The three lodges in Algonquin Park are especially busy during the summer months and should be booked in advance (see chapter 6,

"Lodging & Dining Inside the Park" for more information). If you're planning to rent a canoe and/or camping supplies, then it's also advisable to book ahead. It's not unknown for the busiest outfitters (**Portage Store** on Canoe Lake, **Algonquin Outfitters** on Lake Opeongo and in Huntsville) to run out of canoes, and the guided trips certainly fill up (contact information for all outfitters supplying Algonquin Park can be found in chapter 3, "Exploring Algonquin Park"; for information on guided trips see "Guided Canoe Trips & Hikes" later in this chapter).

Tips Kilometer Markings

Reflective signs along the Parkway Corridor (the stretch of Highway 60 that runs between the West and East Gates) indicate the distance in kilometers from the West Gate. Points of interest in this book that lie along the Parkway Corridor have these kilometer markings as reference. For example, the Visitor Centre is located at K 43.

USEFUL PUBLICATIONS/BOOKS   The Friends of Algonquin Park operate two bookstores in the park (one at the Visitor Centre at K 43, and one at the Algonquin Logging Museum at K 54.5) and put out numerous useful publications about the park, some of which are essential reading. If you are planning a canoe trip in the interior, then you must first get a copy of *Canoe Routes of Algonquin Park* (C$4.95 [US$3.70]). This brochure map shows the entire network of canoe routes in the park, including all portages and campsites. It contains detailed directions for how to get to access points 1 to 29, with information about camping in the interior and park regulations. It is needed before and during any trip, for planning and for orientation. The *Backpacking Trails Map* (C$1.95 [US$1.45]) is the equivalent map for hiking in the interior.

The Friends also put out complete guides to the park's mammals, trees, wildflowers, birds, insects, mushrooms, reptiles, fish, and butterflies, as well as an excellent pictorial history. Each of these is available for between C$1.00 (US$0.74) and C$4.50 (US$3.34), excellent value for the sheer volume of information contained within. They also publish a *Canoeist's Manual* (which will be the best dollar you'll ever spend, especially once you get a look at all the clueless first-timers floundering around Cache Lake in their tippy Kevlars), whitewater guides to the Petawawa and Madawaska rivers, and mini-guides to all 16 of Algonquin Park's interpretive trails (these are themed hiking trails that have information signposts arranged along the full length).

A full list of publications and a printable order form can be found at the park's official website (www.algonquinpark.on.ca). Orders can be taken by mail, phone, fax, or e-mail (P.O. Box 248, Whitney, ON K0J 2M0; © 613/637-2828; fax 613/637-2138; e-mail orders@algonquinpark.on.ca).

If you are interested in camping and canoeing, Bill Mason has written two classic books on these subjects: *Song of the Paddle* and *Path of the Paddle* (Toronto: Key Porter). They are full of canoeing and camping tips from the spiritual master of both arts. For evocative descriptions of Algonquin's changing seasons as well as a personal account of some interior canoeing routes, pick up Joanne Kates's *Exploring Algonquin Park* (Vancouver: Greystone Books). Michael Runtz's *The Explorer's Guide to Algonquin Park* (Toronto: Boston Mills Press) is great for detailed instructions on how to see park wildlife, with elaborate lists of likely locations along the Corridor and at various access points around the park.

2 Reserving a Campsite

Although all you need to enter Algonquin Park is an easily obtained vehicle day permit (for more on vehicle permits see chapter 3, "Exploring Algonquin Park"), if you want to stay at one of the park's many campsites then it's a good idea to book a few weeks ahead. Campsites fill up during the busy summer months, especially over long weekends in July and August.

There are two kinds of campsites at Algonquin Park: **interior sites** that can be accessed only by canoe or by foot, and **car campgrounds** along the Parkway Corridor and around the periphery of the park. Either of these types of sites can be booked up to five months in advance by calling **Ontario Parks** toll-free between 7am and 11pm (© **888/668-7275;** for outside Canada and the U.S., call © **519/826-5290**), or by reserving through the website at www. ontarioparks.com. Reservations can be made using Visa, Master-Card, check, or money order, and include a C$9 (US$6.70) nonrefundable charge. Cancellations or changes must be made at least 24 hours in advance (the fee for this is C$6 [US$4.45]), otherwise you will be charged C$20.75 (US$15.40) for an interior permit, or a night's camping fee for a car campground reservation. A written confirmation of the reservation is sent upon receipt of payment. Discounts are offered for senior citizens (20%) or disabled persons (50%) upon showing proof of eligibility.

CAR CAMPGROUND RESERVATIONS   While 80% of the car campground sites can be pre-booked, it may be possible to find a site on a first-come, first-served basis, especially at the quieter Tea Lake and Coon Lake sites. But the other campgrounds fill up fast. Many of the car campgrounds have electrical hookups and can facilitate trailers and RVs.

The following information is required to book a car campground site:

- name of your preferred campground (information about the park's 12 campgrounds can be found in chapter 6, "Lodging & Dining Inside the Park")
- arrival and departure date
- type of site required (tent or trailer, electrical)
- contact details
- number of people in party
- vehicle license number
- method of payment.

For information about the different camping fees at car campgrounds, see chapter 3, "Exploring Algonquin Park," p. 39.

INTERIOR SITE RESERVATIONS   Interior sites must be booked at least three days in advance, and if you're planning to visit the park over one of the busy summer or fall long weekends it's best to call a good month before your intended arrival date. With more than 2,000 campsites available to choose from in the interior, there are almost always sites available, but the busiest lakes near the busiest access points (Burnt Island, Tom Thomson, Happy Isle, Proulx, Big Crow) definitely fill up. When you call you don't reserve an actual site, you just reserve a spot on a particular lake. It's up to you to get to the lake as early as possible to have your pick of the choice campsites (for more information on choosing a good interior campsite, see chapter 5, "Camping in the Interior").

Before you call **Ontario Parks** (© **888/668-7275**) to make your reservation you must first know your exact route, and that means you need a copy of *Canoe Routes of Algonquin Park* or *Backpacking*

Trails of Algonquin Park in front of you (see "Useful Publications/
Books" above). The people who work at the reservation service are
not trip counselors; if you have any questions about your prospective route, then call the Algonquin Park Information Office
(© **705/633-5572**) before making your reservation. They will be
happy to review individual trips and make helpful suggestions.

With the map in front of you, be prepared to provide:

* trip start and departure dates
* entry and exit access points
* daily travel routes (and any alternative routes in case your original route is filled to capacity)
* contact details
* number of people per party (maximum of 9)
* vehicle license number
* method of payment.

Interior sites cost C$8 (US$5.90) per person, per night. For more
fee information see chapter 3, "Exploring Algonquin Park."

3 When to Go

Algonquin Provincial Park is open year-round, and each season
brings its own rewards. May is an excellent time to visit—the black-
flies and mosquitoes have not yet arrived, and the forest floor is
covered with a tapestry of vibrant wildflowers. Summer is high
season—the vegetation is deep and green, and the lakes are warm
enough to swim in. Fall is the favorite time of year for many. The
crowds (and bugs) are gone, and the deciduous forests blaze with
reds, yellows, and oranges. The days are cool and pleasant, full of the
soothing smell of autumn leaves.

Algonquin is open all winter for cross-county skiing and other
cold-weather activities, accessible from the plowed Highway 60
Corridor that cuts through the southwestern end of the park. This
is also a wonderful time to visit the park—the woods are eerily
silent, the white expanse of snow peppered with wolf and deer
tracks. Visitors still pay a daily vehicle permit, checking in at the
East and West Gates during their winter business hours (West Gate:
9am to 4pm; East Gate: 8am to 4:30pm). The Visitor Centre is
open on weekends from 10am to 5pm, and daily during the Christmas and March breaks. Winter camping is permitted at the Mew
Lake Campground, which also has roofed accommodation in the

form of sturdy, six-sided yurts. Winter yurts can be booked only through the Ontario Parks toll-free number (© **888/668-7275**). It's also possible to camp in and explore the interior—by ski, snowshoe, or dog sled, depending on your level of adventurousness (for information on staying in one of the winter yurts, see chapter 6, "Lodging & Dining Inside the Park"; for information on winter activities and winter camping in the interior, see section 10, "Winter Activities," in chapter 4, "Outdoor Pursuits in Algonquin Park"). For food, gas, and accommodation other than camping, visitors have to go to Dwight or Whitney (6km [3.7 miles] and 5km [3.1 miles] outside the park, respectively). The park puts out a handy *Algonquin in Winter* brochure, which details all winter park fees and includes maps of the cross-country ski trails. To have one sent to you, call the park information line or e-mail in a request (© **705/633-5572;** e-mail: info@algonquinpark.on.ca).

AVOIDING THE CROWDS   Algonquin is most popular from mid-July to mid-August. With school out for summer, families from all over Ontario and Canada take to the park *en masse*, and the European and Japanese tourists descend on the Portage Store. From the park's seven children's summer camps, parties of young canoeists circulate out onto the lakes and streams for overnight trips (for information on children's camps within the Park see "Summer Camp" in chapter 4). It is a busy time for the park, but away from the Highway 60 Corridor the vast forest swallows up its visitors so it's still possible to feel alone in the wilds.

Campgrounds are almost always filled during the four Ontario long weekends (Victoria Day in late May, Canada Day on July 1, the August 1 Civic Holiday, and Labor Day, the first weekend in September), so if you are planning on visiting during these times make sure to book a reservation well in advance. The further you get from the Parkway Corridor the better chance you have of securing a spot. Achray, Kiosk, Brent, and Kingscote all have nice car campgrounds that are slower to fill up.

The most popular interior campsites are on lakes closest to the park's two interior outfitters: the Portage Store on Canoe Lake and Algonquin Outfitters on Lake Opeongo. Other busy access points are at Smoke Lake, Rock Lake, and Galeairy Lake, which extends beyond the park boundaries to Whitney. If you plan to start your trip from one of these lakes then try to leave before Friday—this will improve your chance of finding good sites for the night and you will be deeper into the interior by the time the weekend trippers arrive. Again, far fewer people venture to access points on the east, west, and north sides of the park, so if it's solitude you're after then it's worth traveling the extra distance.

Early mornings at Algonquin are the best time to see wildlife. There is rarely anyone about, the trails are quiet, and out on the water everything is still and shrouded in mist.

CLIMATE & WEATHER   Algonquin Park is located on the highest land in southern Ontario, on a dome of Canadian Shield rock that rises to an elevation of 280 meters (918 ft.) in the east and more than 500 meters (1,640 ft.) in the west. This means that the park's climate is closer to that of northern Ontario than southern Ontario. Summer days are warm, averaging between 18 and 25°C (65–77°F), but the nights are noticeably cooler. Fall temperatures average a fresh but comfortable 10°C (50°F), a perfect hiking temperature. In the winter it gets cold—down to –40°C (–40°F) some nights, though a daily average is closer to –10°C (14°F). Having said that, the winter cold is dry, and when the sun is shining it can be quite pleasant out on the ski trails.

In an average summer month it will rain 10 out of 30 days, but these kinds of showers tend to blow up quickly and then disappear without too much surrounding drizzle. Rains come in off Georgian Bay from the west, so the higher west side of the park receives more rain and acts as a rain shadow for the drier and lower east side. In total, between 75 and 90 millimeters (3 and 3.5 in.) of rain falls in the park per summer month, with slightly more in the fall. Winter snowfall averages about 80 centimeters (32 in.) a month with a month-end snow cover of around 46 centimeters (18 in.).

SEASONAL ACTIVITIES   The park's excellent interpretive program runs from late June to Labor Day. It includes daily conducted walks led by park naturalists, special programs for kids, and film and slide shows every evening at the Pog Outdoor Theatre. In addition, the interpretive staff host a few special events—July's Spirit Walks at the Logging Museum, and the wildly popular public Wolf Howls in August (for more information on the park's interpretive programs, see chapter 4, "Outdoor Pursuits in Algonquin Park").

For animal viewing, each season has its own highlights: moose command springtime in the park. Attracted by the puddles of salt at the sides of the highway, moose can often be seen grazing by the wildflowers along the Parkway Corridor and indeed pose a threat to motorists who don't see the darkly colored animals at night. Summer is a free-for-all, with moose, bears, deer, chipmunks, loons, and the rest of the usual suspects making appearances in the wild. During the fall it's often possible to see beaver foraging for winter food at dusk below the colorful forest canopy. In winter the silence in the woods is complete but for the haunting cry of distant wolves.

A great new addition to park activities is the interactive Opeongo Expedition Research Adventure Program running at Opeongo Lake (6km north from K 46.3 on the 60 Corridor). The Harkness Laboratory of Fisheries Research and Algonquin Park has initiated a hands-on monitoring and researching program that aims to raise money for new research at the Lab. Heading out in a Zodiak into the middle of Opeongo Lake, you are fully educated on water temperatures, fish tracking, and plankton levels and identification. For more information, see chapter 4, "Outdoor Pursuits in Algonquin Park."

4 What to Take

Good trip preparation accounts for not only planned activities but also the range of possible weather conditions in the park. Even at the height of the summer the evenings can be chilly, so it pays to bring some warm clothes—a fleece or sweater, long underwear, and a hat or toque. Rain gear is a must—nice mornings can quickly become rainy afternoons, and if you're 5 kilometers into a 10-kilometer hike then the soggy walk back will seem very long indeed. If you are planning on doing a lot of hiking then make sure you have a sturdy pair of hiking shoes or boots. The trails at Algonquin can be pretty rocky; good ankle support will help with unsteady footing. And when you get back to camp, don't forget to remove your shoes and look after your feet!

Other supplies to pack into your hiking rucksack include a lot of water (for a full day of hiking you should bring 4 liters [4 qt.] per person), food such as energy bars, mixed nuts, and dried fruits or granola, sun block, sun hat, shades, and a small first-aid kit. Insect repellent is imperative in Algonquin Park and its surroundings. Every year the mosquito and black fly populations fluctuate, so there is no safer guideline than to recommend using 90% deet products from May straight through to August if you are that concerned. Be sure not to use any product that contains deet on children younger than 5 years of age, and there are special pet repellents you can get to help protect your dog. Citronella and natural products like tea tree oil do not have the same effect as deet, but also don't have the threat of horrible smells or staying on your clothing after laundering.

The smartest way to weather winter activities in Algonquin is layers. A synthetic shirt made of wicking materials makes an excellent base for cross-country skiing, with extra layers that can be stripped off as you heat up. And heavy winter clothes are of course a necessity: thick hat and gloves, long underwear, ski pants, and good boots with lots of extra pairs of wool socks (trust me: you can NEVER have enough socks!). Talk to someone at your local outdoor store for advice on what gear best suits your activity.

If you're staying in a campground you'll probably want to bring a portable stove of some kind. All of the sites have fire pits, and most have grills, but Algonquin can get pretty dry in the summers—which means there are regular bans on open fires. Cooking on a fire is tricky, consumptive, and ecologically damaging. Considering high-volume, low-impact camping techniques will keep our wilderness areas pristine. Consult one of the many websites or books on "leave no trace" principles or talk to an outdoor expert or park naturalist.

If you're planning on hiking or canoeing in the interior, then there are some additional supplies you will want to bring with you. Chapter 5 contains a full discussion of what to take on an overnight camping trip.

Finally, you will be near a lot of lakes and rivers, possibly even moving around on top of them. Don't forget a swimsuit and some extra footwear (one wet and one dry pair). And fishing gear is a must for many.

5 Getting There

BY PLANE

Visitors to Algonquin can fly into either **Ottawa International Airport** (© 613/248-2125; www.ottawa-airport.ca) or Toronto's **Lester B. Pearson International Airport** (©(terminals 1 and 2) **416/247-7678,** (terminal 3) © **416/776-5100;** www.lbpia. toronto.on.ca). Both airports are serviced by most of the major U.S. and European airlines, including **Air Canada** (© **888/247-2262;** www.aircanada.ca), **American Airlines** (© **800/433-7300;** www. amrcorp.com), **Delta** (© **800/241-4141;** www.delta.com), **Continental** (© **800/231-0856;** www.continental.com), **Northwest Air**

(© 800/225-2525; www.nwa.com), **US Airways** (© 800/428-4322; www.usairways.com), **Lufthansa** (© 800/563-5954; www.lufthansa.com), **British Airways** (© 800/403-0882; www.ba.com), **KLM** (© 800/361-1887; www.klm.com), and **Air France** (© 800/667-2747; www.airfrance.com).

Toronto's airport is further serviced by **LTU** (© 866/266-5588; www.ltu.com) **Korean Airlines** (© 800/438-5000; www.korean air.com), **Cathay Pacific** (© 800/268-6868; www.cathaypacific.com), **Alitalia** (© 800/361-8336; www.alitalia.it), **Singapore Airlines** (© 800/ 387-0038; www.singaporeair.com), **Austrian Airlines** (© 888/817-4444; www.aua.com), and **Mexicana** (© 800/531-7921; www.mexicana.com.mx), among others.

Once you've arrived in Ottawa or Toronto you will have to drive to the park—see below.

BY CAR

The best way to get to Algonquin Park is by car, and for visitors from out of town this probably means renting one. Both the Toronto and Ottawa airports have the following rental agencies located on-site: **Avis** (© 800/272-5871; www.avis.com), **Budget** (© 800/268-8900; www.budget.com), **Hertz** (© 800/263-0600; www.hertz.com), **National Car** (© 800/227-7368; www.national car.com), and **Thrifty** (© 800/847-4389; www.thrifty.com). Check the respective airport website for rental agency direct phone numbers.

Algonquin's Parkway Corridor is about equal distance from Ottawa and Toronto. The car ride from Toronto to the West Gate of the park is about 260 kilometers (161 miles) or 3 hours; from Ottawa to the East Gate of the park it's 250 kilometers (155 miles), also about 3 hours. The Parkway Corridor itself is 56 kilometers (34.7 miles) long and takes about 40 minutes to drive from end to end. Campgrounds are located upon its entire length. To get to the more remote access points takes considerably longer, especially from Toronto. As a general rule, if you intend to visit the southern and western sides of the park Toronto is the closest departure city; if you're going to the northern and eastern sides of the park then Ottawa is closest.

FROM TORONTO   From the airport take Highway 409 East to where it joins with Highway 401, then continue east on the 401 a short distance to Highway 400. Go north on Highway 400 for 90 kilometers (56 miles) to Barrie—roughly a 1-hour drive. Shortly after Barrie the highway splits into Highways 11 and 400—veer right on Highway 11, following the signs to Orillia and North Bay. Huntsville is 125 kilometers (77.5 miles) from Barrie, a little over an hour's drive. The turnoff for Highway 60 is immediately north of town. Turn right on Highway 60, going east toward Dwight and Algonquin Park. The **West Gate** of the park is about 50 kilometers (31 miles) or 40 minutes from Huntsville.

If you are heading to one of the more remote northern access points, do not turn off at Highway 60 after Huntsville but instead continue north on Highway 11. The western side of the park can be accessed by turning east off Highway 11 at Emsdale and South River. For the most northerly access points, around **Kiosk** and **Brent,** continue north on Highway 11 to Callander (just short of North Bay), where it's possible to cut east on Highway 94 a short distance to Highway 17. Highway 17 East follows the Ottawa River down along the whole northwestern length of the park, all the way to Ottawa itself. Keep in mind the distance from Toronto to Brent is considerable—around 480 kilometers (300 miles), about a 6-hour drive.

For Algonquin's southern panhandle, follow Highway 401 East out of Toronto to Belleville, turn north on Highway 62 toward Bancroft, and at Maynooth take Peterson Road (County Road 10) west to the **Kingscote Lake** access point just inside the park (there are a few other potentially faster—but more confusing—ways of getting here from Toronto if you juggle around the access and county roads).

Finally, if you're trying to go from Toronto to the **Achray** access point at the far eastern end of the park, then take Highway 401 East all the way past Belleville to Highway 41 (a distance of 190 kilometers [118 miles]), and turn north toward distant Pembroke (another 230 kilometers [143 miles]). Just before Pembroke turn west and follow Highway 17 for a short distance, then turn left again onto County Road 28. This is the **Barron Canyon Road,** and it leads directly into the park. Follow it for 26 kilometers (16 miles) to the **Sand Lake Gate** at the park boundary. The distance from the Sand Lake Gate to Achray is 24 kilometers (15 miles), which adds up to a total journey time from Toronto of approximately 6 hours. From Sand Lake Gate you can also go up to the **Lake Travers** or **McManus Lake** access points.

FROM OTTAWA   To get to Algonquin Park's **East Gate** take Highway 417 West out of Ottawa. Highway 417 turns into Highway 17 before long; continue west until you see the turnoff signs for Highway 60 and Renfrew (about 100 kilometers [62 miles]). Follow Highway 60 West through Eganville, Barry's Bay, and Whitney into Algonquin Park (another 150 kilometers [93 miles]).

Getting to one of the eastern or northern access points is even easier from Ottawa. Stay on Highway 17 West until you pass Pembroke, a journey time of about an hour and a half (150 kilometers [93 miles]). After Pembroke there are a number of access roads heading west; the furthest of these, Kiosk, is a journey time of about 2 hours from Pembroke (205 kilometers [127 miles]).

BY BUS

The only other way to get to Algonquin Park from Toronto is to take the **Algonquin Park Shuttle Bus,** available between July and August on Mondays, Wednesdays, and Fridays. This is a two-leg trip; **Ontario Northlands** (Toronto Coach Terminal, 610 Bay Street, *©* **416/393-7911**) departs downtown Toronto at 9:15am and arrives in Huntsville at 1:01pm (they have several daily runs to Huntsville, but this is the only one that connects to the second leg of the trip). Once the Ontario Northlands bus has unloaded at the Empire Hotel, passengers switch to a 1:15pm **Hammond Transportation** bus (*©* **705/645-5431;** fax 705/645-3629; www.hammondtransportation.com) that will drop them at Oxtongue Lake (1:50pm), the Portage Store at Canoe Lake (2pm), or the Lake of Two Rivers Store (2:15pm). The same bus takes returning passengers back to Huntsville. The one-way combined fare is C$62 (US$46); no reservations are required.

Taking the bus from Ottawa to the park is a lot more difficult—in fact, it's so indirect it is hardly worth it. You have to take **Greyhound** (*©* **416/367-8747**) from Ottawa to North Bay, then Ontario Northlands from North Bay to Huntsville, and finally Hammond Transportation from Huntsville to the park, a one-way combined fare of about C$107 (US$79.35).

BY HELICOPTER

Helicopter trips to Algonquin Park from downtown Toronto are available year-round. Depart from the downtown Toronto Island Airport direct for the northland. Packages including roundtrip flightseeing, half-day, full-day, and two-day excursions. Fly by jet helicopter and land just south of the park access point, in the forests of the Ontario Leslie Frost Natural Resource Centre. Experienced guides will greet and escort you on your wonderful wilderness trips into the pristine mixed forests of Algonquin Park. The flight time is approximately 1 hour, and operates during daylight hours only. Contact **The Helicopter Company Inc.**, Toronto Island Airport, Toronto, ON M5V 1A1(© **888/445-8542** or **416/203-3280**; www.helitours.ca.) Rates start at C$500 (US$370.80) per person for groups of four.

6 Guided Canoe Trips & Hikes

There are a number of outfitters and private companies that offer guided canoe trips and hikes into Algonquin Park for all levels of ability.

Watermark Canoe Journeys, P.O. Box 131, Dwight, ON P0A 1H0 (© **800/890-1947** or 705/766-0970; fax 705/766-0971) are a little cheaper, with 3-day trips for C$285 (US$211.40), $140 (US$103.85) for children under 12. **Eco-Explorations,** P.O. Box 5559, Huntsville, ON P1H 2L5 (© **888/326-3975;** fax 705/788-2013; www.eco-explorations.com), offers canoe, kayak, and backpacking trips for all levels.

The most reliable trips are probably those run through the park outfitters. **Algonquin Outfitters,** R.R.1 Dwight, ON P0A 1H0 (© **705/635-2243;** fax 705/635-1834; www.algonquinoutfitters. com) has stores at Brent and Lake Opeongo, and charges C$375 (US$278.12) for a 3-day trip. They also offer several guided day-trip options including a "greenhorn service" for canoe novices. **The Portage Store,** P.O. Box 10009 Algonquin Park, Huntsville, ON P1H 2H4 (© **705/633-5622;** fax 705/633-5696; www.portage store.com) offers similar packages, only they depart out of the busier Canoe Lake access point.

For information on guided dog-sledding trips, see section 10, "Winter Activities," in chapter 4, "Outdoor Pursuits in Algonquin Park."

7 Tips for RVers

Unlike some of the serious touring parks in the U.S., Algonquin is not really about RVs on the move. Only a relatively short expanse of highway goes through the park, and the other access points are all one-way trips in.

Most motor home owners will want to camp in one spot and stay, and the car campgrounds dotted along the Parkway Corridor and around the park's periphery are perfect for this. The majority of the campgrounds along the corridor have electrical hookups—only Tea Lake, Kearney Lake, Coon Lake, and the peripheral sites at Achray, Brent, Kiosk, and South Algonquin do not.

Gas is available in the park at the **Portage Store** on Canoe Lake and the **Opeongo Store** on Lake Opeongo. There is a trailer sanitation station 35 kilometers (22 miles) past the West Gate, and for vehicle repairs there are places in both Whitney to the east and Dwight and Huntsville to the west.

8 Tips for Travelers with Disabilities

In recent years, Algonquin Park has done much to make its facilities more accessible to those with disabilities. The Visitor Centre, the Logging Museum, and the Pog Lake Outdoor Theatre are all fully wheelchair accessible. The 1.3-kilometer (0.8-mile) Logging Museum trail is flat and okay for a wheelchair, though one of the grades is a bit steep. The Spruce Bog trail at K43 has a boardwalk and the trail is partially wheelchair accessible—if you're adventurous!

The Canisbay, Lake of Two Rivers, Pog Lake, Mew Lake, and Kearney campgrounds all have wheelchair-accessible sites, with specially designed picnic tables, that are close to the washroom facilities. With the exception of Canisbay (which nevertheless has wheelchair-friendly showers), all the comfort stations at these campgrounds can be navigated in a wheelchair. Of the three lodges in the park, only **Killarney Lodge** is fully wheelchair accessible, and even its washroom doors are a bit narrow—so it's best to phone ahead with the exact dimensions of your chair (© **705/633-5551**). None of the interior ranger cabins or Mew Lake winter yurts are wheelchair accessible.

Fees for camping and vehicle permits are approximately half the regular price for disabled persons, but you may be required to show a **Disabled Parking Permit** (issued by the Canadian Ministry of Transportation) or a **National Identity Card** (issued by the Canadian National Institute for the Blind). You can view their website and obtain a permit at http://www.mto.gov.on.va/english/dandv/vehicle/disabled.htm.

9 Tips for Travelers with Pets

There are a number of regulations concerning pets in the park, and dogs in particular. These exist in large part because of complaints from other campers, but there is also a measure of safety involved for both pets and their owners. There have been a number of cases in the park of temporarily brave dogs racing back to their human companions with an irate bear in hot pursuit.

All pets must be on a leash not greater than 2 meters (6.6 ft.) in length. Leashed dogs are permitted on all the trails except Mizzy Lake, which is the park's prime wildlife-viewing trail. If you're taking your dog on a hike, make sure to bring a poop scoop and a supply of water for the dog. *Don't* leave dogs to asphyxiate in a hot car, which can happen within minutes..

Dogs are permitted in all campgrounds, though a portion of sites at Canisbay Lake, Mew Lake, Pog Lake, and Achray campgrounds have been designated dog-free (and radio-free). Pets are not permitted in ranger cabins, and none of the lodges in the park allow them. There are two kennels in Huntsville for travelers who need somewhere to board their pets, as well as several veterinary clinics including the **Algonquin Animal Hospital,** 869 Highway 60 (© **705/789-5181;** fax 705/789-5133), the **Huntsville Animal Hospital,** 459 Highway 60 (© **705/789-9656;** fax 705/789-1082) and **Van Der Kraan Veterinary Services,** 108 Main St. East, Huntsville (© **705/789-3215;** fax 705/789-6226).

Dogs assisting disabled persons are allowed in all public areas including all park buildings.

10 Tips for Travelers with Children

Algonquin Park is a great place for kids. Both the Visitor Centre and the Logging Museum have cool educational dioramas on the park's history and its animal inhabitants, and the daily naturalist-led hikes provide both kids and adults with a great introduction to the park's wildlife, geology, and human history. Every summer evening around 8 or 9pm (times vary, so consult the notices posted daily throughout the park), there is a free film and slide show at the Outdoor Theatre on some aspect of the park—from wolves to butterflies to insect-eating plants. Additional special events are listed in *This Week in Algonquin Park* (see the note under "Essentials" in chapter 3, "Exploring Algonquin Park"), including the public wolf-howling expeditions—which drive kids feral with excitement.

During the summers, the park interpretive program runs the free **Algonquin for Kids** daily at 10:30am in the Visitor Centre. Children ages 5 to 12 spend an hour or more playing games, listening to stories, and learning about their favorite animals. Two or three times a week kids are invited to participate in the **Park Helper Program**—organized beach and campground cleanups, for which kids receive special buttons. During the rest of the year, **The Friends of Algonquin Park** offer a range of educational programs for school kids. For more information on these programs contact the **Visitor Centre** during normal office hours, Monday to Friday, 8:30am to 4:30pm (© **613/637-2828**; fax 613/637-2138).

For parents with really young children, there are baby-changing stations in most of the campground bathrooms.

11 Alcohol in the Park

Alcohol is permitted only on registered campsites—if you are found drinking alcohol anywhere else in the park, including picnic sites, you could be charged a fine and evicted. Registered campsites include sites in the interior, but keep in mind that the park does not allow you to bring in bottles and cans. So if you need some alcoholic consolation after a long day of paddling, store your 12 ounces in a plastic water bottle to keep at your site.

None of the restaurants in the park are licensed except the one at the Portage Store, but the lodges have a BYOB policy with a limit of one bottle of wine per person. The closest places to buy booze are at the **LCBO** stores (Liquor Control Board of Ontario) in Whitney to the east (© **613/637-2150**) and Dwight to the west (© **705/635-2891**).

12 Protecting Your Health & Safety

Overall, Algonquin Park is generally a pretty benign place, but there are definitely a few health and safety tips you should keep in mind while visiting.

The first concerns wildlife, specifically **black bears** and **wolves.** In May 1978 a bear killed three teenage boys on the east side of the park, and in October 1991 another bear killed a couple on an island in Lake Opeongo. Although there have been two dozen fatal attacks by black bears in North America since 1900, attacks are extremely rare—you have a greater chance of being struck by lightning during your visit to Algonquin than being molested by a black bear. 2003 saw a large increase in the number of bears within the park, which in turn increased sightings—and road-kills—along the 60 corridor.

(Tips) Bear Encounters

Here are a few tips courtesy of the Ministry of Natural Resources on what to do if you find yourself face-to-face with a black bear:

- Don't try to feed it.
- Never come between a mother bear and her cub.
- Immediately pick up any small children.
- Stay calm and don't run. Instead move slowly away from the bear.
- If you are with more than one person then group together and try to look as big as possible. Wearing bright raincoats and raising your arms both help to make you look larger and more intimidating.
- Make as much noise as possible—bang pots and pans, smack your shoes against a rock.
- Avoid direct eye contact—bears apparently find this threatening.
- Try to stand your ground if a bear charges or stands up on its hind legs. These charges are bluffs; they're the bear's way of letting you know you're too close. Speak to it in a strong, firm voice and back away.
- If the bear still tries to approach you, stop backing away and act as aggressive as possible. Yell, throw rocks or sticks, and use bear spray if you have it. Never turn and run.
- If the bear makes actual contact with you then **DO NOT PLAY DEAD**. Fighting back is the best way to persuade a black bear to leave you alone.
- Report any sightings of bears in campsites to park staff.

Most bears want nothing whatsoever to do with us, and venture into campsites only because they smell food. These "campsite" bears rarely pose any threat to humans, and can usually be scared away (see "Bear Encounters" above). The first precaution you should take against having these kinds of bears around is hanging your food. Food packs (which should include litter, toothpaste, and any perfumed products) should be strung up away from your tent, at least 3 meters (10 ft.) off the ground and 2 meters (6.6 ft.) away from the tree trunk. If you're staying in a car campground then make sure to keep your food safely stored in airtight containers in your vehicle. Unlike their infamous Yellowstone cousins, Algonquin bears have not yet figured out how to open car doors.

Wolves are another potentially dangerous animal in the park. There are cases of park visitors encountering aggressive wolves, although this is still *extremely* rare. If you do see a wolf (and you would be part of a lucky minority) then keep your distance. If the wolf approaches the protocol is much the same as it is for a bear—make a lot of noise and try to look as imposing as possible.

Another animal hazard in the park, perhaps improbably, is the **moose.** Every year (particularly in the spring) more than two dozen moose are killed and as many cars damaged in nightly collisions along the Parkway Corridor. These crashes can be avoided if motorists practice more vigilant driving, watch for the glare of moose eyes, and never exceed the 80 kilometer per hour (50 mph) speed limit.

If you're camping in the interior then you need to be aware of **giardia**—or "beaver fever," as it's called by locals. Giardia is a microscopic parasite found in some lakes and streams that is often spread by animal excrement in the water (hence the name beaver fever). If contracted, it can lead to an intestinal illness that can cause nausea, bloating, anorexia, fever, and severe diarrhea. To avoid getting giardia, bring lake or stream water to a rolling boil for 5 minutes before drinking it. Iodine tablets or another water-purification system will also eliminate giardia from your drinking water. Some people continue to drink from Algonquin's lakes without ever getting giardia; if you want to take the still-slight risk, then make sure to fill your water bottle well away from shore in the open water. If you're planning on going on one of the short day hikes, bring along your own water.

Other park hazards include poisonous **berries** and **mushrooms** (make sure to consult a field guide before eating), and **poison ivy** (found only around the Barron Canyon on the park's east side and near Tea Lake Campground along Highway 60). Swimmers need to carefully check the water depth before **diving** in, as many of the lakes have rocky bottoms hidden just a few feet below the murky surface. **Hypothermia** is another concern, and not just when the water is extremely cold in the spring and fall—most cases of hypothermia occur in the summer. Standing around in a soaking-wet cotton T-shirt in the pouring rain will drop your core body temperature quicker than you might imagine. If you're out camping make sure to bring a warm fleece and sleeping bag, preferably protected in waterproof materials. The treatment for hypothermia is to get dry and warm as soon as possible.

Tips Mosquito Bites & West Nile Virus

A great philosopher once said, *"Those who doubt that one person can make a difference have never shared a night in a tent with a mosquito."* Boy, is that the truth. Mosquitoes are, without a doubt, a natural pest within the park that we have no control over. One area of camping you definitely want to look after prior to your arrival to the park is mosquito management.

First detected in the province in birds in 2001 and in humans in 2002, the mosquito-borne West Nile virus has become a concern in Ontario. Human illness from West Nile virus is very rare, even in areas where the virus has been reported. The chance that you will become ill from a mosquito bite is extremely low. To date, West Nile Virus has not been detected within the park or its inhabitants. The mosquitoes that carry the virus tend to stay within larger cities and urban areas. You can further reduce your chances of becoming ill by protecting yourself from mosquito bites:

- Cover up. Wear long sleeves, socks, closed shoes, and a hat.
- Wear light-colored clothing, because mosquitoes are attracted to darker colors.
- Add bug hats and bug jackets to your list of outdoor gear, if you are a serious camper or hiker. Tuck pant legs into your socks and wear elastics on the wrists of your shirt to prevent insects from entering.
- Use a bug-tarp shelter when camping to avoid biting insects. A bug tarp is a light, portable screened shelter that provides good protection.
- Ensure your tent is in good repair and won't let mosquitoes and other biting insects in while you are sleeping.
- Use a proper mosquito repellent with at least 90% deet content. (Deet should not be used on children under the age of 3; consult your health-care provider.)

Finally, avoid open areas during severe thunderstorms. Forked **lightning** is a common sight during the Algonquin summer. Don't ever stand under a tree for protection during a lightning storm, and take care not to stand on exposed roots, as lightning can travel through a struck tree to its roots—and into you. If you are caught on the water during a storm and have no other escape except to ride out the storm use the following guidelines. Make sure not to touch any masted-area of the boat. Stay low and in the center of the boat —avoiding the term "stand-up human lightning mast!" Keep your arms and legs inside the boat—not dangling in the water. Discontinue fishing, swimming, or other water activities when there is lightning or even when weather conditions look threatening. The first lightning strike can be a mile or more in front of an upcoming thunderstorm. Disconnect and do not use or touch the major electronic equipment, including radios, throughout the duration of the storm.

13 Protecting the Environment

Algonquin Park is a place of great natural beauty, but as the numbers of appreciative visitors grow so too do the dangers associated with sloppy camping. To prevent Algonquin Park from becoming a giant garbage heap, there are a few basic **"no-trace" camping rules** you should follow.

Whatever trash you take into the park you should take out with you (remember: there are no cans or bottles permitted in the interior). For campgrounds along the Parkway Corridor, make sure to use the trash cans provided; they are in such abundance there is really no excuse for littering.

Cooking fires can be tricky, consumptive, and ecologically damaging. Keep in mind a low-impact, non-evasive cooking regime to ensure that our wilderness areas remain pristine. When camping in the interior, don't harm any live trees, and don't pollute the lakes and rivers. Algonquin Park has only a thin layer of topsoil covering the granite, so there is little to prevent dysentery-carrying bacteria from leaking down into the water. Each of the campsites in the interior comes with a privy, dug deep enough to prevent this. If you have to go in the woods make sure you are at least 50 meters (165 ft.) from the water and bury both the feces and toilet paper. This same rule applies to the soapy water you use for washing dishes, even if you use biodegradable soap.

Another mantra of park environmentalism is "don't feed the animals." Doing so is in effect signing their death warrants, as they can become infected with human diseases, lose their own survival skills, or—in the case of some of the larger animals—lose their healthy fear of humans and end up crushed by a car or shot as pests. Wild places should be left wild—at the very least because they act as ancestral touchstones for our own increasingly domestic lives.

Exploring Algonquin Park

When people speak of exploring Algonquin Park, they often do so in terms of interior camping: assembling the gear, and either hiking or canoeing into the wilds. The combination of wilderness and solitude that results is a big draw for many visitors, but it's not necessary to go on a 5-day canoe trip to experience this. Algonquin's forest and lakes can also be reached (up to a point) by car, either via the Parkway Corridor, or by driving to one of the access points that wrap around the periphery of the park.

The stretch of Highway 60 that bisects the southern edge of the park provides the most jumping-off points and is bristling with historical, artistic, and natural attractions: the Visitor Centre, the Logging Museum, the Algonquin Gallery, the interpretive hiking trails, and more. The peripheral access points are another way of exploring the park; while some consist of little more than a dusty parking lot with a lakeside view, others—like Kingscote, Achray, and Brent—are actually worth a visit in their own right, regardless of whether you have any intention of penetrating the interior.

1 Essentials

ACCESS/ENTRY POINTS & INFORMATION   Highway 60 is the only roadway that cuts directly through the park, a 56-kilometer (35-mile) stretch of highway known as the **Parkway Corridor.** It runs along the bottom end of the park, neatly separating the southern panhandle from the square majority of the park. For many visitors, there are only two entry points to the park: the **West Gate** (open summers 8am–9pm; winters 9am–4pm), about 15 kilometers (9 miles) east of Dwight; and the **East Gate** (open summers 8am–7pm; winters 8am–4:30pm), 5 kilometers (3 miles) west of Whitney. Neither gate has direct phone numbers available to the public, but the park information officers are located at the West Gate and can be reached daily from 8am to 4:30pm through the park **Information Line** at ⓒ **705/633-5572.**

Algonquin Provincial Park

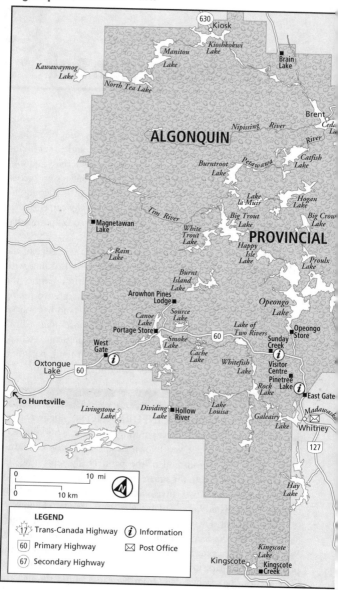

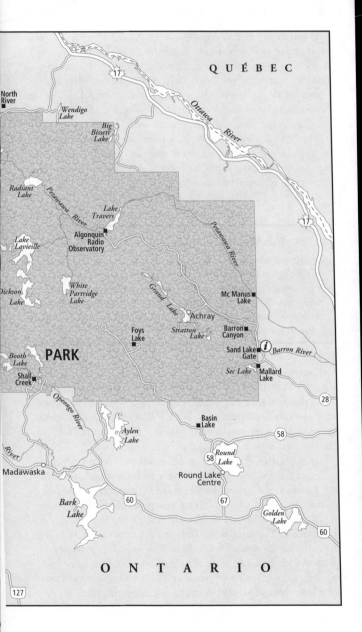

If you intend to visit Algonquin for the day or longer, then you must stop at one of these gates to purchase a **vehicle permit.** There is no need to stop if you're just passing through the park, have a reservation at one of the lodges, or have already reserved a campsite in one of the campgrounds or in the interior (the daily vehicle permit is included in the overnight camping fee; all three lodges provide day permits for all their guests).

The two gates are staffed by park information officers, who dispense permits and answer inquiries—they also provide trip counseling. Both gates have public washrooms and small gift shops that contain, in addition to a selection of books on Algonquin Park, flashy parkland T-shirts and pine tree coffee mugs.

Tips **This Week in Algonquin Park**

During the summer you can pick up a free copy of *This Week in Algonquin Park* at either gate or at the Visitor Centre. An indispensable planner for the Parkway Corridor, the little pamphlet lists all the interpretive hikes, kids' programs, canoeing demonstrations, and nightly films happening that week in the park.

Two other sources of Algonquin information are the park radio station, CFOA **102.7FM,** which broadcasts a looped recording outlining potential fire bans, special events, and general park news; and the free *Parkway Corridor* and *The Park Interior* newspapers, which are published every season by the Friends of Algonquin Park and can be found at both gates and the Visitor Centre.

Algonquin Park also has **29** official **access points** from which to strike out into the interior. Nine of these are located along the Parkway Corridor; the rest are dotted around the periphery of the park. Each access point is serviced by an **access point office,** the locations of which can be found on the *Gates & Access Points in the Park* map in chapter 5, "Camping in the Interior"; for detailed directions see the park's *Canoe Routes of Algonquin Park* map. It is necessary to check in with the access point office staff before embarking on your trip—they will sell you your permit and answer any queries you may have about your trip ("Yep, lots of bear sightings this year...").

An Algonquin Index

Average number of summer visitors: 300,000
Area of park: 7,725 square kilometers (2,982 square miles)
Number of scientific papers based on work conducted here: 1,800
Total number of wolf-howl participants up to year 2002: 111,608
Number of bears in park: 2,000 (1 every 3 square km)
Number of moose: 2,500+
Number of beaver: 10,000+
Number of wolves: 300
Percentage of park area available for logging: 78
Real percentage of area minus lakes and buffer zones: 57
Percentage clear-cut: 5
Kilometers of logging roads that you do not see: more than 2,000 (1,240 miles)
Species of plants in park: more than 1,000
Kilometers of canoe routes in the park: 2,100 (1,302 miles)
Number of lakes that contain brook trout: 170
Total number of lakes: 2,000+
Number of interior campsites: 1,760
Age of sections of Canadian Shield: 1 billion years

VEHICLE PERMITS, CAMPING AND RENTAL FEES   To use the park, visitors must have a park permit displayed on the dashboard of their vehicle. This is true whether you are just visiting the park for a day, camping at one of the car campgrounds, staying at a lodge, or camping in the interior. If your vehicle does not display a permit, you are subject to a C$25 (US$18) fine. Once again, you do not need to purchase a vehicle permit if you have a camping or lodge reservation since any of the car campground office, the interior access point office, or the lodge will give you one for the duration of your stay.

The price for a **daily vehicle permit** is C$12 (US$8.90), with C$10.50 (US$7.80) reduced-price vehicle permits for the Kiosk, Brent, and Achray sites (based on 2003 rates). On most of the fees there is a 20% discount for seniors and a 50% discount for persons with disabilities. Summer vehicle permits are available from April 1 to November 30 for C$65 (US$48.20); winter vehicle permits are C$45 (US$33.40) and annual permits cost C$100 (US$74.20).

Fees for staying overnight in the park range broadly depending on whether you're planning on camping in one of the car campgrounds, camping in the interior, or staying in one of the yurts or in a ranger cabin. Full-price fees for a **car campsite without electricity or showers** is C$22.50 (US$16.70) per group of six people or fewer, C$18 (US$13.40) for seniors, and C$11.25 (US$8.35) for persons with disabilities. Groups are allowed one vehicle; for additional vehicles there is an extra C$9 (US$6.70) charge. **Campsites with showers** cost C$24 (US$17.70) a night, C$19.20 (US$14.25) for seniors, and C$12 (US$8.90) for persons with disabilities. **Campsites with both electrical hookups and showers** cost C$28 (US$20.80) a night, C$22.40 (US$16.60) for seniors, and C$14 (US$10.40) for persons with disabilities. The campsites at Kiosk, Brent, and Tea Lake are available for a reduced rate: C$20 (US$14.85) a night, C$16 (US$11.90) for seniors, and C$10 (US$7.40) for persons with disabilities. The Coon Lake campground is C$21.50 (US$15.95) a night, C$17.20 (US$12.75) for seniors, and C$10.75 (US$8) for persons with disabilities. The park also has 18 **group campsites** at Whitefish Lake; each one can accommodate 10 to 40 people and is available for C$20 (US$14.80) a night plus an additional C$4 (US$3.00) per person ($1 [US$0.74] per person for kids aged 6–17).

The fee for **interior camping** is C$8 (US$5.90) a night per site per person. Kids aged 6 to 17 pay C$3.25 (US$2.40) a night, seniors pay C$6.40 (US$4.75), and persons with disabilities pay C$4 (US$3.00). As with all campsites, there is a C$9 (US$6.70) nonrefundable reservation fee, and a C$6 (US$4.45) change or cancellation fee. For more reservation information, see chapter 2, "Planning Your Trip."

The cost of renting one of the seven **yurts** (each of which can accommodate up to six people) at Mew Lake Campground is C$60 (US$44.50) a night in the summer, C$55 (US$40.80) a night in the winter. Yurts can also be rented for C$350 (US$260) a week. Another rental option is the historical **ranger cabins** of the interior. The majority of the cabins can be rented for C$41.50 (US$30.80) a night for the first person, with an additional C$8 (US$5.90) per person up to a maximum of four (the Kitty Lake and Crooked Chute cabins can handle six). All cabins also have a weekly rate:

C$275 (US$203.95) for the first person, and an additional C$57 (US$42.30) for each subsequent person. The three drive-to cabins at Kiosk, Brent, and Rain Lake—equipped with fridges, stoves, and lights—are more expensive; their nightly rates are C$80.25 (US$59.50), C$75 (US$55.65), and C$61.50 (US$45.60), respectively (C$8 [US$5.90] for each additional person), with weekly rates of C$540 (US$400.50), C$500 (US$370.80), and C$400 (US$296.65), respectively. The Brent cabin has a special group rate of C$75 (US$55.60) a day for up to six people, with C$10 (US$7.40) for each additional person up to a maximum of 12.

PARK RULES AND REGULATIONS   Most of the regulations governing the park are concerned with protecting the park from the very people who have come to appreciate it. The majority of these rules are common sense; if you are properly respectful then you won't be busted by one of the conservation officers or park wardens who patrol the park. Within park boundaries each of these wardens has the authority of an Ontario Provincial Police officer—in a typical year they make 350 or more charges, all punishable by fines or prison.

For a full list of park regulations, see the back of the *Canoe Routes of Algonquin Park* map. Here is a list of some of the higher-profile ones:

- You must have a permit to camp in the interior, and a vehicle permit if you're visiting the park.
- A maximum of nine people are allowed at each interior campsite, with only three tents.
- You must be out of your campsite by 2pm on the day your permit expires.
- No bottles and cans are allowed anywhere in the park except organized campgrounds and picnic areas with regular collection.
- All firearms are prohibited in the park.
- It is forbidden to cut or damage any living tree or plant—this includes such park favorites as picking wildflowers and peeling birch bark.
- Camping is permitted only at designated sites in the interior (marked by an orange sign).
- Motor boats are not permitted on most Algonquin lakes. There are exceptions to this rule; see *Canoe Routes of Algonquin Park* or contact a park information officer for more details.

- No littering in the park—to do so is to endanger the lives of bears and other animals that lose their healthy fear of humans.
- Campfires should be lit only in designated fireplaces.
- Bicycles are only permitted off-road on designated trails. These are marked on the *Canoe Routes of Algonquin Park* map by a red line. In addition, bike helmets are mandatory.
- Most campers are in Algonquin Park to find tranquility; therefore, noise restrictions are enforced. This means no radios, cd or cassette players, or excessive noise like yelling. You can sing around the campfire (or portable stove), but wear a Walkman if you want to listen to music.
- All pets must be on a leash.

For the rules concerning alcohol in the park see chapter 2, "Planning Your Trip."

OUTFITTERS If you're planning on camping in Algonquin Park then there is a good chance you will be paying a visit to one of the area's many outfitters. They supply a range of services, everything from planning and leading individual trips to renting equipment and canoes, organizing pick-up and drop-off points for interior canoe trips, and selling innumerable brands of bug repellent. The outfitters located in the park itself are the most expensive: **The Portage Store** (P.O. Box 10009, Huntsville, ON P1H 2H4; ✆ **705/633-5622;** fax 705/633-5696; www.portagestore.com) on Canoe Lake charges about C$30 (US$22.25) a day for a lightweight Kevlar canoe, and **Bartlett Lodge** (P.O. Box 10004, Huntsville, ON P1H 2G8; ✆ **705/633-5543;** fax 705/633-5746; www.bartlett lodge.com) on Cache Lake rents heavier aluminum canoes for an expensive C$35 (US$25.95) a day. **The Opeongo Store** (R.R.1, Hwy 60, Dwight, ON P0A 1H0; ✆ **888/280-8886;** fax 705/635-1834; www.algonquinoutfitters.com), run by **Algonquin Outfitters** on Opeongo Lake, is a bit cheaper—especially if you rent one of the aluminum canoes (if you're just renting canoes for the day and are not planning any long portages, then it probably doesn't matter what kind you rent). Please note: another name for this store is Opeongo Algonquin Outfitters, not to be confused with **Opeongo Outfitters** (P.O. Box 123, Whitney, ON K0J 2M0; ✆ **800/790-1864;** fax 613/637-2791; www.opeongooutfitters.com) in Whitney, who do not have a store directly on the lake but occasionally say they do, and are thus responsible for untold Access Point 11 canoe rental mix-ups.

All the other outfitters are located east or west of the park on Highway 60 or in one of the gateway towns, or they are located further up on the park periphery. Many of them are located close to or directly on a particular peripheral access point, so if you are planning a trip to a specific part of the park then make sure to select the closest outfitter. The back of *Canoe Routes of Algonquin Park* lists all the outfitters and access points together on a map, and the table overleaf indicates the closest town to each outfitter as well as the specific services each one provides. The least expensive of these outfitters are **Canoe Algonquin** (1914 Hwy 518 East, R.R.1, Kearney, ON P0A 1M0; ⓒ **800/818-1210;** fax 705/636-0017; www.canoe algonquin.com; e-mail gocanoe@canoealgonquin.com) and **Forest Tower Outfitters** (R.R.1, Kearney, ON P0A 1C0; ⓒ **800/716-1643;** fax 705/636-0874; www.foresttoweroutfitters.com), both located outside the park near Kearney. They charge only C$20 (US$14.80) a day for a Kevlar canoe, paddles and lifejackets included (the big operations in the park are the only ones that charge extra for these necessities). Since these outfitters are not located directly on an access point, you will have to either lash the rented canoes to the roof of your vehicle (many of the outfitters rent roof racks for C$8 [US$5.90] or so, an excellent option that can accommodate up to two canoes per vehicle), or pay a shuttle fee to have the canoes dropped off at one of the access points closest to the store. Shuttle fees usually run C$30 to C$40 (US$22.25 to US$29.70) each way. This is the case whether you're moving one or five canoes, so the larger your group the cheaper it is.

All other outfitters to the north, east, and west of the park charge on average somewhere between C$22 (US$16.30) and C$27 (US$20) a day for a Kevlar canoe. They are **Algonquin Outfitters,** which has four locations including the Opeongo Store (in Dwight (Oxtongue Lake) ⓒ **705/635-2243;** in Huntsville ⓒ **705/787-0262;** in Brent ⓒ **705/747-0040;** www.algonquinoutfitters.com); **Tracs Outfitter** (1 Chemical Road, P.O. Box 303, South River, ON P0A 1X0; ⓒ **705/386-0440;** fax 705/386-1370; www.tracs outfitters.com); **Voyageur Outfitting** (P.O. Box 67055, 2300 Yonge Street, Toronto, ON M4P 1E0; 877/837-8889) located right next to the Access Point 1 parking lot; **Canadian Wilderness Trips** (45 Charles St., Suite 100, Toronto, ON M4Y 1S2; ⓒ **416/960-2298;** fax 416/966-4039); **Northern Wilderness Outfitters** (Box 89, South River, ON P0A 1X0; ⓒ **888/386-0466;** www.northern

Outfitting Services In & Around the Park

Outfitter	Closest Town	Canoe Rental	Kayak Rental	Camping Supplies	Food Prep	Trip Guiding	Water-Taxi	Shuttle Service	Fishing Gear	Winter Skis
In the Park										
The Portage Store	Dwight	yes	yes	yes	yes	yes	no	yes	sell	closed
Opeongo Store	Whitney	yes	yes	yes	yes	yes	yes	yes	rent, sell	closed
(Algonquin Outfitters) Bartlett Lodge	Dwight	yes	no	no	no	no	no	no	no	closed
West of the Park										
Algonquin Outfitters	Huntsville	yes	yes	yes	yes	no	no	no	sell	yes
Algonquin Outfitters	Dwight	yes	yes	yes	yes	yes	no	yes	rent, sell	yes
Canoe Algonquin	Kearney	yes	yes	yes	no	no	no	yes	sell	no
Forest Tower Outfitters	Sand Lake	yes	yes	yes	yes	no	no	yes	sell	no
East and Northeast of the Park										
Opeongo Outfitters	Whitney	yes	yes	yes	yes	yes	yes	yes	yes	yes
Algonquin Bound	Madawaska	yes	yes	yes	yes	no	no	yes	sell	closed
Algonquin East Gate Motel & Outfitters	Whitney	yes	just 1	no	no	no	no	no	no	no
Algonquin Portage	Pembroke	yes	yes	yes	no	no	no	yes	no	no
Valley Ventures	Deep River	yes	yes	yes	yes	yes	no	yes	sell	yes
North of the Park										
Canadian Wilderness Trips	South River	yes	yes	yes	yes	no	yes	yes	sell	closed
Northern Wilderness Outfitters	South River	yes	no	no	yes	no	no	no	rent	closed
Tracs Outfitter	South River	yes	yes	no	no	no	no	no	no	closed
Voyageur Outfitting	South River	yes	no	yes	yes	no	no	yes	no	closed
Algonquin North Outfitters	Mattawa	yes	yes	yes	yes	yes	no	yes	rent, sell	closed
Halfway Chute Outfitters	Mattawa	yes	yes	yes	yes	yes	no	yes	no	closed

wilderness.com); **Algonquin North Outfitters** (R.R.2, Corner Hwys 630 & 17, Mattawa, ON P0H 1V0; ☎ **877/544-3544;** fax 705/744-3265; www.algonquinnorth.com); **Halfway Chute Outfitters** (R.R.2, Hwy 630, Mattawa, ON P0H 1V0; ☎ **877/343-8689;** fax 705/744-2155); **Algonquin Bound** (P.O. Box 228, Madawaska, ON K0J 2C0; ☎ **800/704-4537;** fax 613/637-2054; www.algonquinbound.com); and **Algonquin East Gate Motel & Outfitters** (P.O. Box 193, Whitney, ON K0J 2M0; ☎ **613/637-2652;** fax 613/637-5593; www.mv.igs.net/~outfitters/).

There are two outfitters serving the far eastern side of the park at Achray: **Algonquin Portage** (1352 Barron Canyon Road, Pembroke, ON K8A 6W7; ☎ **613/735-1795;** www.algonquin portage.com) and **Valley Ventures** (P.O. Box 1115, R.R.1, Deep River, ON K0J 1P0; ☎ **613/584-2577;** fax 613/584-9016; e-mail vent@magma.ca). Both are even more expensive than the outfitters in the park (they charge upward of C$30 [US$22.25] a day for canoes), but they are the only ones that service the remote area around Lake Travers and the stunning Barron Canyon—destinations popular with independent-minded canoeists. Shuttle service charges are hefty (between C$100 [US$74] and C$200 [US$148]), but the distances involved are considerable, and some of the fees include moving campers' vehicles between drop-off and pick-up points, which allows trippers to select long one-way routes (the east side in general has fewer suitable trip loops than the west side).

2 Tips from a Park Naturalist

Park Naturalist Brad Steinberg's long relationship with Algonquin Park began early: visits to the family cottage were highlights of his childhood summers, contributing to the fascination with flora and fauna he still possesses. Combining his love of wildlife with the desire to educate others, Steinberg has been a full-time park naturalist for almost two years—he spends his days researching and designing new programs for the park, and is always available to answer the public's questions.

While Steinberg is the park's resident reptile and amphibian expert, he maintains that all parts of the park are equally exciting. He loves to spot a moose or hear the wolves howl late at night, but he's equally fascinated by observing the everyday functioning of the ecosystem.

FAST FACTS: Algonquin Provincial Park

ATMs   There are no ATMs in the park itself; the closest machines are east of the park in Whitney, or west of the park in Huntsville. That said, many of the stores and outfitters take debit card payment, so you don't need a lot of hard cash.

Gas Stations   In the park itself, both **The Portage Store** on Canoe Lake and the **Opeongo Store** on Lake Opeongo sell gasoline. There are gas stations all along Highway 60 to the east and west of the park, and by the time you get to Huntsville or Whitney they're all over the place.

Car Trouble/Towing Services   For towing and off-road recovery, **Pretty's Towing** (✆ 800/410-7114 or ✆ 705/635-2173) in Dwight dispatches trucks 24 hours a day. They serve the whole of Algonquin Park, and have a licensed mechanic on the premises.

Emergencies   Dial park staff at ✆ 705/633-5583 (or ✆ 705/633-5070) between 8am and 4:30pm. At all other times contact the Ontario Provincial Police at ✆ 888/310-1122. In case of fire, notify a park warden immediately, or call ✆ 705/457-2107. The Ontario Poison Control hotline is ✆ 800/267-1373. Ambulances can be dispatched from either Huntsville (✆ 705/789-9694) to the west or Barry's Bay (✆ 613/756-3090) to the east.

Medical Services   There is no medical center in the park, but all park offices are equipped with first-aid kits, and there is a trained first-response team that can be contacted by any park employee. The closest hospitals are west of the park in Huntsville and east of the park in Barry's Bay. **Huntsville Hospital** (✆ 705/789-2311) is 43 kilometers (26.6 miles) from the West Gate, and is located at 354 Muskoka Road 3, half a kilometer north of the intersection with Highway 60. **St. Francis Memorial** hospital (✆ 613-756-3044) in Barry's Bay is 55 kilometers (34 miles) from the East Gate, and is located on Siberia Road. To find it follow the signs in town.

Telephones   There are payphones located all along the Parkway Corridor, at all campsites, and at most access points. All of the lodges and outfitters in the park have payphones, as do both gates, the Visitor Centre, and the Logging Museum.

Note that unless you have satellite coverage, your cell phone will not work within park boundaries.

Weather/Fire Bans   Both gates, the Visitor Centre, all the campsites, and all the access points have the latest weather posted on-premises—this is essential for trippers looking to micro-plan their adventures. To hear the latest weather on the radio, tune into the **CBC** at **94.3 FM** on the west side of the park, or **98.5 FM** on the east side. To find out about possible campfire bans in the interior, you can listen to the **park radio station** at **102.7 FM,** or you can ask any park warden.

Photo Supplies   **Cavalcade Color Lab** in Huntsville (34 King William Street; ℂ **705/789-9603;** www.cavalcade.on.ca) is a one-hour photo lab and camera store. On the other side of the park, **Barry's Bay Photo** (19566 Opeongo Road; ℂ **613/ 756-2015**) in Barry's Bay also develops film. There are numerous places in the park itself to buy film, including the Visitor Centre, the Portage Store, and the Opeongo Store.

Post Office   Both the Visitor Centre and the Logging Museum have post boxes where you can mail your letters, though the closest official **Canada Post** offices are in Whitney (ℂ **613/637-2951**) and Dwight (ℂ **705/635-1350**). If it's just stamps you're after, the Visitor Centre, the Logging Museum, and all the park stores (see "Supplies," below) sell them—along with a dizzying array of postcards on which to adorn them.

Supplies   There are three places to get supplies within the park itself. **The Lake of Two Rivers Store** (ℂ **705/633-5728;** K 31), is open summers 7am to 9pm. On top of running a rather colorless snack bar, the store rents bikes and stocks basic groceries, ice, fishing tackle, camping supplies, Mountie book-ends, and wildlife T-shirts. Both the **Portage Store** (ℂ **705/633-5622**) on Canoe Lake and the **Opeongo Store** (ℂ **613/637-2075**) on Lake Opeongo can take care of all your one-stop camping needs. They sell perishable, dried, and canned food; ice; gasoline; fishing gear; lots of camping supplies; and clothing. Other supply shops line Highway 60 east and west of the park, and both Huntsville and Whitney have supermarkets and camping stores. Huntsville also has a **Canadian Tire** (ℂ **705/789-5566**) on the corner of Highway 60 and Muskoka Road 3.

Some of the most interesting residents in the ecosystem are the many rare species of birds that thrive within the park's boundaries—the park has developed a worldwide reputation as an excellent base for birdwatchers. Steinberg suggests that birdwatchers stake out some of the park's best places for bird watching: the airfield behind Mew Lake, the road heading toward Opeongo Lake, the abandoned rail track, and, of course, Mizzy Lake trail.

Steinberg also offers an insider's view on the park's best hiking, camping, and canoeing for the visitor who wants to fully enjoy the park's varied flora and fauna. In his opinion, the best and most accessible hiking trails lie along the Highway 60 corridor. He also notes that most campers stick to the corridor and rarely trek in to the interior sites, like the ones around Big Trout and White Trout lakes—a good thing to keep in mind if you're looking for a relatively isolated site during the summer months.

For a terrific day trip by canoe, Steinberg suggests putting in at the East Beach at Lake of Two Rivers, traveling down the Madawaska, and ending up in Whitefish Lake (approximately 4–5 hours). Hermit Creek (on the south side of Opeongo Lake) is another excellent starting point for a short canoe jaunt; put in at the Outfitters at Opeongo. You're likely to spot lots of wildlife on this route, and you'll also see a fascinating array of lilypads—one of the largest displays in the park.

For many visitors—especially those who are bringing kids—the best time to come is during the summer, to fully benefit from the park's excellent interpretation programs. Most of the naturalists are specialists in areas like fungus and mushroom hunting, bird watching and identification, moose education, or simply identifying the trees along the trails, and they are always willing to share their knowledge or answer questions.

Again offering an insider's view, Steinberg suggests two not-to-miss activities in the park. First is the guided canoe tours—they create a completely different platform for exploring and learning all about the park (see section 6, "Guided Canoe Trips & Hikes," in chapter 2, "Planning Your Trip"). Second is the public wolf howls: these are rare (the naturalists spend weeks tracking the pack), so if you are lucky enough to see one posted drop everything to attend—you're promised some wild excitement as the wolves howl back and forth with the naturalists (see "Howling with the Wolves" in chapter 4, "Outdoor Pursuits in Algonquin Park").

Steinberg encourages visitors to remember that whenever the Visitor Centre is open, there is most likely a park naturalist in the house—if you ever have questions or concerns, or simply would like help planning a canoe route or other itinerary, go on in. If you're confused as to whether to ask for a "park ranger" or a "park naturalist," here's a bit of clarification. The term "park ranger" is a throwback to an older system of park management, in which rangers were responsible for all aspects of running the park (national parks in the United States still have park rangers). In Ontario, the traditional job of the ranger has been divided into three areas: park wardens, park maintainers, and park naturalists. In 1940, Algonquin's first park naturalist center was opened (in a tent!) and today employs two full-time naturalists, seven seasonal naturalists, and many junior naturalists. "Ranger" is outdated and no longer used—but it will get a grin from the naturalists, who realize that for most Canadians the term conjures up images of Yogi Bear, with his pork-pie hat, laid-back attitude . . . and pic-a-nic basket.

3 The Visitor Centre

Opened in 1993, the **Visitor Centre** (© **613/637-2828**) is Algonquin Park's premier educational attraction. It is located south of the Parkway Corridor (at K 43), a 5- to 10-minute drive from the East Gate. The facility is both impressive and free; it's practically impossible to come away from it without having learned something interesting about the park's history and ecosystem. The Centre's observation deck offers a breathtaking and unspoiled view of a typical slice of Algonquin Park—on a clear day, it feels like you can see for kilometers.

Your Algonquin Park education begins with a series of excellent natural history dioramas that neatly divide the park into its separate hardwood, pine, and spruce bog ecological zones. All the animal and plant inhabitants of the park are lovingly detailed in their natural habitats: the black bear, the wolf, the moose—even the beaver, whose cross-sectioned lodge is itself worth the visit. Then comes the park history, reproduced with a full complement of educational tools: short films, photos, models, dramatic recreations, and a talking logger dummy named Emile. Kids especially love Emile; they often make fun of his outrageous French-Canadian accent.

The center has other draws: a small theater, which every 15 minutes or so plays a short introductory film about the park; a large

bookstore run by the Friends of Algonquin Park; a terrific panoramic view of the park itself; and a relatively inexpensive cafeteria (see chapter 6, "Lodging & Dining Inside the Park"). In addition, park naturalists occasionally give talks in the Centre throughout the day—it's usually possible to spot one in a corner, playing around with some bark or a few dead beetles. In the Algonquin Room, the Centre hosts exhibitions of art inspired by the beauty of the park. The Visitor Centre is open daily from 9am to 9pm, from mid-June to early September. In late May and September it's open daily from 10am to 6pm (10am–5pm in early May and October). The rest of the year it's open only on weekends from 10am to 5pm, except during Christmas and Easter breaks, when it's open daily from 10am to 5pm. For exact seasonal hours, call the center at
© 613/637-2828.

4 The Highlights

Algonquin Park is unique in the world for two things: its sheer abundance of wildlife, and the number of connecting lake and river systems. You can experience both of these things while visiting the park by renting yourself a canoe and seeing the landscape (and, if you're lucky, some of its inhabitants) from the water. You don't need to strike out deep into the interior to do this; there are plenty of quiet rivers and lakes accessible from the Highway 60 corridor that can be navigated by rental canoe—see chapter 4, "Outdoor Pursuits in Algonquin Park," for more information about day canoe routes. If you are in the interior there are some broad, vigorous lakes that are considered to be quintessentially Algonquin: **Manitou, Travers, Louisa, Proulx, Cedar, Big Trout, Opeongo,** and **Lavieille,** to name a few. Early in the morning these shorelines (indeed, everywhere in the park) stir with wildlife: moose grazing in the lowlands, otters on the banks, loons trilling on the water. Of the interpretive trails along the Parkway Corridor designed specifically with wildlife viewing in mind, the **Mizzy Lake Trail** is the best.

The **Barron Canyon** on the road to Achray is perhaps the park's most stunning natural feature. Begun as a fault in the earth's crust, the canyon was further excavated by a raging glacial river that at one time poured a volume of water equal to a thousand Niagaras through the narrow outlet. The canyon can be viewed either by canoe from below or from above on the **Barron Canyon Trail** (see chapter 4, "Outdoor Pursuits in Algonquin Park").

Before the arrival of the loggers, the eastern half of Algonquin was bristling with giant white pines over 40 meters (132 feet) tall. A couple of **virgin stands** of these pines still exist, though they're accessible only by canoe. One sits off the **Crow River,** to the east of Big Crow Lake (see the "Opeongo–Proulx–Big Crow–Opeongo" route in chapter 5, "Camping in the Interior," for a fuller description), and the other can be found at the south end of the park near **Dividing Lake.** (There is also a 350-year-old stand of **virgin red pine** at the east side of **Dickson Lake**). For those on the Parkway Corridor, a number of impressive white pines can be seen on the newly opened **Big Pines Trail** across from Rock Lake road at K 40.

5 Driving the Parkway Corridor

The **Parkway Corridor,** also known as the Frank MacDougall Parkway, is a 56-kilometer (34.7-mile) section of Highway 60 that crosses the southwestern edge of the park. It is the only part of the park developed specifically with tourism in mind; from here it is possible to enjoy the park without any of the strenuous concerns of interior camping. Reflective kilometer markers along the Parkway Corridor refer to distances from the West Gate; they are used in this book to refer to the exact location of various services along the highway.

Tips Kilometer Markings

Reflective signs along the Parkway Corridor (the stretch of Highway 60 that runs between the West and East Gates) indicate the distance in kilometers from the West Gate. Points of interest in this book that lie along the Parkway Corridor have these kilometer markings as reference. For example, the Visitor Centre is located at K 43.

On roads leading away from the highway and on the Parkway Corridor itself are a number of organized **campgrounds** and **picnic areas,** most of them located on lakes and rivers with views into the park. This is also where the majority of the park's **interpretive trails** are located; found at the head of each one are mini-guides that describe the standout natural and historic features of the trail. The **Logging Museum,** the **Visitor Centre, The Portage Store,** the **Opeongo Store,** the **Harkness Fish Research Laboratory,** and the three **lodges** are all accessible from the highway. For a full list of activities along the Parkway Corridor see chapter 4, "Outdoor Pursuits in Algonquin Park."

Driving the Corridor is also an excellent way to see **wildlife,** especially if you do so during the prime animal viewing times: early morning and dusk. Low, wet regions are good for viewing moose and beaver, in particular the area around **Eucalia Lake** just west of the Lookout Trail.

6 Out on the Periphery

Although the area surrounding the Parkway Corridor gets the most visitor traffic, it represents only a small portion of the Algonquin landscape. At least 20 other access points are located around the periphery of the park; many of these are worth a visit in their own right. Here are brief descriptions of three of the most popular:

ACHRAY

The east side of Algonquin park is lower and drier than the west side; as a result the forest is mostly pine, with a complement of big oak trees and slender poplars. After the Parkway Corridor, Achray has more facilities than any other area of the park. A lovely **campground** overlooks Grand Lake, with a long beach and spectacular vistas across the lake. The park runs an **interpretive program** here on summer weekends, with kids' programs during the day and guided hikes on the trails. Program information is posted at the Achray campground, at the Sand Lake Gate, and at the Achray Access Office.

There are two interpretive walking trails on this side of the park: the magnificent **Barron Canyon Trail,** located 28 kilometers (17.4 miles) west of the Sand Lake Gate, and the equally beautiful —if more modest—**Berm Lake Trail,** which begins at the Achray campground parking lot. The **Eastern Pines Backpacking Trail** offers hikers a 17-kilometer (10.5-mile) loop past great blue heron and osprey nests, with an optional (and highly recommended) excursion down to the rock pools and natural waterslide of **High Falls.** This side of the park is also an excellent departure point for **canoe trips,** whether they are 2- or 3-day trips around Grand Lake or to Barron Canyon, longer trips along the Petawawa River from Lake Travers, or day trips around Achray. There are no outfitters around Achray; the closest canoe rental place is **Algonquin Portage** on the road in from Pembroke.

BRENT

The Brent access point is located at the far north end of the park on Cedar Lake. Once a bustling lumber town, the site of the Kish-Kaduk Lodge and a stop on the now-defunct Canadian Northern Railway, Brent's fortunes have declined and all that remains now are a few low buildings, an outfitting and supply store, a 29-site drive-in **campground,** and a large historic **ranger cabin.** But there are other reasons to visit the area, notably Cedar Lake itself. The lake is pure Algonquin: rugged and broad, the whitewater Petawawa River draining out of its eastern end.

The road into Brent is also the jump-off point for the **Brent Crater Trail.** The only interpretive trail at the north end of the park, it offers an observation tower that hikers can climb and look out across the outline of a vast crater, formed 450 million years ago when a meteorite crashed into the forest.

SOUTH ALGONQUIN

Bad access has kept a lot of people from visiting South Algonquin in the past, but in recent years the road has improved and a number of new park facilities have sprung up. The combination of excellent scenery and relatively few visitors make this part of the park well worth exploring.

Kingscote Lake is the main leaping-off point for trips into the south Algonquin interior. There is a small **campground** at the southern end of the lake, not far from the access point. The lake itself is ringed with paddle-in campsites. If you're canoeing in the area keep a lookout for red-shouldered hawks; at least three pairs have nests in the area—a bonus for birding enthusiasts since the birds are rare elsewhere in the park. Both Big Rock Lake and Scorch Lake can be reached within a day or two by canoe. Scorch Lake has two hiking trails: the short (under 1 kilometer [0.6 mile]) but steep **Scorch Lake Lookout Trail,** which winds through a gnarled oak forest before ending at a stunning view of the lake, and the 2.5-kilometer (1.5-mile) **Bruton Farm Hiking Trail,** which takes hikers up to the remains of an old farm depot dating back to the 1870s.

There is another access road to the east of Kingscote that leads to a **horseback riding trail,** the **High Falls Hiking Trail,** and the 5-kilometer (3.1-mile) **Byers Lake Mountain Bike Trail.** This area is spectacular in the winter; the **Algonquin Nordic Wilderness Lodge** (© 705/745-9497) maintains more than 80 kilometers (50 miles) of **cross-country ski trails,** which you can read about in chapter 4, "Outdoor Pursuits in Algonquin Park."

For more information about the South Algonquin trails and amenities, contact park information and they'll send you a free *South Algonquin* park brochure.

7 Historical Attractions

Although there are 48 official "historical zones" in the park, most physical evidence of Algonquin's history is hidden away in the park interior, often far from the Parkway Corridor. There are a few exceptions to this—notably the **Logging Museum** and the **Visitor Centre**—but for the most part the past in Algonquin must be sought out. This is not a bad thing. Algonquin Indian vision pits, scattered mill and farm remains, abandoned railway beds, and extinct lodges are stumbled upon suddenly and mysteriously; this adds an element of the unexpected to park explorations, making you feel a little like an amateur archaeologist set loose in the ruins of a once-flourishing civilization. These ruins mark the different stages of the park's history, from native settlement to the arrival of British surveyors in the early 1800s, through to the loggers, the settlers, the rangers, and the pleasure-seekers.

Fun Fact **Algonquin, Tracking a People & a Name**

No one is exactly sure what the word *Algonquin* means, though the interpretation usually given is "the place of spearing fish from the bow of a canoe." This is an appropriate designation given the Algonquin landscape, but it may not be the correct one. The problem is that a derivative of the word *algonquin* exists in the Micmac language (a tribe located 1,500 kilometers (930 miles) east, in the Maritimes), but not in the Algonquin language itself.

The name made its first appearance on paper in the journals of French explorer Samuel de Champlain, who met a group of native peoples on the shore of the St. Lawrence in 1603. These were members of the Montagnais nation who were returning from a victorious raid on the Iroquois, and were in full celebratory mood. Their ritual dancing stopped Champlain in his tracks, and he wrote in his journal: "...suddenly all the women and girls proceeded to cast off their mantles of skins and stripped themselves stark naked, showing their privities, but retaining their ornaments of matachias...." In this account is a clue to the possible origins of the Algonquin name. Hypnotized by the flashing privities and matachias, Champlain may have asked "Who are these people?" His Etchemin translators responded: "*a'llegon kin*," which means in their dialect, "those who are doing the dance." And so the misnomer stuck.

For the French, "Algonquian" became the language group that referred to all 30 of the nations living in northeastern North America, from the Cree to the Ojibwa to the Nipissing. But the true Algonquins were a people who lived north and south of the Ottawa River. The name of that great river was mistakenly used to refer to a tribe further west, and so the Algonquins lost the most direct association with their heritage. This was to be the first of many indignities suffered.

The greatest upheaval in the lives of these relatively peaceful nomadic hunters came in 1647 when they were attacked by the Iroquois, who were seeking to expand their fur-trapping territory in order to meet the demands of their European trading partners. This was genocide; the Algonquin population was almost totally wiped out, its few surviving members scattered across Quebec.

In the 1690s the Iroquois were driven out of Ontario by the Ojibwa, and so the remaining Algonquins slowly returned to the area and resumed their traditional hunting practices. This peace would not last long; disease and alcoholism continued to reduce the tribal ranks, and eventually the Algonquins were pushed out altogether by expanding European settlement (this was a clear betrayal, since after the British defeated the French in 1760 they promised in the "Articles of Capitulation" that the natives could keep their lands and would not be molested upon them).

By the end of the 19th century the Algonquins numbered fewer than 1,300. Their descendants settled at Desert Lake north of the Ottawa River and Golden Lake on the Bonnechere River, in areas that would become reservations. A 1986 census found 5,000 Algonquins living in reservations in Quebec and Ontario, most of them far from their traditional homelands.

Sources: Roderick MacKay and William Reynolds, *Algonquin* (Boston Mills Press, 1995); Peter Hessel, *The Algonkin Tribe* (Kichesippi Books, 1987)

Historical Attractions in the Park

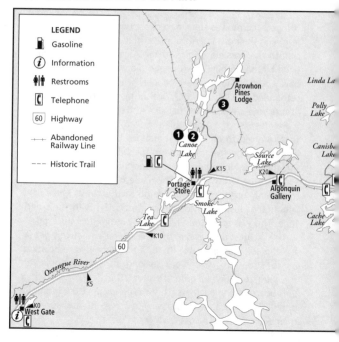

The earliest inhabitants of Algonquin Park were the Laurentian Archaic Peoples, who camped on the shores of Radiant Lake 5,000 years ago. The density of wildlife made the area perfect for seasonal settlement; years later the semi-sedentary Algonquin peoples (for more about the Algonquin peoples, see "Algonquin, Tracking a People and a Name," above) would summer and harvest crops in the milder south, moving north into the park during the winter, the moose and hare tracks easy to follow in the snow.

Across from the Rock Lake campground, just below where the Madawaska River enters Rock Lake, are a group of 31 **Algonquin Indian vision pits,** one of the few remaining traces of the park's oldest inhabitants. During puberty and other significant rites, the Algonquins would lie in these small depressions, fasting and waiting for their spirit totems to bring them visions. The pits themselves are not that impressive; they are filled with debris and are difficult to make out. To find the pits, land your canoe just before the first of the cottages on the west side of the lake and follow the flagging tape

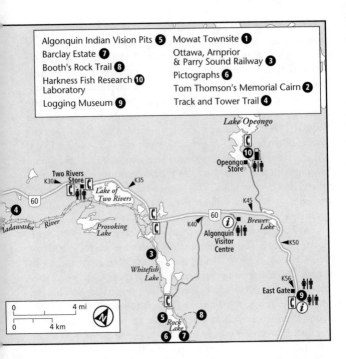

Algonquin Indian Vision Pits **5**   Mowat Townsite **1**
Barclay Estate **7**   Ottawa, Arnprior
Booth's Rock Trail **8**   & Parry Sound Railway **3**
Harkness Fish Research **10**   Pictographs **6**
Laboratory   Tom Thomson's Memorial Cairn **2**
Logging Museum **9**   Track and Tower Trail **4**

north along the shoreline. More dramatic are the rock piles left by the natives to commemorate their visions. These can be found on the ridge to the southwest of the pits, also marked by orange flagging tape (usually).

The Algonquins (though it's possible they may have been Ojibwa) also left evidence of their early presence in the form of **pictographs** painted onto lakeside granite shoulders. They were once visible on the west side of Rock Lake across from the old **Barclay Estate.** And it is still possible to make out a few symbols on the north side of Carcajou Bay below Grand Lake at the Achray access point.

The **Visitor Centre** has many impressive historical dioramas, including one that shows the layout of an Algonquin hunting camp. The excellent educational displays cover the full sweep of park history, from first peoples through to the first rangers in their lonely cabin posts (to read more about the Visitor Centre, see "The Visitor Centre," above).

The area's abundance of enormous white pines drew the next wave of Algonquin inhabitants: the loggers. Fueled by the needs of the British shipbuilding industry, teams of rough-hewn loggers set upon the trees in the 1830s, and ever since the forest has been ringing with their activity (though they're more covert nowadays). Artifacts from the height of the logging era can be found throughout the park: the rotted scaffolding of old log chutes (between Smoke and Ragged Lakes), the silent bulk of a grounded tug boat-type craft silted up by the water's edge (at the south end of Burntroot Lake), the structural tracing of abandoned farm depots. At one time more than half the able-bodied men in Canada spent their winters grappling with the big pines. This way of life has been captured and recreated at what is without the doubt the park's finest historic attraction: the Logging Museum.

The **Logging Museum** is located just inside the East Gate, north of the highway. The museum itself is both a log reception building and a 1.3-kilometer (0.8-mile) trail, with exhibits arrayed along its length. The reception houses a small book and gift shop, four "minidioramas" that detail select aspects of Algonquin's logging history, and a cozy theater. A 10-minute film full of jerky black-and-white footage introduces visitors to the loggers of yesteryear, and brings the discussion up to modern times. At the end of the film the screen and back wall rise to reveal the open trail beyond. Visitors can then walk past relics and reproductions from the logging past: camboose shanties, log chutes, squared timbers, old stables, rickety sleighs, a very cool steam-powered warping tug or "alligator," and lots of plastic horses. Overall the walk is a pleasant one; it winds its way slowly past a pretty lake and through a pine forest (suspiciously devoid of big trees).

The next most conspicuous legacy of Algonquin's logging past is the old Ottawa, Arnprior & Parry Sound Railway, built by Canadian timber baron J.R. Booth between 1894 and 1896. Once the busiest railway line in Canada, all that now remains are cleared sections of forest, some overgrown abutments, and the occasional trestle. The 7.7-kilometer (4.8-mile) **Track and Tower Trail** (with an optional 5.5-kilometer [3.4-mile] side trail) is designed to showcase this period of the park's history. A section of the trail follows the old railway line, passing two wooden trestles and the site of the Skymount fire tower. Much more besides is discussed in the trail guide, including the once-glorious Highland Inn, which at its peak in the 1930s had more than 100 bedrooms filled with chattering socialites. **Booth's Rock Trail** features another once-grand structure, now reduced to cement foundations: the old Barclay Estate. For more about these two trails, see chapter 4, "Outdoor Pursuits in Algonquin Park."

(**Fun Fact**   **The Baron & the Trees**
_____

There is a famous black-and-white photo of a 98-year-old J.R. Booth inspecting an order of timber. With his stern face, full white beard, tightly buttoned greatcoat, and pointed malacca cane he looks every inch the vigorous and self-made lumber baron. At one time, J.R. Booth was at the head of the largest company in the world owned by a single man—it was worth millions of dollars, employed more than 1,500 people, and was responsible for producing more than a million feet of sawn lumber every day.

His relentless business sense changed the face of Algonquin Park—indeed, the park's trees contributed to his success. Booth owned a huge chunk of timber in the area. In 1892, fed up with the slow progress of river drives, he decided to build a faster route to his Ottawa mills—a railway. Getting through 635 kilometers (394 miles) of Precambrian rock was no mean engineering feat, but by 1897 the **Ottawa, Arnprior & Parry Sound Railway** was fully operational. The line soon became one of the busiest in Canada. Wheat and timber were shipped from west to east, at one time so densely packed on the tracks that a train passed every 20 minutes. When the line finally closed in 1959, long after J.R. Booth's death in 1925, the park was a different place. There were more tourists now than loggers. The railway had helped bring them in.

In the northwest corner of Canoe Lake is the old **Mowat Townsite,** once a sprawling settlement of 500 people and the location of the first park headquarters. When the Gilmour Lumber Company went bankrupt at the turn of the 20th century and the mill closed, the spot was claimed by tourist prospectors. Mowat Lodge was opened in 1913; it hired as its most famous guide the doomed painter, woodsman, and Canadian icon Tom Thomson. Unfortunately, Tom's bad luck was passed on to the lodge—it burned down twice, and the site was finally abandoned to ghosts in 1930. Now all that remains are a few crumbling foundations and a scattering of chimney rubble.

Directly across from the site on a narrow peninsula with a spectacular view of Canoe Lake is probably the park's most famous historical landmark: **Tom Thomson's memorial cairn.** Tom drowned in Canoe Lake in July 1917, and his body was recovered not far from where the cairn itself stands. Several months after his death, a group of his artist friends (some of whom would later become known as the Group of Seven) erected a monument to the artist at his favorite campsite. Pilgrims to the cairn can tie up at the small dock and make their way up the footpath. The cairn is located next to a faded totem pole, erected by counselors from a nearby camp in 1930 (for more about "The Life & Mysterious Death of Tom Thomson," see below).

One of the park's most enduring features is the **Harkness Laboratory of Fisheries Research,** which has operated within the park for nearly 75 years. Located at the southern end of Lake Opeongo, it was originally set up by the provincial Ministry of Natural Resources as a research post to collect data for the management of Algonquin's fisheries. It now serves as a base for scientists from around the world who come to conduct research projects involving everything from zooplankton to birds to wetlands (and, of course, fish!). Park guests who visit the lab can get some hands-on experience taking water samples from the lake, testing water temperatures, and tracking lake trout. The hour-long Zodiak trip to the middle of Lake Opeongo is extremely educational—but not to the point of boredom!—and you'll leave with more knowledge about fish and plankton than you'll ever know what to do with (not to mention a free Harkness Labs pin).

The last historical sites of note in the park are the only ones that can be slept in: the **ranger cabins.** In the early 1900s, dozens of cabins were built in the Algonquin interior to accommodate patrolling rangers. Pairs of rangers would spend their summers and winters moving from cabin to cabin, keeping a lookout for poachers and forest fires. When the practice was discontinued in the 1940s, the cabins were left to rot. In the mid-1990s, the park found a way to preserve 13 of them: by renting them to the public. The cabins are scattered around the park, with only three accessible by car and not canoe (Rain Lake, Kiosk, and Brent). Details of each cabin's history can be found in the individual cabins themselves (see chapter 6, "Lodging & Dining Inside the Park," for more details).

8 Art in the Park

In 1885, future Algonquin Park founder Alexander Kirkwood observed a "gloomy grandeur" in the national forest, "the noble pines and stately oaks bespeak the growth of centuries." This "gloomy grandeur" has been one of the magnets of attraction for artists virtually since the park's conception. It is an artistic heritage that's still strong today; there are galleries in and around the park, and several organizations run artist workshops deep in the forest itself.

Tom Thomson was the first artist to celebrate Algonquin Park's distinct landscape, and his enthusiasm was contagious. Between 1914 and 1917, Thomson introduced the park to several friends whom he had worked with in Toronto's commercial art industry: **Arthur Lismer, A.Y. Jackson,** and **Frederick Varley.** He would lead the artists on painting explorations of the interior, their canoes laden with canvas and paints. The vivid impressionist colors and naturalistic style of the paintings that emerged from these sessions were something new in Canadian art; indeed, they led to the formation of the first and best-known Canadian art movement. Initially called the "Algonquin School" to honor the source of their inspiration, those original Algonquin painters banded together with several more friends after World War I and formed the **Group of Seven.** Many of the lakes in Algonquin are still named after some of the founding members: Tom Thomson (who would have been a member had he lived), Lismer, MacDonald, Varley. Since then Canadian artists have ransacked the wilds for inspiration, and Algonquin Park has been high on the list of destinations.

There are several galleries in and around the park. The **Visitor Centre** has a small (free) exhibition space to the left of the entrance that features works of local artists. The very popular **Oxtongue Craft Cabin and Gallery** (© **705/635-1602;** fax 705/635-2183; www.oxtonguecraftcabin.on.ca) south of Dwight is a mecca for seekers of Canadiana. The rustic log cabin itself is practically buried under woodsy trinkets, and the interior is brimming with lovely stained glass, paintings and prints, jewelry, pottery, leather goods, and wood-carved ducks. Prices range enormously, from C$4 (US$3.00) painted stones and C$8 (US$5.90) fridge magnets to C$650 (US$482.10) custom-designed paddles. All works are by

Canadians artists, from sea to shining sea. To get there take Highway 60 west out of the park toward Dwight, turn left (south) on Highway 35 and then right (west) on Fox Point Road. In the summer, the gallery is open Monday to Saturday from 10am to 5pm; Sunday from 1pm to 5pm. Call for spring and autumn seasonal hours.

Fun Fact **The Life & Mysterious Death of Tom Thomson**

In the years since his passing, Tom Thomson's paintings and the facts of his life have ballooned into a national cottage industry of adulation and mythology. In the same way that his paintings seemed a distillation of Algonquin's raw landscape, Thomson's relationship to the wilderness seemed to represent something uniquely Canadian—a spiritual ideal for the nation.

Between 1912 and 1917, Thomson's hand-painted gray-blue canoe was a familiar sight in Algonquin Park. When he wasn't fishing or working as a guide, Thomson could be found somewhere onshore, hunched over a birchbark panel. He loved the land and was comfortable within it; many nights he would sleep in his canoe, noiselessly drifting beneath the stars.

Of his finished sketches he was a bit ambivalent—he'd leave them in the bush as often as not, and gave them away if anyone expressed interest. It is often said he was more proud of his fishing than his artistic abilities. In the end, it was his fishing that doomed him.

On a calm summer morning in July 1917, Thomson was seen leaving Mowat Lodge on one of his solo fishing expeditions. Later that same day his canoe was spotted overturned on Canoe Lake. Of Thomson there was no trace; eight days later his body rose to the surface, a large bruise on his temple and a spool of copper fishing line wrapped 17 times around one swollen ankle.

In the inquest that followed, accidental drowning was judged to be the cause of death. For many this was an unsatisfactory conclusion—Thomson was a strong swimmer and an expert canoeist, and the waters that day were level and smooth. Seeding more doubt was the bizarre nature of the inquest itself—it took place two days *after* the body was buried and then exhumed, and some who carried the casket claimed it was too light to contain a body.

His death triggered a storm of speculation, one that has not abated to this day. Did Thomson commit suicide? Was he murdered? There is some circumstantial evidence to support foul play. Though it was not common knowledge at the time, Tom was seeing a local cottager named Winnifred Trainor, a tall and comely woman who may also have been the object of affection of one Martin Bletcher. The portrait of Bletcher that survives is not terribly sympathetic: mean, hot-tempered, and pro-German (a villainous trait in 1917's pacifist circles). Thomson and Bletcher are known to have argued violently the night before the artist's disappearance, and Bletcher could well have known where Thomson was headed the next day. What's more, it was Bletcher and his sister who reported the upturned canoe to the authorities—two full days after they claim to have first spotted it.

Thomson's 1970 biographer William Little believes Bletcher killed Thomson, either by accident or design. One theory goes that the two men met somewhere on the portage trail and had an argument that ended with Thomson brained by a paddle. Bletcher disposed of the body by binding heavy stones to one leg and dropping it into the lake. But in a shallow lake it's hard to keep a good man down.

There is a final haunting addendum: Tom's restless spirit is said to still patrol Canoe Lake. Witnesses all claim to see the same thing: a gray-blue canoe gliding through the mist, its paddler's gaze fixed on a faraway shore.

For fledgling artists, the park also plays host to two organizations specializing in art courses and workshops. **The Algonquin Academy of Wilderness and Wildlife Art** (© 888/696-4255, ext. **2252** or © 705/789-1751, ext. 2252;) in Huntsville combines "a high level of instruction" with "inspirational wilderness settings." They offer C$25 (US$18.55) sketching hikes every Wednesday in the park, and longer 5-day immersion courses on the portage trail for C$925 (US$686), all outfitting, meals, park fees, instruction, and materials included. **Northern Edge Algonquin** (© 800/ **953-3343;** fax 705/386-1597; www.algonquincanada.com) offers similar trips into Algonquin Park—featuring, in addition to paint-ing, instruction in creative writing, drum making, mixed media, and "yoga and nature sculpture." For experienced artists simply looking for supplies, **North Art** (ⓒ **800/628-5681** or ⓒ 705/788-0726), located at 6 West Street North in Huntsville's town center, sells high-quality paints, canvases, brushes, pastels, frames, and stained-glass materials.

4

Outdoor Pursuits in Algonquin Park

For wilderness enthusiasts, the sheer number of available outdoor activities boggles the mind. Algonquin Park is like a gigantic natural amusement park run by an elite corps of inconspicuous wilderness facilitators. It's big and wild and, metaphorically speaking, full of rides. Your choice of vehicles: the canoe, the hiking boot, the ski, the snowshoe, the mountain bike, the horse, the dog sled, just to name a few.

Although most of the organized activities in the park take place along the Parkway Corridor, basic Algonquin activities—fishing, canoeing, swimming, picnicking, and hiking—can also be done from most peripheral access points. For activities that require specifically designed trails—mountain biking, cross-country skiing, horseback riding—the Parkway Corridor, South Algonquin, or the Barron Canyon road are the main departure points. The park interpretive trails are concentrated along Highway 60, as are many of the best day canoe trips. For information about exploring the park's 2,100 kilometers (1,302 miles) of interior canoe routes or 140 kilometers (87 miles) of backpacking trails, see chapter 5, "Camping in the Interior."

1 Picnicking & Swimming

Okay, picnicking is a fairly sedentary activity, but it's one that's dear to many park visitors. There are six official lunch-consumption spots along the Parkway Corridor, all with sturdy picnic benches, public toilets, garbage cans, and long views of the Algonquin wilderness. If nothing else, you can always cop out and picnic at the East Beach picnic area, with its brand-spanking-new log building and well-sheltered picnicking areas right at the beach on Lake of Two Rivers. Just off the 60 Corridor, with pristine, newly built picnic tables and sheltered overhead, the East Beach offers the not-so-brave individual a haven from the sometimes harsh elements of the park. Many of the campgrounds also have picnic areas, some of them more interesting than the six designated sites—**Rock Lake Campground,** for example, has a great snacking area right on the water. Some of these spots are also excellent swimming locations, so 40 minutes after your meal you can burn a few calories in a bracing freshwater dip.

The best of the six official picnic spots is **Tea Lake Dam Picnic Ground** at K 8. Big stone barbecue pits overlook Oxtongue River and a discreet concrete dam. It's quiet, scenic, and remote, with a river swimming area below the dam. Both the **Lake of Two Rivers Picnic Ground** and **East Beach picnic area** are excellent for swimming, with long sandy beaches leading into the vaguely yellow lake water (caused by high iron content—not a safety concern). The large western site is located right off the highway; the eastern one, located off a short side road, is smaller and more private. The **Canisbay Lake Picnic Grounds** is tucked in next to the campground and is another good site for privacy-seekers. The **Oxtongue River Picnic Ground** is pleasant enough; it's located right at the head of the Western Upland Backpacking Trail, a big grassy open area facing an arching wooden footbridge. If there is one site to skip it's the **Costello Creek Picnic Ground:** no swimming, no view, no space, no thanks. You're much better off eating your lunch at the **Visitor Centre** down the road, standing on the balcony overlooking the park. **The Portage Store** is another good spot; they have a few benches in a screened-in area next to the store. Finally, if you're heading out of Algonquin, consider stopping in at **Ragged Falls Park** a few kilometers west of the West Gate. The star attraction here is a large waterfall tumbling over dark boulders. The falls are a 5- to 10-minute walk from the parking lot, and though I couldn't see any picnic benches, the dramatic scenery more than compensates. It is also an exciting place to swim. There are a number of rock pools formed by the falls, frothy with white water and perfect for dipping.

2 Parkway Corridor Day Hikes

There are two kinds of walking trails in Algonquin Park: the longer overnight backpacking trails discussed in chapter 5, and the shorter self-guided **interpretive trails** discussed here and in the next section. These latter trails vary in length, and take anywhere from half an hour to 5 hours to hike. Fourteen of them are located just off the Parkway Corridor, two near Achray, and one at Brent. There are also three trails in South Algonquin, mentioned briefly in chapter 3's section 6, "Out on the Periphery."

In many ways these self-guided trails are the stars of the park interpretive program. Each is designed to explore some aspect of the park environment, and comes with its own handy trail guide written by former Chief Park Naturalist Dan Strickland. Hikers can consult the booklet at each of the points marked along the trail length. All this context is available for the low, low price of 37 cents, and can be picked up at each of the trailhead dispensers.

The trails range from short, level walks to long, steep climbs, and almost all of them are criss-crossed with malevolent roots. In all cases hiking shoes should be worn and the usual supply of water and trail mix brought along in the accompanying knapsack (see section 4, "What to Take," in chapter 2 for a full description of day-hiking supplies). The blue dots and brown arrows are trail markers, indicating which direction to go when there is some ambiguous fork in the path. The trails arranged along the Parkway Corridor are the busiest; on summer holiday weekends it can sometimes seem as if you are queuing through the woods. This can be avoided by starting a little earlier, or by avoiding the Saturday- and Sunday-after-noon peak times.

Bat Lake Trail   Bat Lake Trail is fairy unremarkable—in fact, its commonness is why it was selected to showcase Algonquin Park ecology (and why it is so quiet—many give this trail a miss). The trail passes through a variety of habitats, from conifer to hardwood forest, spruce bog to acid lake. Kilometer 1 travels through white pine and white spruce, the sandier soil supporting a conifer forest more often found at the park's eastern side. After this it's deciduous: the sugar maple, king of the park, proud owner of an inspiring mantle of autumn colors. An eastern hemlock "cathedral grove" starts just short of kilometer 3, and soon gives way to a bog's char-acteristic black spruce and tamarack, the only trees that will grow in the nutrient-poor peat. A short boardwalk crosses the bog, and the next landmark of interest is naturally acidified Bat Lake around kilo-meter 4. Although the lake cannot support fish, it doesn't conform to our usual expectation of a dead lake. This is because it isn't dead—it's day-glow and healthy, positively crawling with larvae, yellow-spotted salamander tadpoles, crustaceans, and algae. The last

Day Hikes in the Park

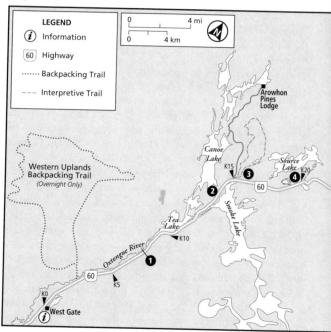

trees of note are the speckled alders, which crowd the final creek-hopping boardwalk. 5 kilometers (3 miles). Easy. Access: Bat Lake Trail parking lot across from Mew Lake (K 30).

Beaver Pond Trail ⚡ *(Kids)*   This trail is fascinating for the insight it provides into the (sometimes) mindlessly industrious life of the beaver. These mammals alter their environment more than any other animal except humans, and this large-scale terra-forming is very much in evidence over the 2-kilometer (1.2-mile) length of the hike. It is a short walk from the parking lot past gnawed beaver stumps to your first view of a beaver pond. To the left is an old dam, and it's possible to make out an overgrown lodge in the clearing. There are better views ahead. A short boardwalk crosses a beaver meadow, grasses and sedges encroaching on what was once all pond and even earlier all forest. It's unlikely this meadow will return to the forest—some busy beaver will come along, rebuild the dam, and flood the area all over again. The result will be a habitat of water-lilies,

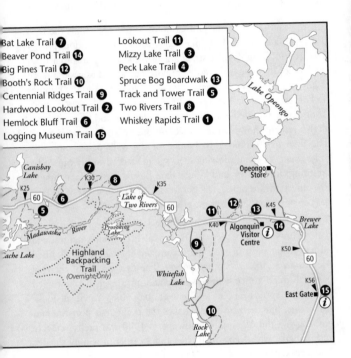

frogs, ducks, great blue herons, moose, dragonflies, and others, all of them flourishing in the unique beaver-created ecosystem. For the next half-kilometer (0.3 mile) or so the walk follows the first beaver pond, crossing over a narrow section just after an impressive beaver dam. The path comes to a point at **Amikeus Lake.** This lake is a more active beaver center. It's possible to make out fresher-looking lodges and, if you're lucky, spot our actual protagonist (look for a narrow V-shape wave in the water). The path continues along the shore before cutting back and up, rising steeply for a few hundred meters to a lovely cliff-top lookout that puts the whole beaver pond habitat in perspective. The final 300 meters (985 feet) are an occasionally steep descent through pine forest to the parking lot. 2 kilometers (1.2 miles). Moderate. Access: Beaver Pond Trail parking lot (K 45).

Big Pines Trail ☆ An easy walk through a very shady forest, the Big Pines Trail passes some 75 full-grown white pines and tells the story of white pine logging in Algonquin Park. Though relatively flat, the trail is a new one and has a lot of roots to tangle the feet. Just under a kilometer (0.6 mile) along is the trail's standout pine: a 37-meter (122- foot) ruler-straight giant. The sitting area that rings the base of the pine is the walk's only rest area, and as good a place as any to ponder your human inferiority complex. About a kilometer farther on, the trail arrives at the remains of an old logging camp. At one time the site held a bunkhouse, cookery, and office, though all that remains now is a rusty stove cordoned off by a wooden fence. The final half-kilometer (0.3 mile) of the walk passes more big pines, many of them showing their age in scars variously caused by lightning, forest fires, and White Pine Blister Rust (a fatal fungus that infects white pines). **2.9 kilometers (1.8 miles). Easy. Access: Big Pines Trail parking lot across from entrance to Rock Lake Road (K 40).**

Booth's Rock Trail ✿   Booth's Rock Trail is a favorite for many park visitors for the variety of its terrain. It combines natural and human-made sites; in fact, the accompanying trail guide is titled *Man and the Algonquin Environment.* The first stretch of the trail passes through a nice hemlock grove and onto a small lake ringed with black spruce (about 1 kilometer [0.6 mile] in). It all looks marvelous, but the trail guide makes the point that post-fire and post-logging the Algonquin landscape of 1900 was pretty scraggly and pathetic, with feeble bent trees and a carpet of wimpy shrubs. The next kilometer wraps past an old farm clearing and a turnoff to **Gordon Lake.** From here it's a fairly steep climb up to the top of Booth's Rock, past a few roots and trees blackened by a 1998 forest fire. The view from the top is amazing—a 180° panoramic sweep over bald rock to **Rock Lake,** an old mill site, and uninterrupted forest. The trail follows the lookout for a while before heading steeply down, a set of stairs making the going a little easier. At the bottom the trail forks right, the left-hand path continuing directly into the architectural remains of the once-sprawling **Barclay Estate** (see chapter 3). The estate, built by a powerful judge and relative of J.R. Booth, is worth checking out. Abandoned in 1953, it's still possible to see the overgrown tennis courts and the large cement dock on Rock Lake where the old judge greeted his guests as they disembarked. Double back to the fork and go left. The last 2 kilometers (1.2 miles) track J.R. Booth's abandoned railway bed all the way to the parking lot. **5.1 kilometers (3.2 miles). Strenuous. Access: parking lot 1 kilometer (0.6 mile) south of the Rock Lake Campground office, 8 kilometers (5 miles) down Rock Lake Road from the Parkway Corridor (K 40).**

Centennial Ridges Trail ★★ *(Finds*   This trail is long and steep
but worth the workout, since approximately half of it is spent on
cliffs with awesome views of the park. If you're training for a
decathlon then you could finish the trail in under 3 hours, but for
most people the total journey time will be closer to 5 or 6 hours.
Centennial Ridges Trail was created in 1993 to commemorate
Algonquin's 100th birthday, and the accompanying guide profiles
11 important personages from the park's history. The trail begins
in a mixed conifer and deciduous forest, and straight away passes a
1.5-billion-year-old chunk of granite. There are so many roots that
you will likely spend more time looking at your nimble sneakers
(that was a test—you should be wearing hiking boots) than the surrounding forest, which is fine as long as you look up before tumbling over one of the fenceless cliffs. The first view is one of the best.
The trail follows this ridge for several hundred meters before cutting
back through the forest to a second, higher ridge and the tallest
point on the hike—170 meters (560 feet) above the parking lot.
The trail continues along this ridge for another 3 kilometers
(1.9 miles) or so, at one point passing through a rare grove of red
spruce. There are more pines along the next cliff before the trail
drops down to the lovely **Cloud Lake** nestled in the woods. After
Cloud Lake the going is a bit swampy for about 2 kilometers
(1.2 miles) before the trail rises again to the last and best lookout of
the hike: the view over **Whitefish Lake.** On these cliffs back in
1994 naturalists tried to re-introduce the peregrine falcon to Algonquin Park. Small box homes were secured to the side of the cliff,
with tubes to feed the young falcons. Over the next 2 years 12 pere-
grines were raised, but the ungrateful punks all took off and no one
knows whether they survived. Currently there are no peregrine
falcons in the park, but pairs of nesting falcons have been reported
from other areas of Ontario, so the program is still considered a
success. The final kilometer of the hike passes a small lake before
rejoining the original trail in and bottoming out in the lot. 10 kilometers (6.2 miles). Strenuous. Access: Centennial Ridges Trail parking lot, 2 kilometers (1.2 miles) in from the Parkway Corridor at K 37. The trail can also be
reached from the Coon Lake Campground.

Hardwood Lookout Trail   The only real reason to walk this trail
is the view, and you can get to this faster by going left instead of
right at the trailhead. If you do go the direction you're supposed to,
then you will pass some fine hardwood trees, the ecology of which

is discussed in the trail guide: sugar maple, yellow birch, beech, and cherry, with a few conifer intruders (white pine and hemlock) to liven things up. When the view of **Smoke Lake** finally arrives after a short but very steep ascent, it's a bit crowded out by those very same hardwoods. 8 kilometers (5 miles). Moderate to strenuous. Access: Hardwood Lookout Trail parking lot (K 14).

Hemlock Bluff Trail   The Hemlock Bluff Trail is a pleasant hour-and-a-half stroll through a mix of hardwood and Eastern hemlock forest. The trail guide discusses some of the research performed at Algonquin Park over the years, an interesting story though one that has little to do with the trail itself. The trail's standout feature is a pretty lookout over **Jack Lake** about a kilometer and a half (0.9 miles) into the hike. The top of the lookout is shady but breezy, an excellent spot for a picnic. The last couple of kilometers are an unremarkable finale. 3.5 kilometers (2.2 miles). Easy. Access: across from Jack Lake and the Hemlock Bluff Trail parking lot (K 27.2).

Lookout Trail ⊛   Another short trail, this one features a stunning view of the park and showcases Algonquin geology—a long story several billion years in the making. The first kilometer (0.6 mile) is pretty uneventful—the trail winds uphill through a combination of deciduous and pine trees, the forest cool and shadowy and a little bit *Blair Witch*. The trail guide reminds us that we are walking on a thin skin of soil between us and the planet, a hide of bedrock under our boots. Eventually the trail tops a rise and comes out onto a broad shoulder of granite, sheer cliff below. The view here stretches 25 kilometers (16 miles) out to the distant **Lake of Two Rivers** and beyond, with **Little Rock Lake** off to the side. It is especially mind-blowing in the autumn, when the forest is a patchwork of reds and yellows, and ravens, broad-winged hawks, and turkey vultures wheel in the sky overhead. The cliff-top is about 525 meters (1,700 ft.) above sea level. The trail follows the cliff closely for another 100 meters (330 ft.) or so before dropping down and away, eventually rejoining the original path in. 1.9 kilometers (1.2 miles). Moderate to strenuous. Access: Lookout Trail parking lot (K 40).

Mizzy Lake Trail ⊛⊛ *(Finds*   The Mizzy Lake Trail is all about the animals (except dogs—they're not allowed on the trail). It is Algonquin Park's wildlife showcase, an excellent 11-kilometer (6.8-mile) hike past nine small lakes and ponds and innumerable habitats. There are no guarantees, of course, that you will see any wildlife, especially if you walk the trail in the middle of a summer day. For best results, visit the trail early in the morning. Most of the inhabitants (moose, beaver, otters, turtles, to name a few) are in low areas: marshes, bogs, and lakesides. This means they are wet; while some of the trail is on a boardwalk there are definitely muddy areas, so make sure your hiking boots are water-resistant.

Most of the trail is through deciduous forest—aspen, sugar maple, beech, and birch, the usual west-side suspects—with concentrations of black spruce and tamaracks in the bogs. Just under 1 kilometer (0.6 mile) inland the trail passes a large beaver dam. Keep an eye out for the expanding-V wake of swimming beaver—the animals are more active at night, but come autumn it's possible to see them out and about almost any time of day. About 2 kilometers (1.2 miles) in is **Mizzy Lake** itself, one possible location for spotting otters wiggling through the lily pads. About 600 meters (2,000 ft.) farther on the trail joins the abandoned **Ottawa, Arnprior & Parry Sound Railway** bed—definitely the best part of the trail for close encounters of the mammalian kind. Over the next 2 kilometers (1.2 miles) your chances of seeing moose and spruce grouse are good. There are even rewards for keeping your eyes on the ground: moose, deer, bear, beaver, and wolf tracks, pressed into the damp forest floor. After **West Rose Lake** (a favorite with local moose populations), there is an optional 2-kilometer (1.2-mile) side trip to some beech-tree bear "nests." The bears feast on calorie-rich beechnuts, dragging down the branches from their perches mid-way up the tree. **Wolf Howl Pond** is at the deepest part of the hike. It was once used as a "rendezvous site" by a pack of wolves, and even now a throaty imitation wolf howl can bring back a distant (or not-so-distant) response. The second half of the hike is a little wetter than the first—there are more boardwalks, including one that crosses a lovely open beaver meadow about 2 kilometers (1.2 miles) from the end of the hike. 11 kilometers (6.8 miles). Easy to moderate. Access: Mizzy Lake Trail parking lot at the bottom of Arowhon Road (K 15).

Peck Lake Trail ⍟ Bring your bathing suit, because this is the perfect trail for a hot day in the park. This easy walk circumnavigates **Peck Lake** in about 45 minutes, and features many good spots to break for a picnic or a swim. The view of the lake itself—with its low pines and boggy corners—isn't particularly remarkable. It is the lake's waters that are exceptional: cold and clear, they're a joy to swim in, and the many sloping rocks along the shore are perfect for drying out in the sun. There are also some good opportunities to see

Algonquin's animal spectacle: painted turtles sunning themselves on the rocks, dive-bombing dragonflies, loons trilling and cackling on the water. More critters are discussed in the trail guide, which is all about the ecology of an Algonquin lake. The best swimming rocks are in the first kilometer (0.6 mile) of the hike, before the section of boardwalk that crosses a yellow bog. Another length of boardwalk passes an old beaver lodge poking above the surface of the lake. After this the trail wraps back to the shadier south side of the lake, ending in a peaceful grove of hemlocks. 2 kilometers (1.2 miles). Easy. Access: Peck Lake Trail parking lot (K 19).

Spruce Bog Boardwalk ★★★ *(Finds (Kids* This trail rocks. It's short (only 1.5 kilometers—under a mile), easy, and very weird. The landscape it intersects could be from another planet—Planet Spruce Bog, combination desert and water-logged sponge. *Lord of the Rings* meets a trip to Jupiter is the feeling you get as you wind through the mossy, squishy trails. About half of the walk is along a boardwalk, which allows you to move through unstable wet areas not normally accessible by foot. Be aware that this trail, although classified as wheelchair accessible, is quite mushy and unbalanced. With moist, rocky, mossy bits sporadically located in between lengths of boardwalk, the trail is definitely not completely wheelchair accessible. In fact, the only areas I would consider taking a wheelchair on are the beginning and the end of the trail itself. The first stretch of boardwalk crosses a bog where two mats of sedge pinch the pond into a narrow band of water. The bog itself supports very little in the way of plant life—the water is acidic and contains almost no oxygen. This means it acts as an excellent preservative; the accumulated peat layers contain leaves and fallen trees that are still intact after thousands of years. Just short of a kilometer (about half a mile) along you enter the strangest part of the walk: a forest of sickly black spruce rising up out of the moss, shadowing the boardwalk and muffling any sounds from the highway. After this a new length of boardwalk cuts over to a second, much smaller bog, this one formed not by a beaver dam (like the previous bog), but by a buried section of stranded glacial ice. When the ice melts it leaves a water-filled hole called a kettle, often quite deep under the mat of sedge (this one goes down 9 meters [30 ft.]). This is a good place for a little bird-watching. Spruce bogs support northern species like the boreal chickadee, the gray jay, the yellow-bellied flycatcher, and the much-sought-after spruce grouse, whose ritualized courting can often be seen in April and May. The last half-kilometer (0.3 mile) of the walk is through forest, with a good view of the whole bog once the trail cuts back along the highway. **1.5 kilometers (.9 miles). Easy. Access: Spruce Bog**

Track and Tower Trail 🌟🌟 *Finds*   The Track and Tower Trail is one of the most interesting in the park; it meanders by relics from Algonquin's past, but is filled too with lovely vistas and a killer view over **Cache Lake.** The trail is one of the park's longest; indeed, it is the longest if you decide to take the optional 5.5-kilometer (3.4-mile) side trail following the railway bed east to **Mew Lake.** This side trail is one-way, so if you take it make sure you either have a vehicle at the Highland Backpacking Trail parking lot or have made arrangements for someone to pick you up. The first kilometer (0.6 mile) of the hike is through hardwood forest, up and down small dips in the landscape, past some big cedars and an overgrown beaver meadow. The initial look at Cache Lake may be the coolest and is certainly the most evocative. Extending out across the bay are the remains of two old railway trestles, spiny and shattered, a poignant contrast with the healthy surrounding forest. Half a kilometer (0.3 mile) farther on is an open grassy area next to a small cement dam, once the location of a log dam and chute dating from the 1880s and now an excellent picnic spot. Over the next half-kilometer there are two places where it's possible to turn left and cut out a portion of the main loop. Don't do it! The upcoming view, though a bit strenuous to reach, is definitely worth it. You don't even need to take my word for it; a score of cheerful descending hikers are sure to tell you this very thing ("Keep going honey, it's worth it!" "Almost there, boy that view makes it all worthwhile," "Worth every step of the way, son," etc.).

The steep portion of the hike is about 300 meters (1,000 ft.) long, and takes about 10 minutes to surmount. The view, once it finally arrives is . . . worth it. Cache Lake shimmers between rolling green shoulders and all evidence of human habitation is hidden by the trees. After this there are a couple more reminders of the park's industrial past. The trail follows the old Ottawa, Arnprior & Parry Sound Railway bed, once the busiest in the country, now just a rise of earth deep in the forest. This human-made hill leads to two concrete abutments on either side of the wide **Madawaska River Valley,** once spanned by a slender steel bridge. After this it's a fairly unremarkable 3-kilometer (1.9-mile) hike back through the woods to the parking lot. **Main loop 7.7 kilometers (4.8 miles), side trail 5.5 kilometers (3.4 miles). Moderate to strenuous. Access: Track and Tower Trail parking lot (K 25).**

Two Rivers Trail   If you don't feel like working for your view, then this is the trail for you. Kilometer 1 is an easy ascent through mixed red pine and birch forest to a lookout over the **Madawaska River Valley.** The forest extending into the blue distance is mostly pine, so this is not the place to come for autumn colors. The trail follows the edge of the cliff for close to a kilometer, with many bald rocks for picnicking, and many very steep drop-offs to steer away from (parents be vigilant). Toward the end of the hike the dark and still **Madawaska River** itself finally becomes visible below. No more than an hour's hike. 2 kilometers (1.2 miles). Easy. Access: Two Rivers Trail parking lot (K 31).

Whiskey Rapids Trail ⍟   Whiskey Rapids Trail is the only walk in the park to follow a river, in this case the very pretty **Oxtongue River.** It is a leisurely and picturesque stroll up and down the sandy river banks (lined with spruce and hemlock) and across sturdy boardwalks. There are numerous places to stop for a bite of lunch or even a cooling dip in the water. Parts of the river are stopped with bleached logs and fallen trees, a modern echo of the logging runs that used to take place on the Oxtongue at the turn of the century. You'll hear the **Whiskey Rapids** themselves before you see them. They're quite modestly sized, and look as if they'd be fun to shoot in a canoe. After the rapids (which are about two-thirds of the way along the hike) the trail switches back into the forest and follows an old tote road back to the parking lot. 2.1 kilometers (1.3 miles). Easy. Access: Whiskey Rapids Trail parking lot (K 7).

3 Achray & Brent Day Hikes

Barron Canyon Trail ⍟⍟⍟ *(Finds*   The Barron Canyon Trail has bar none the most impressive view in all of Algonquin Park. It isn't a long or strenuous hike (see the *Achray Trails & Canoe Routes* map in chapter 5, "Camping in the Interior," p. 106); in fact, the actual hiking part of it is almost incidental. People come here for the oxygen-sucking view of **Barron Canyon,** a gneiss gorge that plunges 100 meters (330 ft.) down to the **Barron River.** The first half-kilometer (0.3 mile) is an easy stroll through a conifer forest. When the trail opens to a view of the canyon, the forest itself seems to sigh with the release. Ten thousand years ago the glacier, which at one time covered most of Canada and parts of the U.S., melted past the northern boundary of Algonquin Park. Meltwater from the glacier had previously formed an enormous lake to the west of the park called **Lake Algonquin**—an ancient precursor to the upper Great Lakes. When the retreating glacier exposed a low channel of land through which Lake Algonquin could drain, the waters came a-thundering through. Known by geologists as the **Fossmill drainage outlet,** the Barron River was part of this system. Picture Niagara Falls multiplied a thousand times pressing through the canyon, sculpting the rock walls and removing all obstructing glacial debris. The result is before you—now quiet but still dramatic. The trail follows the edge of the canyon for the next half-kilometer (0.3 mile) and is unfenced—so be careful not to get too close to the edge, and keep a very wary eye on children. The canyon is home to some fascinating flora and fauna. If you look across to the other side of the canyon you will see a brushing of rusty orange on the rock. This is a lichen called Xanthoria, and it survives on the lime that seeps from tiny fissures in the canyon walls. Deep in the river below, four species of crustaceans and the prehistoric-looking deepwater sculpin—normally found only in Arctic regions—all survive in cold waters left over from the glacial age. There is also considerable activity in the air as red-tailed hawks, ravens, and turkey vultures tumble on the overlapping air currents. It is a half-kilometer (0.3 mile) back to the parking lot from where the trail finally cuts away from the canyon edge. 1.5 kilometers (0.9 mile). Easy. Access: the parking lot 11 kilometers (6.8 miles) west of Sand Lake Gate on the Barron Canyon Road. Approximately a 3-hour drive one-way from Parkway Corridor.

Berm Lake Trail ⟨✦⟩   Berm Lake Trail is the perfect embodiment of an easy afternoon hike. The trail loops gently through pine forest and around **Berm Lake,** an undemanding 2-hour walk (see *Achray Trails & Canoe Routes* map in chapter 5, "Camping in the Interior," p. 106). The trail begins with a stand of white pine, sun refracting through the gauzy pine needles. The trail guide, which is about pine forest ecology, explains how this stand is characteristic of the drier east side of the park. Less rain and snow and a large quantity of glacier-deposited sand make the area a conifer paradise. Over the next 2 kilometers (1.2 miles) the trail passes more stands of white and red pine and the occasional jack pine. Both the red and jack pine depend on forest fires for renewal—the red pine for the suitable seed beds that result, and the jack pine for the release of its seeds from their tight cone casings. There is some research to indicate that the park's policy of fire-suppression is responsible for the decline in new populations of these trees, so now is the time to get a good look at what may be a species on the way out. On the far side of Berm Lake, another kilometer farther on, the trail passes through a blueberry patch and into a mixed pine and red oak forest. Most of the last 1.5 kilometers (0.9 mile) follows a well-traveled portage trail. 4.5 kilometers (2.8 miles). Easy to moderate. Access: at end of Achray parking lot to left of stone building. The Achray site is located 5 kilometers (3.1 miles) south of the Barron Canyon Road, 38 kilometers (23.5 miles) west of the Sand Lake Gate.

Brent Crater Trail   This trail features a walk into the 450-million-year-old remains of the **Brent Crater,** one of only 100 or so fossil meteorite crater sites in the world, and, according to the trail guide, one of the most intensively studied. Visitors to the crater climb an observation tower before heading down to the eroded rim of the crater itself. Park information officers say the descent down the sloping crater wall is occasionally a bit steep. The 2-kilometer (1.2-mile) loop takes about an hour and a half to walk. It is located at the far northern edge of Algonquin Park, a 4- to 5-hour drive from the Parkway Corridor. 2 kilometers (1.2 miles). Moderate. Access: Observation tower parking lot 32 kilometers (20 miles) south of Deux Rivières on the Brent Road.

4 Day Canoe Trips

For many, the only way to see Algonquin Park is by canoe. You don't have to be a bush-whacking *trappeur* to do this; the park has plenty of facilities for inexperienced paddlers who just want to spend an afternoon on the water. There are several options if you are a novice canoeist or you simply want to brush up on your J-stroke. From Tuesdays to Fridays during the summer the Ontario Recreational Canoe Association (ORCA) stages free canoe demonstrations at one of the Parkway Corridor campgrounds. After the morning demonstrations, everyone is invited to attend lessons in the afternoon, provided they bring their own canoe, paddle, and lifejacket. The park also organizes weekly nature canoe outings on an Algonquin lake or river, which include some canoeing and camping skill instruction (times for both of these are listed in *This Week in Algonquin Park*, available at the park gates and the Visitor Centre). Canoes, lifejackets, and paddles can be rented by the day at three places in the park (and numerous other places outside the park): **The Portage Store** on Canoe Lake, the **Opeongo Store** on Lake Opeongo, and **Bartlett Lodge** on Cache Lake (see "Essentials" in chapter 3, "Exploring Algonquin Park," for details on rates for these and other outfitters). Both **The Portage Store** (✆ **705/633-5622**) and **Algon-quin Outfitters** (✆ **705/635-2243**) offer canoe instruction in the form of 1-day guided canoe trips. The Portage Store charges C$40 (US$29.70) for a day of instruction, which includes canoe, paddle, lifejacket, and a packed lunch. Algonquin Outfitters charges C$35 (US$25.95), but asks that you call ahead and reserve. For all canoe trips, you are required to have a lifejacket, a spare paddle, a bailing device of some kind, and a 15-meter (50-ft.) length of rope in the canoe with you. In general, creeks and rivers are the best places for beginner paddlers, since they are calm, shallow, and relatively easy to navigate.

If you're renting canoes, there are some excellent routes around the outfitters themselves. The **Canoe Lake** area has much to recommend it. Canoe Lake itself is a popular destination. It's not remote and there is considerable cottage and camp traffic on the lake, but there are also some interesting historical sites at the north end of the lake, including **Tom Thomson's burial cairn** (for more details, see "Historical Attractions" in chapter 3, "Exploring Algonquin Park"). It is also possible to canoe from Canoe Lake over to **Bonita Lake,** through **Tea Lake,** and on to the **Oxtongue River** ☞. The river itself is the desired destination here; it winds picturesquely past bristly spruce and fir, with only two short portages between the river entrance and the **Oxtongue River Picnic Ground.** If you have transportation, you can also put in directly at the Oxtongue River Picnic Ground and paddle either east toward the **Tea Lake Dam** or west toward the **Split Rock Rapids** and a small nature reserve zone that follows the river.

From **Lake Opeongo** and the boat launch at the Opeongo Store there are some very good canoe routes, and the area is generally less busy than elsewhere on the Parkway Corridor. **Costello Creek,** ☞ just to the south of the Opeongo Store, is considered one of the best places to see wildlife in the park. Otters, beaver, great blue herons, and gray jays all make the occasional appearance, and the wide-open bogs and rising cliffs to the east give the route a scenic value difficult to match elsewhere in the park. The only problem is the short distance—it takes only an hour to get from the store to where the creek hits the Opeongo Road—so you may want to combine this outing with some paddling around the dramatic Lake Opeongo itself. For those interested in getting a little deeper into the interior for the day, the Opeongo Store offers a very popular **Hailstorm**

Other Outdoor Pursuits in the Park

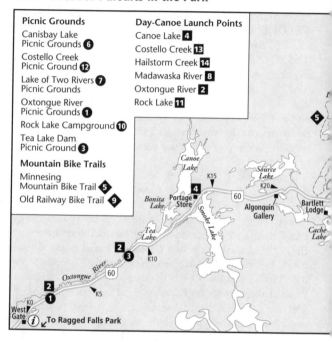

Picnic Grounds

Canisbay Lake Picnic Grounds **6**

Costello Creek Picnic Ground **12**

Lake of Two Rivers Picnic Grounds **7**

Oxtongue River Picnic Grounds **1**

Rock Lake Campground **10**

Tea Lake Dam Picnic Ground **3**

Mountain Bike Trails

Minnesing Mountain Bike Trail **5**

Old Railway Bike Trail **9**

Day-Canoe Launch Points

Canoe Lake **4**

Costello Creek **13**

Hailstorm Creek **14**

Madawaska River **8**

Oxtongue River **2**

Rock Lake **11**

Creek ✦✦ package day trip for C\$50 (US\$37.10). The price includes canoe rental and a return water-taxi up to the far-north arm of Opeongo (paddling the distance can take upward of 5 hours depending on the headwinds, and the often-choppy character of the lake makes it unsuitable for beginners). A huge bog and nature reserve zone, Hailstorm Creek offers some of the best wildlife-viewing opportunities in the park. Moose are plentiful in the area, and some rare nesting birds—the bobolinks and the savannah sparrow—can also be spotted.

Other popular day canoe routes along the Parkway Corridor are **Rock Lake**—very scenic, with possible investigations of the **native vision pits** and the remains of the old **Barclay Estate** (see "Historical Attractions" in chapter 3, "Exploring Algonquin Park")—and the **Madawaska River.** For the latter, put in at the **Lake of Two Rivers** east beach picnic area, and canoe south through **Pog Lake** and into **Whitefish Lake.** There is only a single short portage.

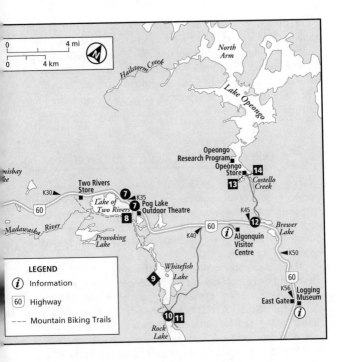

Stumpy dams and views of the abandoned **Ottawa, Arnprior &
Parry Sound Railway** are some of the highlights of this trip.

For more adventurous canoeists, the park's remote east side has
some amazing day trips, though you would do best to stay in the
area the night before since traveling distances are so large. **Algonquin Portage** (☏ 613/735-1795) on Barron Canyon Road rents
canoes for the day, and can also arrange transportation to and from
your departure point (for information on rates, see "Essentials" in
chapter 3, "Exploring Algonquin Park"). The most popular day trip
is to the stunning **Barron Canyon** ✿✿✿. Canoeists can put in at
Brigham Lake and paddle the **Barron River** east through the
canyon to **Squirrel Rapids**—about 3.5 hours of paddling time.
During the busy summer days and weekends it is often possible to
get a car ride back with another park visitor, though to be on the
safe side you can have **Algonquin Portage** outfitters move your
vehicle for a fee.

Long and thin **Grand Lake** is also a marvelous spot to do some paddling. It feels more like a river than a lake, with dramatic scenery that was the subject of more than one Tom Thomson painting (*Jack Pine* and possibly *West Wind*). To paddle all the way to the lake's north end and back takes about 8 hours, so time your trip accordingly.

For general information about canoeing in Ontario, check out the **Paddling Ontario** website at www.paddlingontario.com.

 One Canoe, One Couple, Two Directions

Canoe Lake and Lake Opeongo have been the scenes of some pretty funny canoeing gaffes—not hard to believe when you consider that a large number of the tourists who come to the park are doing so as part of their first wilderness experiences. Deep in the woods the boundaries of common sense can seem very far away.

There is something surreal and strangely pleasing about watching two people get into the bow and stern of a canoe facing each other. There is usually a long pause, one or the other of the couple cocking their head to the side. It's rare to see anyone actually start paddling, though two strong right-handed paddlers could probably spin the canoe in circles at a good clip.

Belly up to a wizened park ranger and listen to his epic tale (ahem):

"I've seen men sittin' on the gunnels,
and women in the drink,
pitched battles with the paddles,
and top-loaded vessels straight-up sink.
I seen darn near thirty tourist in choppy Opeongo Bay,
And thirty more a join 'em on a windy summer day.
I seen fellas tied to wood-stoves get dragged straight off their feet,
an' people standin' minglin' in their boats like they was at a cocktail meet!"

---

5 Whitewater Canoeing & Kayaking

Although Algonquin Park is generally thought of as a flat-water destination, there is one excellent whitewater river at the north end of the park: the Petawawa. The stretch of **Petawawa River** that drains south out of **Cedar Lake** through **Radiant Lake** and **Lake Travers** and into **McManus Lake** practically gave birth to whitewater canoeing in Canada; it is beloved by many and still very popular today. That said, you shouldn't even consider shooting Petawawa's many sets of rapids unless you are an experienced whitewater paddler. Rivers change every time you run them, whether it's hour to hour or day to day, creating very different conditions. Be accountable for your safety and don't rely on others' judgment. Scout every time, and if you are not comfortable walk around the edge of the water. If you do decide to paddle the Petawawa, you'll need a copy of the Friends of Algonquin Park's *Petawawa River Whitewater Guide*, available for C$5.95 (US$4.40) at all park bookstores.

There are other good whitewater rivers to the east and south of the park. Two of these are detailed in another Algonquin Park publication, *The Madawaska River/Opeongo River Whitewater Guide*.

6 Mountain Biking Trails & Family Biking

Bicycles are permitted only off-road on designated trails, of which there are three in Algonquin Park, marked on the *Canoe Routes of Algonquin Park* map by a dotted red line. For visitors without bikes, the **Lake of Two Rivers Store** (© **705/633-5728**) just east of **Lake of Two Rivers** (and next to the entrance of the **Old Railway Bike Trail**) rents them in the summer for C$12 (US$8.90) for a half-day, C$18 (US$13.35) for a full day. All of the park's bike trails are open from mid-June to early October. Bike helmets are mandatory. See the *Other Outdoor Pursuits in the Park* map earlier in this chapter for bike trails.

The most demanding of the three trails is the **Minnesing Mountain Bike Trail,** located 23 kilometers (14.3 miles) from the West Gate. The full length of the trail is 23.4 kilometers (14.5 miles), a riding time of approximately 3 hours, but there are three shorter loops of 17.1 kilometers (10.6 miles), 10.5 kilometers (6.5 miles), and 4.7 kilometers (2.9 miles). The trail passes three scenic lakes, and has a lot of ups and downs that account for its "moderate" technical rating.

Bikers looking for a more casual ride or something for kids should try the **Old Railway Bike Trail,** which runs southeast from the Mew Lake Campground to **Lake of Two Rivers** through to **Pog Lake** and on to a **Rock Lake Campground** finish. The total one-way distance is 10 kilometers (6.2 miles), an easy hour-and-a half ride along the historic Ottawa, Arnprior & Parry Sound Railway bed. This trail is reputed to have better wildlife viewing opportunities than the Minnessing Trail, and it's one the whole family can enjoy.

Byers Lake Mountain Bike Trail is the park's third trail; it's at the southern tip of the Algonquin Park panhandle, accessible from the **High Falls Hiking Trail** parking lot, 20 kilometers (12.4 miles) west of Maynooth off Peterson Road. The trail follows an old logging road 5 kilometers (3.1 miles) to **Byers Lake** through a deer yard. Halfway to Byers Lake there is a short side trail down to **Gut Rapids**—which is worth the walk, though you will have to leave your mountain bike back on the trail.

(Kids Summer Camp

Shipping the kids off to summer camp is a great Canadian tradition, one with a very prolific Algonquin arm. Founded in 1906, Camp Northway-Windigo (for girls) on Cache Lake was Algonquin Park's first camp. Since then 15 camps have sprung up and disappeared inside park boundaries, with 8 operating today. It's been close to 100 years and more than 100,000 dirty little boys and girls, including two Canadian prime ministers. Camp Tamakwa, the park's most famous (and expensive) camp for kids, has even been the setting of *Indian Summer*, a Hollywood movie that features characters based on real campers—including the creators of Roots, the infamous Canadian clothing company.

For information about Algonquin Park camps, the Toronto-based **Ontario Camping Association** (© **416/485-0425**; www. ontcamp.on.ca) maintains an information-packed website dedicated to helping parents find exactly the right fit. Parents can conduct searches based on region, cost, gender, and offered activities, complete with mini-summaries of camps.

7 Interpretive Program

Algonquin Park has an excellent interpretive program, one that has been looked to as a model by parks around North America. Terrific for kids, the program is in full swing during the summer months—from late June to Labor Day weekend in early September—and both the conducted walks and the evening program continue during fall weekends. The rest of the year **The Friends of Algonquin Park** cater to adult, school, and youth groups, but they charge for the naturalist walks, overnight activities, and special programs. For a complete off-season education program brochure, or to book one for a group (there is usually a minimum of 12 people or so), contact The Friends at the **Visitor Centre** (✆ **613/637-2828;** fax 613/ 637-2138) during normal office hours (Mon–Fri, 8:30am–4:30pm).

Every day during the summer the park stages five or six free events along the Parkway Corridor. Most of these happen at different times and locations, so if you're interested in attending, first consult the latest issue of *This Week in Algonquin Park*—available at both gates and the Visitor Centre and posted throughout the campgrounds—or call **Park Information** at ✆ **705/633-5572.** Usually the first event of the day is a **conducted walk** ⍟⍟, with a second walk in the early afternoon or evening. These 1.5- to 2.5-hour walks are led by a park naturalist and focus on some Algonquin theme— insects or mushrooms, trees or birds, history or ecology, to name a few. These are excellent outings, full of natural-history gossip and an easy camaraderie on the trail. The aquatic equivalent would be the weekly **canoe outings** ⍟⍟ that have both a biological and a practical focus. Trip leaders point out features of lake or river ecology, and also provide camping and canoeing tips with an eye on preparing visitors for canoe journeys of their own. These outings are from 10am to 4pm; if you're interested make sure to bring your own paddle, lifejacket, canoe, and lunch. For inexperienced paddlers, the Ontario Recreational Canoe Association (ORCA) holds free **canoe and camping demonstrations** at different campgrounds along the Parkway Corridor from 10am to noon, Tuesdays to Fridays. These are followed by 3-hour **canoe lessons** in the afternoon, for which visitors must bring their own canoes and equipment.

The hour-and-a-half **evening program** ⍟⍟ usually takes place just after sundown at the cozy **Outdoor Theatre,** near the Pog Lake Campground at K 35. Visitors follow a lit path from the parking lot to a small amphitheater in a quiet forest glade. Once they're seated on the open benches, there is a short film, a slide show, and a naturalist-led talk about some lively Algonquin critter (wolf, bear, moose, beaver, blood-sucking mosquito, artist). If it's raining then the whole program moves indoors to the Visitor Centre at K 43. It's great for kids.

Algonquin for Kids is the name of the park's kids' program. Children aged 5 to 12 come to the Visitor Centre daily at 10:30am to hear stories, play games, and poke at various creatures live and dead. The other big draw for kids is the park's **special events.** In July the Logging Museum is the site of an annual **Spirit Walk** 𝓕𝓕. This is a chance for children and adults to meet with historical figures from the park's past—the loggers, rangers, trappers, and so on. The interpretive staff all dress up in period costume and park themselves somewhere along the trail for excited interactions with kids. The last Saturday in July is **Loggers' Day** at the Logging Museum. Silviculture experts hold demonstrations, wail shanty songs, and discuss the issue of logging in the park. Admission is C$1 (US$0.74) per person, with an optional old-time loggers' lunch at the sawlog cookery for C$6 ($4.45). The following Sunday evening is a rowdy concert at the **Outdoor Theatre** by the **Wakami Wailers,** whose songs and stories celebrate 150 years of white pine logging in Ontario. Admission is C$1 (US$0.74).

The last and most noteworthy of special events are the **Public Wolf Howls** 𝓕𝓕𝓕 in August. These immensely popular gatherings have been going on for close to 40 years. Wolves permitting, naturalists howl into the Algonquin night and receive spine-tingling replies from the park's most famous animal inhabitants. For more information, see "Howling with the Wolves," below.

Howling with the Wolves

The dramatic climax of the **Public Wolf Howl** goes something like this: one or two lanky park naturalists, illuminated by the stars, raise their cupped hands to their mouths and howl out their best wolf imitation. Shortly after their calls die away comes the eerie response, a mingled pitch of wolf voices echoing above the forest. The adult wolves sound mournful in contrast to the pups, who yipyap in the higher frequencies. The public, standing by their cars, are mesmerized.

The first Public Wolf Howl took place in 1963, not long after researchers in the park discovered that wolves would respond to human imitations of their calls. This was big news for the researchers; wolves that could be located by howling could also be studied. The first tentative invitation in the *Raven* to "an evening of wolf listening" drew an overwhelming response, and since then there have been close to 90 Public Wolf Howls involving more than 112,000 participants.

The operation itself is massive. On Tuesdays and Wednesdays the naturalists look for wolves by howling into the edge of the forest. Wolves with young pups establish a "rendezvous site" where they leave their young for days at a time while they're off on the hunt. Wolves howling one night from a rendezvous site can be expected to return. If a suitable pack is found not far from the Parkway Corridor—and often no pack is located—then word goes out on Thursday morning that the operation is on. That evening, after a slide show at the **Outdoor Theatre** near Pog Lake, an enormous convoy of cars travels slowly through the dark down the closed highway to the designated spot. Twenty or so park staff manage upward of 2,000 people, directing traffic and coordinating with ground control on their car radios and walkie-talkies. Visitors get out of their cars and stand silent by the side of the road. Once the naturalists howl there's about a 70% chance of hearing a return wolf howl.

Why do wolves howl? There are some obvious explanations: to maintain contact with the rest of the pack, and to warn strange wolves of their presence and therefore defend their territory. Many naturalists also believe the howling has some larger social significance—a soulful group sing-along, lupine bonding sessions under the moon. This relates directly to the last, most poetic possibility (and surely the one that draws us in): music for its own sake, unbidden and wild.

8 Fishing

Algonquin Park is known worldwide for its outstanding fishing, especially of **lake and brook trout** (and **splake,** a hybrid of the two). The predominance of these fish is a legacy of the park's glacial past. Algonquin's lakes are cold, high, deep, and low in nutrients—perfect for cold-water species like trout. Early spring is the best time to catch them, as the lakes are uniformly cold from top to bottom and the trout are all over the place. Later in the summer they hunker down low, so intrepid anglers need deepwater techniques to get at them. **Smallmouth bass**—introduced in the park at the turn of the last century—are another popular species, and small numbers of **walleye, muskie,** and **pike** can also be lured from the deep. The one indispensable guide to angling in the park is The Friends of

Algonquin Park's *Fishing in Algonquin Provincial Park*. Available for C$1.95 (US$1.45) at all park bookstores, the book details how and where to catch each species.

To fish in the park you need a **license.** These are not too difficult to come by; they can be bought at private issuers outside the park, at most **access points** in the park, and at **both gates.** There are several kinds of licenses available at a range of prices (all rates for 2003 season). For Canadian residents, the cheapest of these is the 1-day fishing license for C$10 (US$7.40), though if you're planning on fishing more than once in the next year then the 1-year conservation license, at C$18.75 (US$13.90)—which includes the mandatory **Outdoors Card**—is far better value. Non-residents of Canada can buy a 1-year conservation fishing license for C$36 (US$26.70), or a 7-day conservation fishing license for C$22.50 (US$16.70). The Portage Store and the Opeongo Store both sell some fishing gear, and the Lake of Two Rivers store sells worms and fishing tackle.

The **fishing season** in Algonquin Park depends on the species of fish. For lake trout, brook trout, and splake, the season runs from the beginning of May to the end of September. There is a **quota** of **five** of these fish per day, of which only **two** can be lake trout. Bass season runs from the end of June to the end of November, with a limit of **six** fish per day. **Live bait fish** are prohibited in all lakes.

Good fishing is fairly uniform in the park, and this includes the easily accessible Parkway Corridor; 150 lakes in the park support lake trout, including Opeongo (the most heavily fished lake in the park), Canoe, Cache, Canisbay, and Smoke. Brook trout, despite the name, can be found in 230 lakes, including Dickson, Lavieille, Proulx, Big Crow, and Redrock. Finally, if it's bass you're after, then try Bonita, Opeongo, Galeairy, Cache, or Joe lakes. Many of the old-timers in the park know which lakes have secret burgeoning stocks, but getting it out of them is like prying bent nails from a two-by-four.

If angling for and reeling in a whopping lake trout on a line hooked with some shiny trinket-like lure isn't exactly your thing, consider trying out the **Opeongo Expedition Research Adventure Program** 🐟🐟. Being whisked to the middle of Opeongo Lake in a Zodiak, a glorified rubber dinghy with a massive motor on the back, is but one of the highlights of the actual adventure—and adventure is putting it lightly! You'll be asked to take part in aquatic and wildlife surveys, and participate hands-on in taking water temperatures, measuring plankton levels, and tracking tagged lake trout.

You'll also get a behind-the-scenes look at Harkness Fish Laboratories, which has been a venerable research lab at Opeongo since the 1940s: researchers come from all over the world to study here and are accommodated in the small cabins lining the shore of the grand lake. The tours run in July and August, and the money raised goes straight back into funding new research. The 1-hour-plus trips are C$20 per person (US$14.85) and can be booked through **Nature Trails** by calling ⓒ **866/421-6909;** www.naturetrails.on.ca.

9 Horseback Riding

Though you rarely see them, there are horses and riders in Algonquin Park on at least four sets of horseback riding trails. Trails for the most part consist of hard-packed earth or gravel—there are no corrals or shelters on any of the trails. The largest trail network is the **Leaf Lake Horse Trail** on the east side of the park. Used for cross-country ski routes in the winter, this network has about 50 kilometers (31 miles) of trails, though the main run is a 16-kilometer (10-mile) stretch of trail beginning 1 kilometer (0.6 mile) east of the East Gate at the **David Thompson Ski Trail** entrance, and following Highway 60 into the park. The David Thompson parking lot is the one suitable place for camping with your horse; all horse manure must be shoveled into the log composting crib before leaving the site.

The **White Partridge Lake Horse Trail** is a 16-kilometer (10-mile) "cart trail" (you can see it on the canoe route map) that begins south of **Lake Travers** and extends all the way to **White Partridge Lake.** The only suitable camping spot is in a field at the northeast corner of White Partridge Lake. The field can accommodate five parties with nine people on each site; there are fire pits for cooking and two privies at opposite ends of the field. Permits are by reservation only and must be picked up at the **Sand Lake Gate** at the far eastern edge of the park.

The **Lone Creek Riding Trail** is also on the east side of the park, located just off the **McManus Lake Access Road** near Access Point 21. The 30-kilometer (18.6-mile) trail is along an old logging road, and is considered excellent for viewing wildlife. There are four campsites at the trailhead itself; permits can be picked up at **Sand Lake Gate.**

There are more than 50 additional kilometers (31 miles) of horseback-riding trails available for day-use in the **South Algonquin** panhandle. They begin at the **High Falls parking lot** and follow old logging roads north past the remains of **Bruton Farm**. **South Algonquin Trails** (© 800/758-4801; www.southalgonquintrails.com) offers guided trail rides, and is responsible for maintaining the routes.

10 Winter Activities

A park winter shows the Algonquin landscape at a beautiful extreme: wiped clean with drifts of snow and ice, never more raw and clear. It is an excellent time to visit. The number of activities that take place in the park during the winter season attest to a large population of visitors, whipping through the snow on skies, snowshoes, and dog sleds. About the only two activities not permitted in the park are **ice fishing** and **snowmobiling**—though the latter is possible on the hydro line that crosses the southern panhandle of the park.

There are far fewer services in the park during the winter season; chapter 2, "Planning Your Trip," details most of these in section 3, "When to Go." The only **heated accommodations** in the park at this time are the **eight yurts** at the Mew Lake campground, described in chapter 6, "Lodging and Dining Inside the Park." **Winter camping** in the interior is another possibility, though you should be aware that winter temperatures in the park can plummet to –40° Celsius and Fahrenheit. Well-bundled campers can ski in on one of the groomed trails but cannot camp in sight of these trails; nor can they camp at any of the designated summer sites or within 30 meters (100 ft.) of any lake, trail, or portage. This still leaves plenty of space; low, sheltered areas with a good supply of dead firewood are best. Make sure to use extreme caution if traveling over ice and frozen streams.

Cross-country skiing attracts the largest number of visitors in the winter; there are three trail networks designed specifically for the sport. Before embarking make sure you have a copy of the park's *Algonquin Provincial Park in Winter* brochure, available for free from both gates. The brochure contains a map of all the trails, and notes the difficulty level of the various sections and the locations of shelters and telephones on the trail. All of the ski trails along the Parkway Corridor have shelters and emergency barrels (except **Minnesing**), with telephones at the extreme far end of most circuits. For information on ski-trail conditions (or to have a brochure sent to you), call either the park **Information Office** (© 705/633-5572) from 8am to 4:30pm or the **Park Administrative Office** (© 613/837-2780).

The **Fen Lake Trail** begins at the West Gate, where there is a heated comfort station and shelter. The system has four loops of easy and intermediate difficulty, the longest of which is 13 kilometers (8 miles). Look for moose tracks as you pass under the bare hardwood trees. The **Minnesing Wilderness Ski Trail,** located just under 23 kilometers (14.3 miles) from the West Gate, is meant for backcountry skiing and is a little wilder. None of the trails are groomed, and there are some difficult passages throughout. The four loops of the trail are the same as the summer mountain-bike loops: 4.7 kilometers (3 miles), 10.5 kilometers (6.5 miles), 17.1 kilometers (10.6 miles), and 23.4 kilometers (14.5 miles). The **Leaf Lake Ski Trail** network at the east end of the park is the most extensive along the Parkway Corridor. Starting at the **David Thompson entrance** just east of the park boundaries, it contains loops through pine forest from 5 to 50 kilometers (3–31 miles) in length, with all levels of ability from novice to advanced accounted for.

The **Algonquin Nordic Wilderness Lodge** (© 705/745-9497) in South Algonquin maintains more than 80 kilometers (50 miles) of groomed trails in the park, though the lodge itself is located on a secluded lake outside park boundaries. This is probably the best bet for visitors looking to complement nighttime comfort with their daytime exertions. The lodge is open weekends in the fall and all winter from late December to mid-March.

Snowshoeing is another popular activity in the winter. You can slap those tennis rackets on your feet and go pretty much anywhere in the park, ski trails excluded. If you're looking for some boundaries to all that freedom, most of the short interpretive trails along the Parkway Corridor can be walked, and there is a special 8-kilometer (5-mile) overnight snowshoeing trail that departs from the **Minnesing Ski Trail parking lot** over **Canisbay Lake** and onto **Linda Lake.**

Finally, for real adventurers: **dog sledding.** This is an awesome way to see the park, a real chest-thumping throwback to the frontier days of old. There are two sets of dog-sledding trails in the park, though long trips go all over the place. The **Sunday Lake Dog Sled Trails** are located 40 kilometers (25 miles) west of the West Gate and wind north to **Hiram** and **Redfox** lakes in the north. The other set of trails are at the north end of the park near the town of **South River.** Of course, most people don't have their own team of huskies running circles in the backyard, so the only way to experience dog sledding is to go with one of the commercial operators outside the park. Dog-sledding season starts after Christmas and runs straight through to the end of March. Most of the expedition companies in the south part of the park offer rates for everything from 2-hour and 1-day trips (on average about C$80 [US$59.30] and C$160 [US$118.70] respectively) to week-long and 10-day trips (call for exact rates). They include **Algonquin-Way Kennels** in L'Amable (© 613/332-4005; www.mwdesign.net/mush); **Forest Trail Dogsled Tours** in Maynooth (© 613/338-1026); **Call of the Wild** in Markham (© 800/776-9453; fax 905/472-9453; www.call-wild. com); and **Trailbreaker Dog Sledding Adventures** in Novar (© 705/788-2495). Be aware that some of these companies go into Algonquin itself only for the day trips; longer trips happen somewhere south of the park. **Nastawgan Adventures** in Temagami (© 705/783-0461) do all their trips in the park. They charge C$200 (US$148.30) per person, per day, and can accommodate trips of up to 10 days in length. They also do "ski-support" trips, which combine cross-country skiing and dog sledding (everyone takes turns at both) and cost only C$120 (US$89) per person, per day. **The Mad Musher** in Whitney (© 613/637-2820; www.mad musher.com) partners accommodations and restaurant meals with dog-sledding expeditions. Packages are available (prices not available at press time). See Section 1, "Whitney", in chapter 7, "Gateway Towns."

Chocpaw Expeditions in South River (© 705/3860344; e-mail chocpaw@on.aibn.com) is the only company that goes into the north end of Algonquin. It is a large operation and also a very popular one (many clients return annually)—book ahead if you want to guarantee a spot. Chocpaw has 12 full-time guides. In the fall the company sets up heated tents in the park interior so everything is ready for the winter rush. Expeditions, which include all food and equipment, start at C$355 (US$263.30) for 2 days and go up to C$455 (US$337.45) for 3 days, C$705 (US$522.90) for 4 days, C$885 (US$656.35) for 5 days, and C$1060 (US$786.15) for 6 days.

5

Camping in the Interior

Camping in the interior is hands-down the best way to experience Algonquin Park. People disappear and trees loom on shores and around trail bends. The whole landscape rears up and whisks you in. Days are spent walking along pine-scented ridges or paddling on the open water, skin taut and warm in the sun. Hikers and canoeists lunch on the rocky shoulders of lakes and take cooling swims in clear waters. Days are ambitious or lazy, passing kilometers or just passing time, feet propped up on the bow of a canoe with a water-stained paperback in hand. Meals feel hard-won and taste delicious; afterward, hypnotic campfires prompt rambling discussions. The stars are bright and immediate. Loon calls serenade the sleepers.

The interior of Algonquin Park can be accessed by foot or by canoe. There are three backpacking trails in the park covering more than 140 kilometers (87 miles) of ground. Canoe route variations are almost infinite; routes extend for 2,100 kilometers (1,302 miles) in a network that criss-crosses the whole of the park. Whether you go for one night or ten, your interior camping experience will never be forgotten.

1 So You're Going on a Camping Trip

Camping trips require advance planning. You could just up and run off into the bush with your tent, but you'd get hungry and probably wet and you wouldn't find a good campsite. Get it together! Plan ahead. The first thing you need to figure out is when to go. For both hiking and canoeing, prime season is early August to mid-October. May is also a good time, but you have to time your trip before the blood-sucking-insect assault of late May and early June. July isn't bad, though the humidity can be a drag and the park is often crawling with young campers and their counselors. The water starts to get cold in the fall, but the colored leaves make up for it as do the absence of people and bugs. Only highly experienced trippers should consider canoeing in November, so close to the winter freeze.

It is possible to camp in the interior during the winter, though you'll have to trade in your hiking boots for snowshoes or cross-country skis (for more information on winter camping, see section 10, "Winter Activities," in chapter 4, "Outdoor Pursuits in Algonquin Park").

Once you've decided when to go, the next thing to do is to get yourself a copy of either *Canoe Routes of Algonquin Park* or the *Backpacking Trails Map*, depending on whether you're traveling by canoe or by foot. Both of these maps, especially the former, are packed with wise camping tips, not to mention all the canoe and hiking routes. Chapter 2, "Planning Your Trip," explains how to get copies of these maps and also discusses everything you need to know about your next move: reserving campsites in the interior.

In brief, interior sites can be booked up to 5 months in advance by calling **Ontario Parks** toll-free between 7am and 11pm (© **888/668-7275**; for outside Canada and the U.S., call © **519/826-5290**, or by booking through the website at www.ontarioparks.com. Reservations can be made using Visa, MasterCard, check, or money order, and include a C$9 (US$6.70) nonrefundable charge. Cancellations or changes must be made at least 24 hours in advance (the fee for this is C$6 [US$4.45]), otherwise you will be charged C$20.75 (US$15.40) for an interior permit. A written confirmation of the reservation is sent upon receipt of payment.

Before you call Ontario Parks to make your reservation you must first know your exact route, and that means you need a copy of your map in front of you. Remember, the people who work at the reservation service are not trip counselors; if you have any questions about your prospective route then call the Algonquin Park Information Office (© **705/633-5572**) before making your reservation. The staff there will be happy to review individual trips and make helpful suggestions.

With the map in front of you, be prepared to provide the trip start and departure dates, the entry and exit access points, your daily travel routes, and any possible alternative routes in case your original route is filled to capacity. You will also need to provide contact details, the number of people per party (maximum of nine), your vehicle license number, and a method of payment.

Interior sites cost C$8 (US$5.90) per person, per night. This chapter deals with camping on individual sites in the interior. There are also four interior campgrounds on the periphery of the park (see section 4, "Campgrounds," in chapter 6, "Lodging & Dining Inside the Park").

Overnight camping trips—especially long ones in a canoe—are serious business and should be undertaken only with someone experienced in tow. You have to be totally self-sufficient, with all your food and equipment on your back or in your canoe. You need to know how to read a map and possibly use a compass. You have to be prepared for bad weather. This means waterproofing all your stuff, but it also means feeling confident about paddling across a windy lake with four-foot-high waves crashing over your plunging bow. If you're unsure of your abilities, the park does maintain some **paddle-in campsites** on Crotch and Canisbay lakes. Another option is to hire a guide through one of the outfitters. Rates for this are competitive, and can involve meeting new people if you decide to join in with an existing group. Outfitters can also help if your group wants to go on a trip alone but would prefer if someone else planned the route, assembled all the gear, and packed all the meals. For information on guided trips see chapter 2, "Planning Your Trip"; for a list of outfitters and the services they provide see chapter 3, "Exploring Algonquin Park."

Once your route is mapped out and your interior campsite reservations are made, you're ready to start assembling your equipment: food, clothing, shelter, and all the peripherals. Canoes, lifejackets, paddles, and bailers (if you're canoe tripping) can be rented collectively from an outfitter or brought from home. The best canoes are the lightest canoes, especially if you're planning to do a lot of portaging. Don't bring a cedar-strip or a heavier aluminum canoe if it can be avoided. Kevlar and lightweight Royalex are the lightest, with tough plastic hulls that can take a good beating.

Looking for equipment at a modern camping store can be a bit overwhelming—gear is coming out at you from all directions and there's a real danger of walking out of the shop with a 200-watt revolving headlamp and matching sets of mosquito body-armor. There's a list of suggestions below in the "Camping Gear Checklist," but in the end a lot of this is subjective—how comfortable, exactly, do you want to be? Your best bet is to put together a basic (or elaborate) list of what you need (or think you need) and have a local outfitter go over it to help you avoid overloading yourself with unnecessary paraphernalia—or leaving out something as essential as, say, the map. Once you get some experience under your belt, you'll be able to figure out the extras without spending a king's ransom on gimmicks and garbage.

Bill Mason's *Song of the Paddle* (Toronto: Key Porter) is the camping and canoeing preparation bible. Consult it for the Real Low Down. One thing you should do is waterproof everything— wrap your clothes, sleeping bag, and mattress in plastic garbage bags or in your groundsheet. You'll be happy you did if it rains or you dump your canoe. Zip-lock bags do a tremendous job not only of keeping clothing like socks and underwear dry, but also of keeping in liquids in the event that a package or container bursts.

As far as food goes, both Bill Mason's book and the back of the park's canoe routes map provide some sample menus. The most important thing to remember is the longer the trip the hungrier you will get, so whatever you pack should be high in nutritional value. Because bottles and cans aren't permitted in the interior, you will have to pack all your food into zip-lock bags and plastic containers. A good idea is to prepare one or two meals beforehand (chili, maybe a pasta sauce) and freeze them. By the last days of your trip they will have thawed, all the while having kept whatever food was packed against them (cheese, etc.) nice and cool. Don't drink water directly from the lake (though many do). Fill up water bottles before you go and bring along some iodine tablets for water gathered en route. If you're boiling lake water, be sure to keep it rolling for 5 minutes. You can always fill up your water bottles with hot water before you collapse into your sleeping bag for the night. Dehydration is (literally) a killer, so you should be drinking water constantly while canoeing or hiking. Remember that by the time you feel thirsty, you are already dehydrated.

All canoe trips depart from one of the 29 numbered **access point offices,** and all hiking trips depart from one of four **trailheads.** Before you head into the wilds you must register with a park warden and pick up your interior camping permits, *at least 3 hours before sunset.* Canoeists register at the access point office closest to their departure point; west-side backpackers pick up their permits at the **West Gate,** the **East Gate,** or at the **Rain Lake access point** office in Kearney; east-side backpackers pick up their permits at the **Sand Lake Gate** or the **Achray Campground** office. At each office a park warden will review your route with you and confirm which lakes you will be staying on each night you are in the park. Keep your copy of the permit, as a rambling park warden could ask to see it when you are in the interior (if you are caught in the interior without a permit you will be fined). Also hold on to the yellow garbage bag they bequeath to you. This will help you follow the one true path of **"no-trace camping,"** taking out with you all the refuse you brought in. It's worth reviewing the park regulations in chapter 3, "Exploring Algonquin Park," or on the back of the canoe routes map; the most important of these is the prohibition of cans and bottles in the interior.

(Tips Camping Gear Checklist

- Small first-aid kit—with gauze pads and antiseptic
- Tent with waterproof fly
- Sleeping bag (thick one in autumn)
- Thermarest or foam mattress
- Groundsheet and extra tarp for dinner area, to cover your pack in the canoe, and to use as a makeshift sail if you're feeling really lazy
- Extra garbage bags and zip-lock bags for waterproofing
- Clothes (see "What to Take" in chapter 2, "Planning Your Trip")
- Hiking shoes and water shoes or sandals
- Rainsuit
- Sun hat and sun block
- Lightweight stove and fuel
- Cooking utensils (pots, bowls, cups, cutlery, scouring pad)
- Toilet paper (and zip-lock bags to pack out your used paper)
- Biodegradable hand soap and dish detergent
- Toiletries (toothbrush, toothpaste, etc.)
- Insect repellent
- 10-meter (33-ft.) nylon rope for food hanging and clothesline
- Extra matches in waterproof container
- Pocket flashlight and pocket knife
- Water bottle(s)
- Iodine tablets or water-purification system
- Backpack (for hikers, backpacks should have internal or external aluminum frame and waist belt to help distribute the weight)

Gates & Access Points in the Park

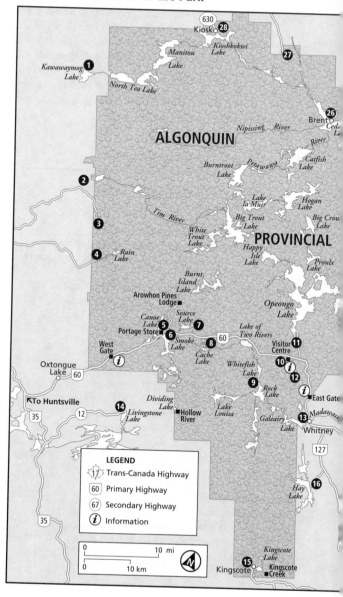

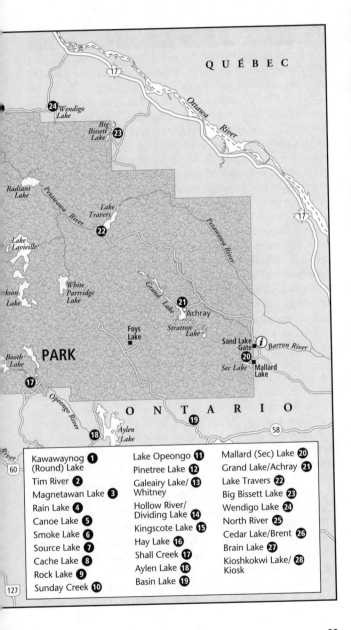

QUÉBEC

Ottawa River

17

17

24 Wendigo Lake

Big Bissett Lake 23

Radiant Lake

Petawawa River

Lake Travers 22

Petawawa River

Lake Lavieille

White Partridge Lake

Grand Lake

ckson Lake

21 Achray
Stratton Lake

Foys Lake

Booth Lake

PARK

Sand Lake Gate ■ *i* Barron River

17

Opeongo River

Sec Lake 20 ■ Mallard Lake

18

Aylen Lake

O N T A R I O

19

58

River

60

127

Kawawaynog (Round) Lake **1**	Lake Opeongo **11**	Mallard (Sec) Lake **20**
Tim River **2**	Pinetree Lake **12**	Grand Lake/Achray **21**
Magnetawan Lake **3**	Galeairy Lake/ Whitney **13**	Lake Travers **22**
Rain Lake **4**	Hollow River/ Dividing Lake **14**	Big Bissett Lake **23**
Canoe Lake **5**	Kingscote Lake **15**	Wendigo Lake **24**
Smoke Lake **6**	Hay Lake **16**	North River **25**
Source Lake **7**	Shall Creek **17**	Cedar Lake/Brent **26**
Cache Lake **8**	Aylen Lake **18**	Brain Lake **27**
Rock Lake **9**	Basin Lake **19**	Kioshkokwi Lake/ Kiosk **28**
Sunday Creek **10**		

2 At the Campsite

Campers in the interior can stay only at designated sites, identified by an orange campsite poster. Canoeists must stay at canoeing campsites and hikers must stay at backpacking campsites (occasionally a lake will have both, as at **Stratton Lake** near Achray). These are identified on your canoe or backpacking map by a solid red triangle for canoeing campsites and an open red triangle for backpacking campsites. I have found that canoe maps from different years show some slight variation in the location of campsites—it's worth having an up-to-date map to avoid paddling out of your way to a campsite that no longer exists.

When you review your route with the park warden, you select a lake but you do not select an actual site (almost all of the backpacking campsites are on lakes). Campsites are taken on a first-come, first-served basis—and, since not all sites are created equal, it pays to arrive in the early afternoon for the pick of the crop. All sites are supposed to be vacated by 2pm, unless of course a group plans to stay at a site for multiple nights. Nine people are the most that can stay at a site, though sometimes it's possible to find two sites next to each other for larger groups.

There are a few tricks to choosing a good site. Often the best sites are on high ground or on jutting peninsulas where it's too windy for insects and rainwater can't pool (though more exposure means you can get raked by storm winds). Islands are also great for lack of bugs and the excellent views, but tricky for firewood—so you'll probably have to scavenge on shore if you want a campfire. A good swimming area is also important, be it a shelf of exposed rock or a sandy beach.

Each maintained campsite in Algonquin Park has several tent clearings (usually three), a fire pit, and a wooden privy some distance from the site. A few of the sites are filled with funky handmade furniture, courtesy of the inveterately handy spring anglers. Campfires are permitted only in the designated fire pits. If you do have a fire, make sure it's fully extinguished before you go to sleep— a fire should never be left unattended. Every year a few campsites are destroyed that way. Obviously, fires are not allowed when a fire ban is on; use your portable stove instead. After you've eaten and cleaned up (in strict accordance with chapter 2's "Protecting the Environment" no-trace camping suggestions, of course), you'll want to hang your food, garbage, and any perfumed toiletries. Find a spot well away from the tents, and throw your rope over a high sturdy tree limb. Packs should be hung at least 3 meters (10 ft.) off the ground and 2 meters (6.6 ft.) away from the tree trunk.

3 Overnight Backpacking Trips

Algonquin Park has three backpacking trails that explore the forests and lakes of the interior—including a few lakes unknown to most canoeists. The trails aren't too difficult, though they are all quite hilly, with some particularly steep sections on the Western Uplands Backpacking Trail. Hikers are meant to follow the direction arrows on trails—usually clockwise—to ensure fewer encounters between parties. Watch for colored trail markers and consult the map often—the trails all intersect with portages or logging roads at various points, so it's easy to head off in the wrong direction. A fit hiker can cover anywhere from 15 to 25 kilometers (9.3 to 15.5 miles) a day, though contour lines on a map mean vertical distance in addition to horizontal, so judge accordingly. The two most important pieces of equipment are your hiking boots (preferably worn-in prehike) and your pack, which should have an internal or external frame to distribute the 25 or so kilograms (55 lb.) of weight.

All three of the trails have loops that can be hiked in a single day, though at 32 kilometers (20 miles) you will need to start early and really go hard if you want to finish the first **Western Uplands Backpacking Trail** loop. In general, the **Eastern Pines Backpacking Trail** is the best for hikes of one or two days, the **Highland Backpacking Trail** for hikes of two to three days, and the **Western Uplands Backpacking Trail** for hikes of anywhere from two to six days (it is the only one that can accommodate long hikes). The **Highland Backpacking Trail** is the most crowded, the **Western Uplands Backpacking Trail** the least. All of them are beautiful—with fine lookouts over lakes, dips into wildlife-rich rivers and boglands, and haunted stretches of deep forest.

WESTERN UPLANDS BACKPACKING TRAIL   This longest of the three trails has loops of 32 kilometers (20 miles), 1 to 2 days; 55 kilometers (34.1 miles), 3 to 4 days; and 71 kilometers (44 miles), 5 to 6 days. There are two access points for this trail, one at **Rain Lake** east of Kearney, the other on Highway 60 just before K 3. Trips departing from Rain Lake have an 8.4-kilometer (5.2-mile) walk-in to the main loops and are therefore longer; the longest loop is 88 kilometers (54.5 miles). One of the highlights of this hard-wood forest trail is the number of fantastically clear lakes: **Maple Leaf Lake** (just 3 kilometers [1.9 miles] from the Parkway Corridor), **Maggie Lake** (with roomy, much-loved campsites), and **Lupus Lake** (deep and glacial-hued). **Islet Lake** at the top end of the longest loop is also quite scenic. It was once the site of an enormous wooden railway trestle from the **Ottawa, Arnprior & Parry Sound Railway.** Now it's just a long mound of earth at the north end of the lake.

HIGHLAND BACKPACKING TRAIL This trail has some steep sections, but compensates with some fine views. It is the busiest of the trails, and **Provoking Lake** in particular is a popular spot with campers not interested in straying too far into the interior. Hikers looking for some peace and quiet are better off continuing on to **Heads Lake** or further on still to **Harkness Lake.** The **Highland Backpacking Trail** has two loops, one of 19 kilometers (12 miles) that circles **Provoking Lake,** and another of 35 kilometers (21.7 miles) that rolls out to **Mosquito Creek** in the southeast before wrapping parallel to **Head Lake** and back past **Faya Lake,** a tiny glacial hole in the Algonquin carpet.

EASTERN PINES BACKPACKING TRAIL This is a trail worth going out of your way to hike—it's on the much quieter east side of the park, and it passes some superb natural attractions. There are two loops, both of which share their beginning and end sections with the **Berm Lake Trail** (see "Achray & Brent Day Hikes" in chapter 4, "Outdoor Pursuits in Algonquin Park," and see *Achray Trails & Canoe Routes* map later in this chapter). The first is a 7-kilometer (4.3-mile) walk through pine forest and around **Johnston Lake,** home of ospreys and great blue herons. This can easily be walked in one day. The second loop is about 15 kilometers (9.3 miles) all around, with an optional 2-kilometer (1.2-mile) round trip down to **High Falls** that is absolutely worth doing. The falls have a series of overflowing rock pools with a natural waterslide for hours of fun. It's a perfect weekend excursion—one morning to one of the three campsites near High Falls, an afternoon of frolicking, and a return hike the next day. **Stratton Lake** also has some nice sites, though make sure you don't stay in one of the canoe sites to be found on both sides.

4 Overnight Canoe Trips

Canoeing, in my opinion, is the one true way of traveling Algonquin—and the more variety in your chosen water terrain the better. Rivers are especially good for novices, with lots of twisting and cleaving through the bright purple pickerelweed. Generally rivers take twice as long to run as you'd expect, so take this into account when you're working out your distances. They are worth seeking out, as often a river is really just an open ribbon of water through peat-encroached bog, classic habitats for great blue heron and grazing moose. Lakes, of course, will take up the majority of your paddling time. They range from small, shallow, and marshy to gigantic and wind-swept. Sticking to the shores on the big lakes will get you to your destination faster if there's a headwind, and shore views are better for spotting wildlife. Most people try to minimize the amount of portaging they do; it's more difficult to appreciate nature with a canoe on your head, and portaging is quite tiring. Portages are indicated by yellow signs tied to trees at either end, with distances marked in meters. Try to do portages in one trip if you can (with a canoe and a smaller pack on)—it's not such a big deal to make multiple trips if the portage is short, but it gets tedious storming back and forth on a 4-kilometer trail hauling multiple loads. Portage techniques (well, there's really just one: lifting) are discussed in the Friends of Algonquin Park's *Canoeist's Manual*, available at all park bookstores and most access point offices for a bargain-basement C$1 (US$0.74).

Tips Stroke It to the Left

Basic canoeing skills are a breeze to learn, though they take practice to perfect. If you are just learning, make sure to get yourself a copy of either the *Canoeist's Manual* by park legend Omer Stringer, or Bill Mason's *Song of the Paddle* (or his more comprehensive *Path of the Paddle*). The following summary of three basic strokes is inspired by readings from both expert canoeists. The technique for sharp turns follows.

The J-Stroke
The basic canoeing dynamic is that the bow provides power and the stern steers. The canoe will always veer away from the stern paddler's side, so to correct this he or she uses the

J-stroke. The paddle is pulled back as in a regular stroke, but when the lower hand reaches the hip the canoeist twists the flat of the paddle out and pries away from the canoe using the paddle as a lever against the gunwale. This is usually done in one smooth motion, and is impressive to behold as paddlers combine casual cool poise with breathless results.

The Sweep

This is a pretty easy stroke, used to turn the canoe away from the side you are paddling on. The paddle is extended out in front of the paddler, flat side down, and swept in an arc out to the limit of the paddler's range and around to the stern, paddler rigid in the center like a pivot. Don't lean over too much, and make sure the entire blade of the paddle is immersed horizontally in the water.

The Draw

Also fairly easy. The draw does the opposite of the sweep: it pulls either end of the canoe in to the side you are paddling on. The paddler extends the paddle out and draws it in toward the canoe, a small wedge of drawn water splashing into the side.

Combination Left and Right Turns

For the sharpest turns, persons in both the bow and the stern should be engaged. To turn sharply away from the stern-side paddler, the bow person should do a draw on their side, and the stern person should do a sweep. To turn the other way, toward the stern-side paddler, the bow person should do a sweep and the sterner should continue with a regular J-stroke.

In the noble quest to avoid portages, people have come up with all kinds of idealized canoe routes—both one-way and loops. Loops are the most common at the southwest and central parts of the park. The most lakes are located here, and it's quite possible to string a large number together without too much time spent portaging. On the other hand, everyone else has the same idea, so the **Canoe Lake–Joe Lake–Burnt Island Lake–Tom Thomson Lake** circuits are not very private in high season. Trips departing from **Lake Opeongo** and heading into central Algonquin's big lakes (**Proulx, Happy Isle, Big Crow, Lavieille, Dickson**) encounter fewer people, but the longer distances and the longer portages mean they take longer to complete. While it's possible to do loops on the park's more isolated north and east sides, many trippers just do one-way routes and park a car at either end, or arrange to have an outfitter shuttle drop them off. The **Barron Canyon, Petawawa River,** and **North Tea–Manitou Kioshkokwi–Mink–Cedar Lake** runs all are often done this way. Generally you can expect to cover between 15 and 25 kilometers (9.3 and 15.5 miles) a day including portages— a traveling time of between 4 and 6 hours.

Below I have detailed three canoe trips in three different areas of the park—all of them some distance from Canoe Lake and the park's busiest routes. The first is a 2- to 3-day trip, the second a 3- to 4-day trip, and the third a 4-day trip. I have also suggested ways in which each of the trips can be shortened (or lengthened, in one case) to fewer days, or made easier by less paddling.

GRAND LAKE–STRATTON LAKE–BARRON RIVER (2–3 DAYS)

The **Barron Canyon** is one of the standout sites of the park, a huge rock cut more than 100 meters (328 ft.) high in places. Canoeing beneath it is amazing; you feel like a tiny wet pinball in an enormous geological machine. It's a very popular trip, especially with people coming from Ottawa, since Achray is closer to Ottawa than either the East Gate or the Parkway Corridor. This one-way route takes 2 to 3 days to complete, and is suitable for all skill levels (though there is considerable portaging, so bring your hiking boots). Canoeists should either leave a second car at the Squirrel Rapids parking lot or arrange to have one of the local outfitters pick them up.

The access point office is right by the **Achray Campground** on **Grand Lake** (you can stay the night at the campground if you want to get an early start). On Grand Lake go southwest along the shore past a string of beaches until you reach the entrance to the **Barron River,** no more than an hour's paddle. There is a short 30-meter (100-ft.) portage around a low dam; **Stratton Lake** is just beyond. Stratton Lake is long and narrow, with rock shoulders on both sides and deep green depths. It is a wonderful paddling lake, and has excellent campsites dotted along the north side, especially at the far end of the lake. You can spend your first night at one of these sites, or take another short 45-meter (150-ft.) portage down into **St. Andrews Lake** and stay at one of the six campsites there (when

Achray Trails & Canoe Routes

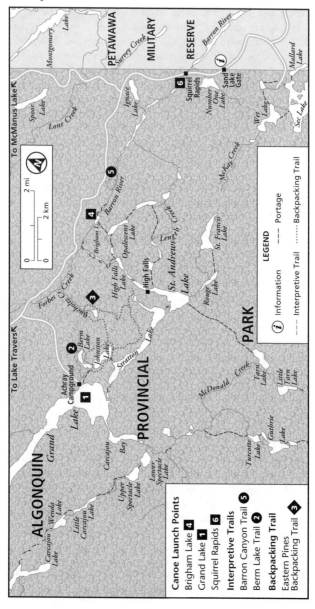

Canoe Launch Points
Brigham Lake 4
Grand Lake 1
Squirrel Rapids 6

Interpretive Trails
Barron Canyon Trail 5
Berm Lake Trail 2

Backpacking Trail
Eastern Pines
Backpacking Trail 3

LEGEND

i Information
--- Portage
--- Interpretive Trail
...... Backpacking Trail

(Map labels:)

To McManus Lake
To Lake Travers

ALGONQUIN

PETAWAWA
MILITARY
RESERVE

Montgomery Lake
Survey Creek
Barron River
Mallard Lake
Spoor Lake
Lone Creek
Ignace Lake
Squirrel Rapids 6
Sand Lake Gate *i*
Number One Lake
Wet Lake
Sec Lake
McKay Creek
Barron River 5
Brigham L. 4
Opalescent Lake
Len's Creek
St. Francis Lake
High Falls L.
High Falls
St. Andrews Creek
Forbes Ck. Creek
Buchanan Lake
Rouge Lake
Berm Lake 2
Johnston Lake
Stratton Lake
Achray Campground 1
PROVINCIAL
McDonald Creek
Tarn Lake
Little Tarn Lake
PARK
Grand Lake
Carcajou Bay
Lower Spectacle Lake
Upper Spectacle Lake
Little Carcajou Lake
Wenda Lake
Carcajou Lake
Turcotte Lake
Guthrie Lake

N

0 — 2 mi
0 — 2 km

Stratton is full it's often possible to secure one of these sites). Either way, you'll want to unload your stuff and then get back into your canoe for a visit to **High Falls** at the far northeastern end of Stratton Lake. You can pull up your canoe and hike over to the falls for a scenic picnic, or just flop around in the descending pools of water.

Day two begins at St. Andrews Lake. From the top of the lake there are two portages; take the second, higher one into **High Falls Lake.** At the north end of High Falls Lake there are a couple of different portage routes to **Brigham Lake.** The portage that involves the least amount of loading and unloading is via Opalescent Lake and the Brigham Chute (an old logging flume that no longer exists), a total portaging distance of 2,170 meters (7,160 ft.). This haul can't be avoided, but it's worth it when you reach the canyon (for a geological history of the canyon, see section 3, "Achray & Brent Day Hikes," in chapter 4, "Outdoor Pursuits in Algonquin Park"). The next 2 hours are the highlight of the trip: the gentle current takes you down past the steep cliffs and the circling ravens and red-tailed hawks high overhead. You can either finish the trip at Squirrel Rapids, or you can camp at one of the half-dozen or so Barron River sites and pull out in the morning.

ALTERNATIVES

For an even shorter trip, you can put in at Squirrel Rapids and paddle into Barron Canyon for the day (or stay one night at one of the river campsites). Another option is putting in at the Brigham Lake Access (33 kilometers [20.5 miles] down the Barron Canyon Road) and paddling one-way down to Squirrel Rapids (you'll need a ride back to the car). For a more demanding 3-day paddle, you can always do a full circuit from Achray, staying 2 nights at St. Andrews or Stratton Lake and visiting the canyon in a day trip.

OPEONGO–PROULX–BIG CROW–OPEONGO (3–4 DAYS)

This trip is a one-way dip into **Big Crow Lake** at the center of Algonquin Park—a solid 3 to 4 days of paddling through wide-open bodies of water and narrow rivers with very little portaging and an afternoon's excursion to one of the park's last (and its largest) stand of **virgin white pines** just off the **Crow River.** The possible waves of Opeongo make it unsuitable for beginner paddlers—unless a water-taxi is arranged to shuttle the party back and forth to the **Proulx Lake** portage (see "Alternatives," below).

Access Point 11 on Lake Opeongo is the departure point, a short drive from the Parkway Corridor just past K 46. It is serviced by one of the two outfitters in the park, the **Opeongo Store.** Trippers can rent canoes and gear here, and even pick up prepared menus if pre-arranged. Opeongo itself is Algonquin's largest lake, a broad Y that splits into a north and an east arm. To paddle from the access point to the top of the north arm takes a good 5 hours, more if the lake is windy, since the headwind is usually from the north. Unless you are a confident paddler, you do not want to navigate Opeongo on a windy day when the waves are up. Canoeists should stay to the left side of the lake; the portage into **Proulx Lake** is in a protected bay at the top of the north arm.

The two portages leading into Proulx are relatively easy; they add up to just over a kilometer if you canoe across the tiny lake between them—though once you have the canoe on your back you may as well just walk the whole thing and follow the path around the lake. Proulx is a lovely lake, with different shades of evergreen lapping down the surrounding hills. There are some nice campsites along the northeast side of the lake where the shore dips in and out, forming slight outcroppings. The **Crow River** leads out of the north end of Proulx and takes a couple of hours to paddle. Its drowsy switchbacks are hypnotic, occasional stands of tamarack inching toward the gliding canoe. **Little Crow Lake** is an excellent place to lunch; one of the campsites on the east side has a large rock landing—perfect for swimming and lounging in the sun. Coming out of the narrow passage between Little Crow Lake into **Big Crow Lake** is a shock as a lot of space seems to rear up very suddenly. The lake is dominated by high cliffs on its south side, pines crowded perilously close to the edge. The last remaining **fire tower** in Algonquin Park sits high above the lake, looking fragile next to the heavy crowns of trees. The campsites on the east side of the lake near the eastern outlet of Crow River are amazing. Two of them are set back on sandy beaches, sheltered by pine and hemlock.

The 2-hour excursion into an area of **old-growth white pine** is worth going out of the way for. Paddle east a short distance down the inlet of Crow River to the entrance of the trail (look for the beaver dam to the right of the portage entrance). Around 35 minutes along the path is the main event: a dozen 300-year-old white pines towering above the canopy. Spared by a far-sighted early park superintendent, the trees are now in their senescence, and many of them are dying. A small yellow sign indicates when you've reached the end of the trail. On your return, watch for bear claw marks on the beech trees where they climb to get at the beechnuts. Canoeing (and portaging) all the way from Big Crow Lake to Lake Opeongo will take 5 hours or so. There are plenty of good campsites in the north arm on both sides of where the portage exits, especially on the islands. The canoe journey back down Lake Opeongo is usually faster than the ascent.

ALTERNATIVES

For a longer 4- to 5-day trip, continue on Crow River to **Lake Lavielle,** on to **Dickson Lake,** and around to the East Arm of Opeongo. The Crow River can get pretty low, especially in the fall, so you will almost certainly have to do all the portages and may even have to drag your canoe over some exposed rocks. Lavielle and Dickson are large lakes smack in the center of an even larger wilderness zone. It's a solid day's paddle from where the Crow River enters Crow Bay through Lavielle to Dickson, with nary a portage in sight. Both these lakes are wild and relatively barren of campers, mostly because they are protected by a tear-inducing 5-kilometer (3.1-mile) portage into Bonfield, Wright, and finally, Opeongo.

An alternative for beginner (or simply relaxed) paddlers is taking a water-taxi to and from Opeongo's north arm. The Opeongo Store charges C$21 (US$15.60) per person each way, a price that includes all gear and canoes (up to three canoes at a time). On busy weekends the boat is going back and forth all day, so make sure to make a reservation if you want to be dropped off and picked up at a designated time.

NORTH TEA–BIGGAR–THREE MILE– MANITOU–NORTH TEA (4 DAYS)

This is a great route that is often overlooked by trippers—even though the town of South River (due east of North Tea Lake) is only an hour or so farther up Highway 11 from Huntsville. The route passes through big rugged boreal lakes with long beaches and heavy green forest. It's a fairly demanding four days of paddling, though there are ways to shorten the route (see "Alternatives," below). Be aware that both **North Tea** and **Manitou** can occasionally have quite a headwind, though this doesn't prevent the lakes from being suitable for a range of paddling abilities. All it does is slow you down.

Access Point 1 is 18 kilometers (11.2 miles) east of South River on **Kawawaymog Lake,** a few kilometers outside the park's western boundary. There are a few outfitters located on this lake, all of which rent canoes and equipment (the outfitters and some general rates are listed in section 1, "Essentials," in chapter 3, "Exploring Algonquin Park"). Getting from the launch point to the entrance of the **Amable du Fond River**—one of the eight rivers whose headwaters originate in the park—takes about a half hour of paddling. Although the river isn't officially in Algonquin Park it feels wild enough, with great blue herons staked out at many of the bends. Canoeing the river and hopping the two short portages is two hours of easy work. **North Tea Lake** is long and pinched in the center, creating a natural division between the east and west arms. There are some broad beaches on the north side of the lake, contours parallel to the undulating line of pine above. It takes about 2 hours to paddle the length of North Tea to where it narrows and becomes **Mangotasi Lake.** This marshy low area is excellent moose habitat; they graze on the tubers and roots in the mud, or munch on the leaves of aquatic plants.

There are three easy portages into **Biggar Lake,** bringing the total distance covered from Kawawaymog Lake to more than 20 kilometers (12.4 miles). The campsites on Biggar Lake (especially those on the south side) are better than those on Mangotasi, so it's worth pushing on that extra bit. Biggar Lake is ringed with cedar, trimmed evenly along the waterline by foraging deer. There are some serious portages between Biggar and Manitou Lake—just under 6 kilometers (3.7 miles) worth. The first set of portages, broken up by the tiny Sinclair, Kawa, and Upper Kawa Lakes, can be done in over an hour, *providing you can manage it in one trip.* Doing a portage in one trip is a key skill to learn, especially in a portage-dense area like this. The best way to arrange it is to divide all the gear into a smaller and a larger pack. One person takes the canoe and the small pack, the other the large pack and any other small bags or gear lying around (paddles can be carried or slipped under the thwarts of the upside-down canoe). When the first person gets tired they can teepee the canoe either on one of the crossbars installed between trees on the portages or on the raised arms of their companion. And so it goes.

Three Mile Lake is nice and isolated, a good place to stay the night. It takes about an hour to cross the length of Three Mile to the 2,800-meter (9,240-ft.) portage into Manitou. Load up on high-calorie gorp before this one; although most of the portage is along a flat logging road, 2.8 kilometers (1.9 miles) is still a long way to carry a canoe. Once into Manitou, there is a sweet swimming area on the beach across from the portage exit. This is also an excellent campsite (fire pit sheltered behind a big rock), with a long view down Manitou to the setting sun.

Manitou is one of my favorite lakes in the park. It is wide and clean, with a steep wedge of green shoreline between the blue of the sky and the blue of the water. There must be 50 campsites on the lake, but at no time does it seem crowded. The portage from Manitou back into North Tea starts steep but ends easily enough. North Tea Lake has even more campsites than Manitou, the best of them scattered across rough little islands and peninsulas, particularly at the far southwestern end of the lake.

ALTERNATIVES

You can shorten the trip to 3 days (and avoid most of the portages) by cutting out Biggar and Three Mile lakes and heading directly into Manitou from North Tea. This would also be a nice and relaxed 4-day trip, with plenty of time to bake on the rocks and explore the shoreline. An even shorter route would be into North Tea Lake and out, an easy 2-day paddle.

6

Lodging & Dining Inside the Park

Staying in Algonquin Park is the best way of exploring it. You become attuned to some of the surrounding natural rhythms, the cascade of animal sounds from dawn to dusk, the changing contrast of light and shadow in the forest. Accommodation inside the park runs the full gamut from luxurious lodge to basic campground and tent. The yurts and ranger cabins lie somewhere between these two extremes, both in price and in comfort level. Although each type of accommodation provides the visitor with a different experience, the Algonquin landscape is always center stage. Lodges are all tucked in the woods off Highway 60, cabins and screened porches looking out over quiet lakes. Yurts and ranger cabins provide rougher but more inexpensive sleeping facilities, solid shelters without the rain hazards and space issues of nylon. The ranger cabins add an interesting historical dimension to your stay in the park, and they are the only roofed lodging located in the park interior. Finally, there are 12 campgrounds in the park and many hundreds of tent sites, some private, others in more sociable areas. The majority of campgrounds are along the Parkway Corridor, though there are some out on the park periphery as well.

Everyone staying in Algonquin Park is required to display a vehicle permit on the car dashboard. Permits are included in the camping, yurt rental, and ranger cabin rental fees—visitors are given permits when they check in at the appropriate access point or campground office. All lodges provide vehicle permits for their guests.

For information on camping in the interior, consult chapter 5, "Camping in the Interior." Winter camping is another option at the park; for more details, check out section 10, "Winter Activities," in chapter 4, "Outdoor Pursuits in Algonquin Park."

⎛Tips⎞ Kilometer Markings

Reflective signs along the Parkway Corridor (the stretch of Highway 60 that runs between the West and East Gates) indicate the distance in kilometers from the West Gate. Points of interest in this book that lie along the Parkway Corridor will have these kilometer markings as reference. For example, the Visitor Centre is located at K 43.

1 Lodges

The lodge era in Algonquin Park began with the coming of the Ottawa, Arnprior & Parry Sound Railway in 1896. Though hauling logs was its primary concern, it wasn't long before entrepreneurs figured out how to make room for tourists and address the Canadian enthusiasm for authentic "wilderness living." Of course, apart from the bumpy train ride, conditions were far from rough. Places like Hotel Algonquin, the Highland Inn, and Mowat Lodge had lavish spreads that accommodated huge numbers of city socialites. Things are not so very different now. Though the big lodges of yesteryear have all burned down or been demolished, three smaller, slightly newer lodges remain. The focus is still on that much-sought combination of comfort and rustic forest credibility—only now the attire is a little less formal, and the guests come more for the peace and quiet than the social buzz.

Arowhon Pines ✷✷✷ *Finds*   This is the most remote and the most elegant resort within the park, with excellent dining and superior facilities. The word has spread that Arowhon is *the* place to stay! Visited by individuals, couples, and families from all over the globe, this resort could probably be successful without ever advertising simply because so many of its guests return year after year. The resort manages to strike a perfect balance between wilderness and comfort; the spare decor of the buildings melds with the surrounding forest but does not diminish its charm. The fulcrum of the Arowhon spread is a stunning six-sided log dining room with central fireplace that rises above the red shingle roof like a Byzantine turret—there's an incredible view from the outside veranda, where guests retire after meals to eat desserts and drink tea. Inside it looks more like a grand old European lodge, with high-quality food served

Lodging & Dining in the Park

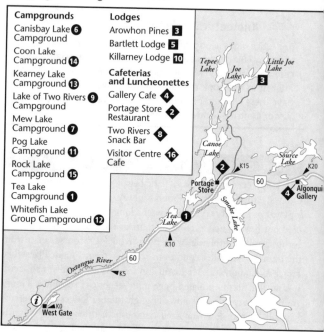

Campgrounds
Canisbay Lake **6**
Campground
Coon Lake
Campground **14**
Kearney Lake
Campground **13**
Lake of Two Rivers **9**
Campground
Mew Lake
Campground **7**
Pog Lake
Campground **11**
Rock Lake
Campground **15**
Tea Lake
Campground **1**
Whitefish Lake
Group Campground **12**

Lodges
Arowhon Pines **3**
Bartlett Lodge **5**
Killarney Lodge **10**

**Cafeterias
and Luncheonettes**
Gallery Cafe **4**
Portage Store **2**
Restaurant
Two Rivers **8**
Snack Bar
Visitor Centre **16**
Cafe

on candlelit buffet tables (for a review of the amazing food at Arowhon Pines, see "Dining in the Park" later in this chapter). The central buildings date from the 1930s, and even the peripheral cabins have an aged feel about them of the kind usually associated with ancestral cottages. Guests can choose to stay in tastefully furnished private cabins in remote corners of the woods (complete with fireplace), or they can stay in larger multi-group log cabins closer to the resort's hub. These cabins are less expensive and more social, filled with return guests who chat by the wood-burning fireplaces in the shared lounges. Depending on the size of the cabin, 2, 3, 4, 8, or 12 rooms radiate out from the central area, each one decorated with antique pine furniture, each with its own bathroom. Extended families can rent whole cabins; there are daily and weekly rates. Apart from the usual flotilla of canoes and sailboats at the waterfront, there is a tennis court, sauna, and four specially maintained trails through the forest. **Summer:** P.O. Box 10001, Huntsville, ON P1H 2G5.

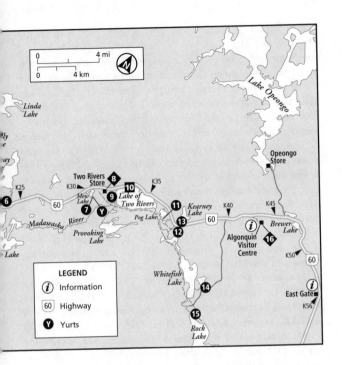

C 705/633-5661; fax 705/633-5795; **Winter:** 297 Balliol St., Toronto, ON M4S 1C7. *C* 416/483-4393; fax: 416/483-4429. www.arowhonpines.ca. 49 units, incl. 3 private cabins; C$190 (US$140.90) double in shared cabin; C$246 (US$182.45) 2-bedroom cabin; C$314 (US$232.90) private cabin (double). 15% discount May 30–June19; 10% premium July 4–Aug 28. Children under 12 half double rate when sharing w/ 2 adults. All meals included. MC, V. Open May 30–Oct. 13. At the end of Arowhon Pines Road off Highway 60 (K 15). **Amenities:** Restaurant, screened porch at main lodge, sauna, tennis courts, games room, movie night, hiking trails, canoes, kayaks, sailboats, rowboats, open-launch cruiser, lake swimming, dock. No pets.

Bartlett Lodge ℛ   Rustic Bartlett is the oldest existing lodging in the park and the only one you need a boat to access (guests call from the courtesy phone at the **Cache Lake** landing). This relative isolation will set the tone of your stay. The peninsula is deeply wooded and there are private cabins in the trees. Bartlett seems to attract a mostly European clientele; they meet in the newly built

lounge just off the dining room, poking at the models of the old Highland and Algonquin Inns. The cabins themselves are a mixed bag. Some are log, others tongue and groove, some are located right on the water (the best ones), while others are set back in the woods on the far side of the main trail. Cabins can accommodate families large and small; five of the cabins have two bedrooms, one has three, all have bathrooms. For die-hard home cooks, there are two house-keeping cabins that come with their own pots, stove, and fridge. Groups tend to stay for a week or more, which, along with the plain decor, gives the whole place something of a congenial camp feel— as you might expect of owners who also run a summer camp for kids. Each of the cabins comes with its own canoe, with kayaks and paddleboats provided on request. The Bartlett dining room is famous throughout the area, its excellent cuisine attracting a cluster of locals every evening at the landing. For a full review of the food at Bartlett Lodge, see "Dining in the Park" later in this chapter.
Summer: P.O. Box 10004, Huntsville, ON P1H 2G8. ⓒ **705/633-5543**; fax 705/633-5746; **Winter:** 297 Lakeshore Road East, Suite 2, Oakville, ON L6J 1J3. ⓒ **905/338-8908**; fax: 905/338-3039; www.bartlettlodge.com. 12 units, 5 with 2 bed-rooms, 1 with 3 bedrooms. For "Modified American Plan" cabins: July–Sept C$199 (US$147.60) per person; June–Oct C$175 (US$129.80) per person; May C$145 (US$107.55) per person. 2 meals included. For housekeeping cabins (no meals): July–Sept C$140 (US$103.85) per person; June–Oct C$110 (US$81.60) per person; May C$90 (US$66.75) per person. Children under 10 C$65 (US$48.20). MC, V, debit. Open May–Oct. The Cache Lake parking lot is at K 23, across from the entrance to the Canisbay Lake campground. **Amenities:** Restaurant, canoes, kayaks, paddle-boats, lake swimming, dock, bike rental, motor boat rental for fishing. No pets.

Killarney Lodge ⓡ   Tucked just off the Parkway Corridor on a peninsula overlooking Lake of Two Rivers is a modest and uniquely set resort complete with cozy-looking traditional cabins that have been recently renovated and decorated (and are now chic and invit-ing). The wholesome black and red-trim cabins peek out from among the sheltering pines, surrounded by bushels of colorful flow-ers. Everything about Killarney Lodge is delightful, from the friendly staff, crackling dining room fireplace, and log cabins straight on down to the immaculate shuffleboard set. All guests stay in small cabins with full bath, most of them private, some with two bedrooms (for large groups or families), and some with a shared veranda. The decor is "sophisticated country," with shiny hardwood floors and thick-quilted beds. Each cabin comes with its own canoe, which intrepid paddlers can launch from beneath their little porches or from the small stretch of sandy beach by the entrance to the lodge. The main lounge and games room has a strict TV ban, a welcome silence that is unfortunately breached on occasion by sounds from the nearby highway. Nevertheless, the more expensive cabins at the far side of the peninsula feel isolated enough, especially when the sun sets to the cry of loons on the water. The dining room serves hearty country fare in big portions—perfect after a day spent on one of the nearby trails. **Summer:** P.O. Box 10005, Algonquin Park, ON P1H 2G9 ℂ 705/633-5551; fax 705/633-5667; **Winter:** ℂ and fax 416/482-5254; www.killarneylodge.com. 37 units. All cabins on the water run from C$139–C$179 (US$103.10–US$132.75) in the spring (May 9–June 26); C$184–C$229 (US$136.50–US$169.85) in high season (June 27–July 10; Sept 1–4; Sept 7–11; Oct 13–19); and C$209–C$259 (US$155–US$192.10) in the peak season (July 11–Aug 31; Sept 5–6; Sept 12–Oct 12). Two-bedroom cabins are at a rate of C$129–C$139 (US$95.70–US$103.10) in the spring; C$164–C$189 (US$121.65–US$140.20) in the high season; and C$184–C$209 (US$136.50–US$155) in the peak season. All 3 meals included. MC, V. Open May 12–Oct 15. South of Highway 60 at K 33. **Amenities:** Restaurant, games room, shuffleboard, canoes, beach, lake swimming. No pets.

2 Yurts

You may be thinking, "What the heck is a yurt?" After extensive research, I can tell you that it's not an alpine pack animal, nor is it a type of cheese curd, or even a shameful social habit ("And then he produced a rather *dreadful* yurt. You can imagine our embarrassment..."). A yurt, according to the *Oxford English Dictionary*, is "a circular tent of felt, skins, etc., on a collapsible framework, used by nomads in Mongolia and Siberia." Well, yurts are also used by Canadians, and these ones aren't made of stinky pelts. They're 100% army-surplus canvas, and, being heated, they're also the only roofed winter accommodation you'll find in all of Algonquin Park (unless you count the dog-sledder shelters). In the summer there are eight yurts in the park: one at Achray and seven at the Mew Lake campground. Come wintertime the Achray yurt closes, but the Mew Lake yurts stay at capacity—cross-country skiers are all over them, and kids dig the bargain-basement Ikea-style metal bunk beds.

Each six-sided yurt can house up to six people; inside are six chairs, a table, cooking gear, a propane barbecue, and two sets of bunks with singles on top and double futons on the bottom (but make sure you bring your own sleeping bag, pillows, and linen). There is an outdoor fire pit—in fact, all cooking has to be done outside—and all pets have to stay outside too since they cramp a funky yurt's style. In the winter the park employees remove all the pots and pans, so you have to bring your own. You also have to bring your own 15- to 30-meter (50- to 100-ft.) extension cord to plug in the block heater. Don't forget, there are 24-hour heated washrooms at the West Gate all winter long.

For a breakdown of yurt rental fees, see "Vehicle Permits, Camping and Rental Fees" in chapter 3, "Exploring Algonquin Park."

3 Ranger Cabins

At one time in the early part of the century, Algonquin Park had a large number of interior cabins, all of them stocked with provisions for the roving bands of rangers. As park policy changed, the cabins went unused and eventually began to fall apart. Tourism saved them. When it was discovered that visitors would pay to stay in these remote cabins, the park resuscitated 13 of them. Now they are an excellent way of immersing yourself in the wild without immersing yourself in discomfort. The cabins are particularly popular with anglers, who come in the spring to fish the surrounding lakes and rivers. Others like the idea of staying so close to an old fire tower (like the one standing less than a kilometer [a half-mile] behind the Big Crow Cabin), or simply like being self-sufficient in the wilds.

Most of the cabins are rustic log constructions equipped with wood-burning stoves, tables, chairs, and outside toilets. They are often located either on a lake or a river, though some are so remote there's not even any water access. All of the cabins can sleep at least four people, some as many as eight, and it is always possible to pitch an extra tent outside. The three drive-in cabins—at Rain Lake, Brent, and Kiosk—are larger and more comfortable, with multiple bedrooms (Brent has four, plus a cool wooden porch), full mattresses, electric fridges, and propane stoves for cooking. The interior cabins are not so plush; in fact, they're really just a roof in the woods. Most of them are large open-concept single rooms, where visitors sleep on double or single bunks—no padding, just hard board under the behind, so make sure to bring your own b-b-bedding. None of these cabins have cooking stoves—though some come with their own aluminum canoe, a fair consolation. All cooking happens outside on the campfire or on the visitor's own portable stove. For the full scoop on each of the cabins and their respective histories and amenities, call the park **Information Office** (© **705/633-5572**) and ask them to send you a free "Old Ranger Cabin Rentals" brochure.

All of the ranger cabins are very popular, especially the drive-in ones, which should be reserved up to 5 months in advance (all of the cabins close for the winter in mid-October and open again in time for the spring fishing season). Renters have to check in to the closest access point office between 2 and 5pm to register, pay, and pick up the keys. Some of the cabins (like Birchcliffe) take more than one day to reach, so be prepared to spend at least one night in the interior (a separate permit and expense). All cabins must be locked and vacated by noon on the day of departure. And there are no pets allowed.

Rental rates for Algonquin's ranger cabins are listed under "Vehicle Permits, Camping and Rental Fees" in chapter 3, "Exploring Algonquin Park." More about the history of the ranger cabins can be read in "Historical Attractions," also in chapter 3.

4 Campgrounds

PARKWAY CORRIDOR CAMPGROUNDS

Most of those who visit Algonquin Park do so by staying at one of the nine campgrounds along the Parkway Corridor. This is a way of immersing yourself in nature without going to all the hassle of an interior trip. There is a range of privacy both among campgrounds and within the campgrounds themselves, so it's up to you to choose how social or how isolated you want to be. The campgrounds aren't just places to lay your tent; they are places to come and have fun quite apart from what the rest of the park itself may offer. Most of the sites have good beach facilities where families can swim, play volleyball (some have nets), or canoe. Other people prefer simply to stake out a spot in the sun, or hang around the campfire grilling burgers and sipping beers.

Campers can expect moderate increases to the prices quoted in this section year over year. With the exception of Rock Lake, all of the campgrounds are run by private contractors who maintain a small office on-site. This is where you come to pick up your permit once you've made a reservation (though you can show up and hope for the best if you don't have a reservation—there are usually vacancies during the week). Some of the campgrounds share an office; the bulletin board will indicate where to go if you arrive at a campground with no office on-site. All of the campgrounds have cold running water and some kind of toilet facilities—however primitive—and many have comfort stations with hot water and showers. Each campground has between 40 and 300 sites, all on level clearings. Most of them have fire pits (with grill) and picnic benches, and many of them have electrical hookups, though you pay more for these and must specify "electrical" when you make your reservation. Six people in up to three tents and a single vehicle are allowed per site (second vehicles pay an additional C$9 [US$6.70]). Canisbay Lake, Mew Lake, Pog Lake, and Achray all have dog-free and radio-free sites for campers intent on silence. In all other areas dogs must be on a leash. For information on reserving a campsite, see section 2, "Reserving a Campsite," in chapter 2, "Planning Your Trip."

Canisbay Lake Campground ⚓   Because of its distance from the highway and the large dispersed grounds, Canisbay is one of the quieter campgrounds. There is good swimming at the large unsupervised beach. Canisbay also maintains **16 paddle-in campsites** at the far side of the lake for campers who want that extra privacy without the serious paddling or portaging. There is a day-use picnic ground at the far west end of the grounds, just above the dog- and radio-free zones. The closest firewood available is at Mew Lake Campground, 7 kilometers (4.3 miles) east of Canisbay, open in the summer from 10am to 8pm. Located at the south end of Canisbay Lake, 1 kilometer (0.6 mile) north of Highway 60 at K 23. 242 sites maintained by Whiskey Jack Park Services. Rates for up to 6 C$24 (US$17.80) with no hookups, C$28 (US$20.80) with hookups. Open May 17–Oct 8.

Coon Lake Campground   This nice little campground, often overlooked on the drive up to busier Rock Lake Campground, has some good views looking out over Coon Lake. There are picnic tables by the water, not far from the backdoor path up to Centennial Ridges Trail. A good campground for hikers seeking privacy. Both the campground office and the woodyard are located at the Rock Lake Campground area. Located 5 kilometers (3.1 miles) south of Highway 60 on Rock Lake Road at K 40. 49 sites maintained by MNR. Rates for up to 6 C$21.50 (US$15.95), no hookups. Open June 7–Sept 3.

Kearney Lake Campground   A modest-sized campground in the woods, Kearney is usually one of the last sites to fill up when the rest of the park is teeming with visitors. It features two small beaches on either side of a narrow river, with the best campsites located on

Algonquin Park Campgrounds

Campground	Distance West Gate	Total Sites	RV Hookups	Flush Toilets	Pay Phone	Relative Seclusion	Laundry Showers	Good Beach	Wheelchair Sites	Open
Parkway Corridor Campgrounds										
Canisbay Lake	23 km	242	67	yes	yes	good	yes	yes	yes	May 17–Oct 8
Coon Lake	40 km	49	none	no	no	average	no	yes	yes	June 7–Sept 3
Kearney Lake	K36	103	none	yes	yes	average	no	yes	yes	June 7–Sept 3
Lake of Two Rivers	K32	241	162	yes	yes	low	yes	yes	yes	May 17–Oct 8
Mew Lake	K31	131	66	yes	yes	average	yes	yes	yes	year-round
Pog Lake	K37	286	81	yes	yes	good	yes	yes	yes	June 7–Sept 3
Rock Lake	K40	118	71	yes	yes	low	yes	yes	yes	April 26–Oct 8
Tea Lake	K11	42	none	no	yes	average	no	no	no	April 26–Sept 3*
Group Campground										
Whitefish Lake	K37	18	none	no	no	good	no	no	yes	April 26–Oct 8
Peripheral Campgrounds										
Achray	n/a	39	none	yes	no	good	no	no	yes	April 26–Oct 8
Brent	n/a	29	none	no	no	good	no	no	yes	April 26–Oct 8
Kiosk	n/a	17	none	yes	no	good	no	no	yes	April 26–Oct 8
South Algonquin	n/a	6	none	no	no	good	no	no	no	April 26–Oct 8

Note: Tea Lake Campground closed May 22–June 6

*Note: Tea Lake Campground closed May 22–June 6

the hill above the northernmost beach, nestled amongst the white pines. Campers register and get firewood across the highway at the Pog Lake Campground office. Located just off Highway 60 at K 36. 103 sites maintained by PKW Campground Services. Rates for up to 6 C$24 (US$17.80), no hookups. Open June 7–Sept 3.

Lake of Two Rivers ⊛   The oldest and one of the largest campgrounds in Algonquin Park, Lake of Two Rivers is also the most social, with big groups and families cavorting on the excellent beach. The beach is probably the main draw; on summer days it can feel like Daytona in here, with oiled teenagers launching themselves across the volleyball court while Mom and Dad bob in the roped-off swimming area. Two Rivers is the best campground both for RVs (more than half the sites have hookups) and for people with disabilities (the two comfort stations are fully handicapped accessible). At the Two Rivers Store adjoining the campground, campers can rent bikes and sneak in some fast food at the snack bar. Firewood can be purchased at the Mew Lake woodyard 1 kilometer (0.6 mile) west of Two Rivers. Located just south of Highway 60 at K 32. 241 sites maintained by Algonquin Park Services. Rates for up to 6 C$24 (US$17.80) with no hookups, C$28 (US$20.80) with hookups. Open May 17–Oct 8.

Mew Lake Campground   This campground covers quite a large area—it wraps itself almost entirely around tiny Mew Lake, with only a meager beach to show for it. It is the only campground open year-round, though staff are on premises only until Canadian Thanksgiving (the second Monday in October). Winter campers can pick up their permits at either the East or West gates, or at the campground's self-serve fee station. The woodyard is located just beyond the campground office and is open from 10am or noon until 8pm, with wood available on a self-serve basis in the winter. Mew Lake also maintains 37 dog- and radio-free sites, and seven yurts year-round (see "Yurts," above). The Two Rivers Store is a few minutes' walk from the campground. Located south of Highway 60 at K 31. 131 sites maintained by Algonquin Park Services. Rates for up to 6 C$24 (US$17.80) with no hookups, C$28 (US$20.80) with hookups, C$60 (US$44.50) a night for a yurt (up to 6 people). Open year-round.

Pog Lake Campground   Pog Lake is a big campground in a pine forest bang in the center of the Parkway Corridor. It's unexpectedly quiet for its central location and large size, with many remote corners (especially on the southwestern peninsula). The Old Railway Bike Trail cuts to the south of the campground; the abandoned railway bed it follows is suitable for walking as well as cycling. There are two small, unsupervised beaches on Pog Lake. The northernmost one is next to a dog- and radio-free zone, so it tends to be quieter. Firewood is sold behind the campground office. Located south of Highway 60 at K 37. 286 sites maintained by PKW Campground Services. Rates for up to 6 C$24 (US$17.80) with no hookups, C$28 (US$20.80) with hookups. Open June 7–Sept 3.

Rock Lake Campground 🌲🌲   Rock Lake has one of the nicest campgrounds in the park, with sites in both the pine forest and in an open grassy area right on the water. The views across Rock Lake from both beaches are excellent. It is located in a hub of activity, between the Old Railway Bike Trail on the one side and Booth's Rock hiking trail on the other. In between is a busy boat launch for interior trips into the lakes south of the Parkway Corridor. Rock Lake itself is fun to explore in a canoe, with native vision pits and faded pictographs not far from the grounds. Firewood can be purchased at the Rock Lake Campground office. There is also a sanitation station off to one side where RVs can empty their holding tanks. Located 8 kilometers (5 miles) south of Highway 60 at the end of Rock Lake Road at K 40. 119 sites maintained by the Ministry of Natural Resources. Rates for up to 6 C$24 (US$17.80) with no hookups, C$28 (US$20.80) with hookups. Open Apr 26–Oct 8.

Tea Lake Campground   Tea Lake is a tiny little campground squeezed between the highway and Tea Lake itself. The sites closest to the highway get a lot of noise from the road, though the ones further in on the lake are quiet and quite scenically located. Since the tiny beach and swimming area have little to recommend them, the main reason for camping here is the canoeing. Tea Lake connects to the Oxtongue River on one side and Canoe Lake on the other, with all kinds of potential day journeys to choose from. Campers who want to purchase firewood have to drive to Mew Lake Campground 20 kilometers (12.4 miles) further east. There are no hydro hookups for RVs. South of Highway 60 at K 11. 42 sites maintained by Whiskey Jack Park Services. Rates for up to 6 C$20 (US$14.85) with no hookups. Open Apr 26–Sept 3, closed May 22–June 6.

Whitefish Lake Group Campground   This is the only campground in the park that caters exclusively to large groups (groups of less than 10 cannot use the grounds). Eighteen sites can each handle between 10 and 40 people, with large grassy areas to pitch multiple tents. Although the campground was developed with youth groups in mind, any group may use the site, from extended families to sprawling bridge clubs. Most amenities—including a woodyard, comfort stations, and phone—are located just to the west at Pog Lake Campground. Reservations must be made well in advance. South of Highway 60 at K 37. 18 sites maintained by PKW Campground Services. Rates are C$20 (US$14.35) per night flat rate, with an additional C$4 (US$3.00) per person per night, C$1 (US$0.74) for kids aged 6–17. Open Apr 26–Oct 8.

PERIPHERAL CAMPGROUNDS

Achray Campground ★★ *Finds*   Achray is an excellent campground in an excellent part of the park. Its 39 sites are evenly distributed along the shore of Grand Lake, broad beaches alternating with rocky points. Though it feels wild and remote, the campground is relatively busy for the park's east end. Both the Berm Lake Trail and the Eastern Backpacking Trail begin next to the parking lot, and canoe trips into Grand Lake and beyond start at the dock next to the picnic area. There is also a construction of some historical note in the center of the campground next to the large stone building: the **Out-Side-In Cabin,** so named by former resident Tom Thomson. There are eight dog- and radio-free sites at Achray, and one summer yurt. Firewood can be purchased from the campground contractors. 50 kilometers (31 miles) west of the junction of Barron Canyon Road and Highway 17 (9 kilometers [5.6 miles] west of Pembroke). 39 sites maintained by Paul Smith and Jessica Poff. Rates for up to 6 C$22.50 (US$16.70) with no hookups, C$60 (US$44.50) a night for the yurt (up to 6 people). Open Apr 26–Oct 8.

Brent Campground   Once a busy lumber town, Brent is now a mostly empty lakeside clearing best known for its excellent ranger cabin out on a point east of the **Brent Store.** The campsites are all located in a fairly open area, some right on the water, all with long views of the neighbors. The other reason to come to Brent is beautiful and wind-swept **Cedar Lake**—which can get quite rough, so novice canoeists beware. The Brent Store sells basic supplies and rents canoes and camping equipment. Camping permits can be picked up at the **Wendigo Gate Office** (✆ **705/747-0039**), 16 kilometers (10 miles) south of the Highway 17 turnoff. Hikers can visit the **Brent Crater Trail** 8 kilometers (5 miles) north of Brent, or walk the abandoned CN Railway line that cuts through the campground. Firewood can be purchased from the contractor.

40 kilometers (25 miles) south of Highway 17 (just west of Deux Rivières). 29 sites maintained by Dana Jennings under contract with Ontario Parks. Rates for up to 6 C$20 (US$14.90) with no hookups. Open Apr 26–Oct 8.

Kiosk Campground   Kiosk is a small campground, the northernmost in Algonquin Park. If you want remote this is it: it boasts 17 sites, one ranger cabin, a tiny beach, and one big lake. Like Brent, Kiosk was once a happening logging town, but now it's just a ghost on the abandoned rail line. Firewood can be purchased from the contractor. At the end of Highway 60, 31 kilometers (19.2 miles) south of Highway 17, 19 kilometers (11.8 miles) west of Mattawa. 17 sites maintained by Dana Jennings under contract with Ontario Parks. Rates for up to 6 C$20 (US$14.90) with no hookups. Open Apr 26–Oct 8.

Kingscote Lake   The small cluster of six sites at the south end of Kingscote Lake (Access Point 15) in South Algonquin are the most primitive sites in the whole of the park—in fact, the "campground," though car-accessible, is actually considered to be a group of interior sites, and campers accordingly pay cheaper interior fees. The sites are located at the edge of a hardwood forest, and have no access to running water or firewood (like interior campers, visitors have to scrounge for deadwood and twigs). This is a lovely—and relatively quiet—area of the park. There are paddle-in sites all around Kingscote Lake for campers with canoes. Permits can be picked up at **Pine Grove Point Lodge,** on Elephant Lake Road, half a kilometer (0.3 mile) west of where the road branches into Kingscote Lake Access Point Road. 58 kilometers (36 miles) northeast of Haliburton. From County Rd. 648 (1 kilometer [.6 mile] east of Harcourt), take Elephant Lake Rd. north for 12 kilometers (7.4 miles), then turn left on Kingscote Lake Access Point Rd. Follow this road for 6.5 kilometers (4 miles) before turning right and driving 0.6 kilometers (0.4 mile) to access point. 6 sites maintained by Pine Grove Point Lodge under contract with Ontario Parks. Interior rates apply: C$8 (US$5.90) per person, no hookups. Open Apr 26–Oct 8.

5 Dining in the Park

There are two kinds of dining experiences available in the park: fine dining at one of the three lodges, or speedy cafeteria-style eating everywhere else. The former varies from exquisite and expensive to, er, hearty and expensive. The latter varies in quality from limp and greasy to tasty and filling. Basically you can't go wrong eating dinner at one of the lodges, though you will have to fork it out if you want to fork it in. All of the lodges have set menus, and each of

Storm Watching

There is a way of watching storms in the area around Algonquin that I have honed over the years. It began when I was young, not far from the park borders at our family cottage. Either my brother or I would remark on it first: the eerie calm, the still leaves, the whole forest tense as if holding its breath. We'd race down to the dock to watch the clouds mount across the lake, a lead-colored anvil waiting to descend. The hairs on the backs of our necks would stir before any ripples were visible on the water. And then the winds would start—the gust front—racing ahead of the storm like barking scouts of war.

This is when you had to dig in. The cedars would bend back and the padded foam on the deck seats would be ripped into the air and flung across the bay. The distant snarl of thunder would get louder and the fork lightning would suddenly leap up all around us, great corrosive bolts burning the air, sometimes twisting into pinwheels. Soon the forest would be roaring with wind and electricity. And still we'd sit (as you should sit—as low as possible), terrified but waiting for the big payoff: the Wall of Water. It would sweep across the lake like a dense gray curtain, frothing over obstacles and blocking out the light. We would wait until the last possible moment before turning and running for the cottage, our heels wet with the licks of rain but our faces dry in the receding cell of empty air. And I have done this too in Algonquin, and my tent has seemed very fragile indeed. But the wind dies and the heavy rain passes and half an hour later the sun comes out, or the day fades into drizzle. With a spectacle so short, you have to be attentive to the build-up.

Environment Canada calls late-April to mid-October "summer severe weather season" in Ontario. Severe thunderstorms blow in off the Great Lakes, on average 150 a year. Of these, 15 or so produce the necessary wind rotations for tornadoes, huge pipes of striated air whose winds whip across the land at 200+ kilometers (124+ miles) an hour. Algonquin bears the scars of these tornadoes in the form of felled trees—wide swaths of wilderness razed to the ground. But don't get paranoid. The park gets only half a dozen or so severe thunderstorms a summer, and a tornado touches down once every few years.

For the most part these storms are an observer's sport, loud but safe, often distant. The scale of the landscape is so huge in Algonquin that it's sometimes possible to watch multiple storm systems move slowly across opposite ends of the horizon like buffalo on a prairie. They rumble ominously as they graze, and their dark bellies are shot through with lightning.

If you are caught on the water during a storm and have no other escape except to ride out the storm use the following guidelines. Make sure not to touch any masted-area of the boat. Stay low and in the center of the boat—avoiding the term "stand-up human lightning mast!" Keep your arms and legs inside the boat—not dangling in the water. Discontinue fishing, swimming or other water activities when there is lightning or even when weather conditions look threatening. The first lightning strike can be a mile or more in front of an upcoming thunderstorm. Disconnect and do not use or touch the major electronic equipment, including radios, throughout the duration of the storm.

For the latest weather updates, Environment Canada has all the details at http://weatheroffice.ec.gc.ca or try www.the weathernetwork.ca.

them is open for more than just dinner: Arowhon Pines serves breakfast, lunch, and dinner; Bartlett serves breakfast and dinner; and Killarney serves lunch and dinner. *Please note:* None of the lodges are licensed, so patrons are encouraged to bring their own bottle of wine.

THE LODGES

Arowhon Pines ✹✹ CANADIAN/CONTINENTAL   If the mind-expanding beauty and symmetry of the six-sided dining room doesn't get you, then the high standard of the cuisine surely will. Owners Eugene and Helen Kates closely guard the lodge's reputation for culinary excellence; they circle the huge central fireplace like revolving ceiling fans, smiling at the guests and inspecting the dishes as they make their way out of the kitchen. Although the menu at Arowhon Pines changes daily, the use of fresh seasonal ingredients (local if possible) and the careful presentation of the dishes are a constant. All dinners begin at 6pm with a buffet of hot appetizers and salads: avocado with red pepper, wild rice salad with mango, deep-fried eggplant, and deviled eggs with tapenade. The soup and entree courses are a la carte. The cornmeal-encrusted salmon-trout with orzo, red pepper, and basil is a great combination of texture and flavor, and the New York steak is suitably thick and juicy. Dessert is another buffet table, this one weighted down with a dizzying selection of cheeses, pies, cakes, and chocolate and sugared confections. Combine the excellent food with the professional service (from staff who return year after year just so they can serve the repeat guests) and the fine view over Little Joe Lake and you have a perfect wilderness dining experience. Apparently it only gets better on the weekends, when the barbecue is wheeled out for the massive lunch buffet. **Summer:** P.O. Box 10001, Huntsville, ON P1H 2G5. ℂ **705/ 633-5661;** fax 705/633-5795; **Winter:** 297 Balliol St., Toronto, ON M4S 1C7. ℂ **416/483-4393;** fax 416/483-4429; www.arowhonpines.ca. Reservations recommended. Breakfast served 8–10am, set menu C$18.50 (US$13.70); lunch served 12:30–2pm, set menu weekdays C$31 (US$23), weekend buffet C$42 (US$31.15); dinner served 6pm sharp, set menu C$60 (US$44.50). All set menu prices excluding 15% tax and 15% gratuity. MC, V. Open June 1–Oct 8. At the end of Arowhon Pines Road off Highway 60 (K 15).

Bartlett Lodge ⭐⭐ *(Finds* CANADIAN/CONTINENTAL   Bartlett Lodge is one of the best dining experiences of the three resorts along the park's corridor off Highway 60. When you arrive at the boat landing on the opposite side of Cache Lake, hail a boat from the lodge via direct telephone. As you are whisked away on the antique boat, watch the romantic sky to witness a fabulous sunset or starry night on Cache Lake (depending, of course, on whether your reservation is 6pm or 8pm).

The interior of the dining lodge is very traditional—it's basic, but still somehow lush and comfortable. While you wait for your table, get a sense of the history of the lodges that used to exist in the park by checking out both the miniature models kept under glass in the waiting area and the surrounding walls, which are adorned with historical memorabilia and photographs in a seriously non-cluttered arrangement. The cozy atmosphere is rounded out by curtain rods made of canoe paddles and tables that state in burnt effect what type of wood they are made from.

Waitstaff are from all over the world and are very knowledgeable about the food, the lodge, and the park itself. A set menu allows you to choose from among five starters and five entrees—your meal includes a soup, starter, sorbet, main course, and dessert. And, like the other lodges in the park, it's BYOB—but here, the server will open your bottle *and* pour for you (unlike other lodges where the waitstaff watched me struggle not to elbow the closely seated guests to my right as I uncorked!). The Bartlett is a definite park tradition and well worth the price. **Summer:** P.O. Box 10004, Huntsville, ON P1H 2G8. Ⓒ 705/633-5543; fax 705/633-5746; **Winter:** 297 Lakeshore Road East, Suite 2, Oakville, ON L6J 1J3. Ⓒ 905/338-8908; fax 905/338-3039; www.bartlettlodge. com. Reservations always required. Breakfast served 8–9:30am, set menu C$13 (US$9.65); dinner served 6 and 8pm, set menu C$45 (US$33.40). All set menu prices excluding 15% tax and 15% gratuity. MC, V, debit. Open May–Oct. The Cache Lake parking lot is at K 23, across from the entrance to the Canisbay Lake campground.

Killarney Lodge AMERICAN/HOME COOKING   Though it doesn't have the gourmet reputation of the other lodges, the kitchen at Killarney nevertheless produces four courses of good country-style food. Like the lodge itself, the dining room—with its low pine-beam ceiling and well-shellacked hardwood floors—is warm and cozy, full of middle-aged couples smiling drowsily into their bark menus. The repeat guests depend on a reliable menu, so there have been few changes in the weekly meal rotation over the years. Saturday's dinner begins with watery beef soup and a standard Caesar salad. The entree distinguishes itself immediately by its great size: a heaping plate of tender roasted chicken, with baby corn, broccoli, and potatoes on the side. The sirloin steak is equally well prepared and equally voluminous beneath the mountain of potatoes and sautéed mushrooms. Those with room for dessert can try a Killarney specialty: the delicious homemade pecan pie with its crunchy caramelized top, which you're more than welcome to enjoy on your private porch overlooking Lake of Two Rivers. Killarney also serves a three-course lunch that includes a soup, an entree (chicken souvlaki, beef pot pie, etc.), and a dessert. **Summer:** P.O. Box 10005, Algonquin Park, ON P1H 2G9 Ⓒ 705/633-5551; fax 705/633-5667; **Winter:** Ⓒ and fax 416/482-5254; www.killarneylodge.com. Reservations recommended. Lunch served 12–2pm, set menu C$21.95 (US$16.30); dinner served 6pm sharp, set menu C$43.95 (US$32.60). All set menu prices include 15% tax and 15% gratuity. MC, V. Open May 12–Oct 15. South of Highway 60 at K 33.

CAFETERIAS & LUNCHEONETTES

The Gallery Cafe 🏷️ *Value* CAFE   Located on a large open-air patio adjacent to the Algonquin Gallery, this cafe is the best place to get a casual bite to eat outside of the more expensive lodges. Hungry patrons can enjoy fat venison sausages topped with mushrooms and onions with a side salad or fries—all the while taking in the forest view. The other fare is less exotic (and features no other Algonquin wildlife ingredient that I know of); a mix of burgers, fries, veggie wraps, and hot dogs. The tuna salad, also delicious, is served on Henrietta's Pine Bakery warm walnut bread. The Gallery Cafe is one of only two places in the park that serve beer (the other is the Portage Store restaurant), and the only one that serves wine. In keeping with the sophisticated arty context of the cafe, they also serve cappuccinos, espressos, and frothy cafe lattes. © **705/633-5225.** Open June 26–Oct 14 every day from 10am–6pm. Lunch items C$3.95–C$6.95 (US$2.90–US$5.15), tax and gratuity not included. MC, V, debit. South of Highway 60 (K 20).

The Portage Store Restaurant AMERICAN   More expensive than the rest of the cafeterias, this place is really a restaurant, with real live waitresses coming to your table. Plus there's beer. This is where you come after a 5-day canoe trip and you're sick of eating stale bagels and peanut butter. You unload your canoe downstairs and race up here for some hot steaks or back ribs, and pound back beers until you're good and drunk and civilized again. Okay, so you don't have to do this, but the Portage Store *wants* you to do this, otherwise they wouldn't charge C$16 (US$11.90) for the steak. Go for the tasty 4-oz char-grilled burgers instead (try the "Tom Thomson," with mushrooms): they're made from a 25-year-old recipe that has stood the test of time. The top-end breakfasts are big and hearty; they range from a single egg and toast to blueberry pancakes and bacon. Even better than the food is the view of Canoe Lake through the big paned windows. Happy German tourists and campers bathed in sunlight reflecting off the bright tabletops. © **705/633-5622.** Spring and fall hours 8am–7pm; summer hours 8am–9pm. Breakfast until 11pm, C$6.25–$9.95 (US$4.65–$7.40); lunch and dinner items C$5.95–$15.95 (US$4.40–$11.80), tax not included. MC, V, debit. Open Apr 28 to Canadian Thanksgiving (2nd Monday of Oct). North of Highway 60 (K 14).

Visitor Centre Cafe CAFE   Also known as the Sunday Creek Cafe, the cafe in the Visitor Centre, with its view over a great swath of Algonquin Park, is a pleasant place to enjoy an afternoon meal. The food is decent and hearty—ski lodge fare, a feeling echoed in the high beamed ceilings and the sturdy wood tables built to withstand winter boots and cross-country ski poles. Indeed, during winter weekends the cafe is the only place in the park to get a hot lunch: a reasonably priced rotation of roast beef and gravy sandwiches, quiche, and hamburgers. They also serve homemade soups, fresh sandwiches, and larger dinner-sized meals of roast beef or chicken. Breakfasts consist of bacon, eggs, and home fries. ℂ 613/ 637-9947. Open spring and fall every day 10am–6pm; summer every day 9am–9pm; winter on weekends only 10am–6pm. Breakfast until 11pm, C$5.95 (US$4.40); lunch items C$5.95–C$6.95 (US$4.40–US$5.15); dinner items C$9.95 (US$7.40), tax and gratuity not included. MC, V, debit. Open year-round. South of Highway 60 (K 43).

The Two Rivers Snack Bar FAST FOOD Your garden-variety fast-food outlet, this snack bar—with its pale interior and cheap plastic tables—even looks like a McDonald's. The food isn't very good, but it's the cheapest in the park, and it attracts a slightly shamefaced stream of late-night campers who couldn't get their campfires going and are looking for a big greasy bang for their buck. The C$4.50 (US$3.35) daily specials are probably the best bet, with selections ranging from the ever-popular hot roast beef sandwiches to chicken wraps and souvlaki. Burgers, onion rings, and fish and chips round out the menu selection. Breakfasts—an offering of bacon, eggs, pancakes, and French toast—are served until 11am. ℂ 705/633-5728. Spring hours 7am–7pm; summer and fall hours 7am–9pm. Breakfast until 11am, C$2.85–C$4.85 (US$2.10–US$3.60); lunch and dinner items C$3.95–C$6.85 (US$2.90–US$5.10); tax not included. Debit advance from store. Open May 1 to Canadian Thanksgiving (2nd Monday of Oct). Next to Lake of Two Rivers Campground, south of Highway 60 (K 31).

7

Gateway Towns

Although Algonquin Park is the area's premiere attraction, the great outdoors doesn't suddenly end at the park borders. The rugged surrounding countryside continues apace, it's just shot through with a little more development. The area all around the park—particularly to the south and west—is considered to be prime Ontario cottage country. Throughout the year (summers especially) it attracts urban refugees looking for a slice of their natural heritage. Other provincial parks like **Arrowhead** north of Huntsville and **Bonnechere** north of Barry's Bay are destinations for hikers, canoeists, and campers. The **Madawaska River** east of Whitney is a serious whitewater canoeing and kayaking center, and the **Ottawa River** off to the east is famous for whitewater rafting. Once the winter snow falls practically the whole countryside is opened up for cross-country skiing.

Huntsville is the most significant gateway town to Algonquin Park. It manages to encompass both beautiful scenery and an enviable list of tourist amenities: world-class golf courses, sprawling resorts, homey little bed-and-breakfasts, sophisticated dining, nearby nature trails, and a bustling waterfront. **Whitney** and **Dwight,** both closer to the park, are geared more toward servicing park visitors; what attractions they do have are usually related to the park itself. The best example of this is the housekeeping cabins that can be rented all along Highway 60 both east and west of the park. These cozy homesteads modestly reproduce the whole cottage experience, and are best appreciated after a day's exploration in Algonquin. They're more affordable than the lodges, and less at the mercy of the weather than camping.

1 Whitney

3 km east of Algonquin Park's East Gate on Highway 60.

Situated on the rushing **Madawaska River** and with five access points into the park, Whitney is a great place to start or finish your trip. More than 40% of park staff hail from this border town, and the locals are definitely proud as peaches of their hidden gem. At first glance Whitney is quite deceptive in what it has to offer the park enthusiast, but don't be fooled—it's the main town coinciding with the largest snowmobile trail in the area, and boasts excellent kayaking, canoeing, hiking trails, outfitters, horseback riding, camping, and fishing. Five minutes by car from **Galeairy Lake,** Whitney can serve as either a base for day trips into the park or as a stocking-up town (and yes, it has an LCBO). If you need to pick up a few amenities on the way into the park, then the gateway town of Whitney is for you.

ESSENTIALS

All of Whitney's amenities are centered around the nexus of Highway 60, Ottawa Street, Post Street, and Haycreek Road. It takes 5 minutes to walk the full circuit, with the **Shell gas station** as the spiritual hub. Whitney is part of the **Bancroft Chamber of Commerce** (© 613/332-1513; www.commerce.bancroft.on.ca), which maintains a website about Whitney, Madawaska, Barry's Bay, and the surrounding area. If you're starting an overnight canoe trip into the park from Whitney, you can pick up your interior permits at the **East Gate.**

TD Bank (© 613/637-2711) is the only bank in Whitney, with a branch on Highway 60 across from the Shell station. For groceries, **Russell's Food Mart** (© 613/637-5353) at 41 Post St. stocks produce, deli meats, and fresh bread and has an ATM on site. The **Whitney Post Office** (© 613/637-2951) is on Haycreek Road, directly across from the **LCBO** (© 613/637-2150), the first right after the bridge.

CAMPING SUPPLIES   Opeongo Outfitters (© 613/637-5470; www.opeongooutfitters.com) on Highway 60 between Whitney and Algonquin Park's East Gate carries a full range of camping and fishing supplies. They're open from the beginning of fishing season in late April to the end of October.

WHAT TO SEE & DO

There are loads of activities to take in and experiences to be had in and around Whitney—to the general passerby they do tend to seem hidden, but all you have to do is ask. Outfitters within the town are very approachable and are more than willing to help you map out your trip! As well, many of the small-establishment owners are the town's own marketing and advertising reps! Wilno to the east is a nice little town—one of Ontario's founding Polish communities. The **Madawaska Kanu Centre** (© **613/756-3620;** www.owl-mkc. ca/mkc; open May 5 to August 31) south of Barry's Bay is an internationally renowned **paddling school** and whitewater vacation hot spot. The school offers weekend kayak and canoe clinics, 5-day certification courses, and 5-day adventure programs on whitewater rivers around Canada. For **whitewater rafting, Owl Rafting** (© **613/646-2263;** www.owl-mkc.ca/owl), way east in Forester's Falls, organizes weekend and week-long adventures on the mighty **Ottawa River. Bonnechere River Provincial Park** (© **613/757-2103;** www.bonncherepark.on.ca), north of Barry's Bay, follows the Bonnechere River from where it exits Algonquin Park down to Round Lake. It is a lovely, flat canoe corridor with campsites along the river and collected around where the river enters Round Lake.

WHERE TO STAY

If you are planning on basing yourself in Whitney for park explorations, then **Riverview Cottages** is probably the best place to do this—you can paddle from the lakefront below your cabin directly into the park. **Algonquin East Gate Motel and Outfitters** rents canoes and can help you get your trip started fairly quickly. The other motels in the area are okay to rest your head for a night but generally you can find nicer places west of the park.

Algonquin Parkway Inn   This is a nondescript little motel on the **Madawaska River.** It has basic rooms available at inexpensive rates, a quality that has endeared it to many repeat guests, especially winter snowmobilers. The picnic area out back overlooks a gentle set of rapids perfect for tumbling and swimming. Units have one or two bedrooms, with every possible combination of double and single bed imaginable. There is one family unit with two bedrooms and an adjoining bathroom; all other units have private bathrooms and showers. The best rooms are the ones facing out onto the river, thin floral curtains clashing slightly with the flower pots hanging outside. Breakfast is served in the mornings for an extra charge. P.O. Box 237, Whitney, ON K0J 2M0 © **613/637-2760;** fax 613/637-5272; www.algonquin parkwayinn.com. 14 units. Family unit has shared bathroom. Double C$54–$61 (US$40.05–$45.25), double w/ 3rd person C$71 (US$54.90); Two-bedroom family unit C$67–$93 (US$49.70–$69). Seniors 10% discount. **Amenities:** River swimming. *In-room:* TV, coffeemaker. AE, MC, V. No pets. North of Highway 60 in Whitney, 3 kilometers (1.8 miles) east of Algonquin Park's East Gate.

The Mad Musher   New in April 2003, The Mad Musher combines accommodations with a restaurant-cum-Internet-hub. (Get your fix here, because it's the only public Internet access on either side of the park!) Owner Steve Dunsford—probably single-handedly the town's best marketing tool—saw potential for a hostel-style establishment and took over the restaurant, which was previously a fast-food joint. (For more on the food, see "Where to Dine," below.) The accommodations downstairs resemble a smaller, upscale youth hostel, with a modern, centrally located, and fully equipped kitchen, TV room with cable, and four guest rooms (three private and one shared). The beds were crafted locally in Whitney and still resemble the trees they were built from. All in all, very clean and comfortable.
P.O. Box 89, Whitney, ON K0J 2M0 ✆ **613/637-2820;** www.madmusher.com. 4 units. Shared bathroom. Double C$60 (US$44.50); single C$45 (US$33.40); dorms C$25 (US$18.55). **Amenities:** River view, laundry facilities, cable TV, full kitchen, TV room, full restaurant, Internet access. MC, V. No pets. North of Highway 60 in Whitney, 3 kilometres (1.8 miles) east of Algonquin Park's East Gate.

Algonquin East Gate Motel and Outfitters   All of the rooms in this highway motel are clean and, like the Algonquin Parkway Inn down the road, inexpensive. Owner David Kay is also an artist; he sells oil, acrylic, and watercolor landscapes of Algonquin Park out of his little studio behind the motel—high-end park souvenirs that have made their way onto many European living room walls. Most of the rooms are in the two main buildings facing the highway, but there is a quieter housekeeping cabin that sleeps four at the rear of the property. Breakfasts are an additional C$4 (US$3) or so, and are served in the cute little breakfast room adjoining the main check-in area. It's possible to rent canoes at the motel for C$25 (US$18.55) a day—taxes, lifejackets, and paddles included. Paddlers put in across the highway on **Galeairy Lake.** P.O. Box 193, Whitney ON K0J 2M0 ✆ **613/637-2652;** fax 613/637-5593; www.algonquineastgatemotel.com. 12 units. 1 bedroom, 1 double bed C$50 (US$37.10); 1 bedroom, 2 double beds C$59–$69 (US$43.75–$51.20); housekeeping cabin C$69 (US$51.20). Extra person C$3.50 (US$2.60). Cot C$10 (US$7.40). **Amenities:** Breakfast room, canoe rental, lake access. *In room:* A/C, TV. AE, MC, V. North side of Highway 60 just before Whitney, 3 kilometres (1.9 miles) east of Algonquin Park's East Gate. Pets C$10 (US$7.40).

Bear Trail Inn Resort   Like an episode of *Fantasy Island* ("Tattoo, show our guests to the celestial suite"), the over-the-top kitsch of this "Ultra Luxury Couples Resort" provokes more laughter than wonder. The resort caters to lovers and newlyweds, and that apparent newlywed need to cram a lifetime's worth of pampering into a single weekend. To this end, Bear Trail Inn has pulled out all the stops, providing an arm's-length list of romantic activities (water skiing, air hockey, ping pong, billiards, darts, ATV off-roading). They've even hired Toronto's Art Shoppe to come up with the resort's unfortunate Louis XIV decorative theme. This decor is seen to best effect in the small lakefront rooms, which are so crammed with cream armoires and four-poster beds that you can hardly make it through to the fake-looking fireplaces. On the upside, there appear to be free copies of *Bridal* magazine in the foyer, and every guest has his or her own terry-cloth bathrobe reserved at the front desk. Accommodation ranges from regular hotel rooms to bridal suites to fantastically cheesy "Honeymoon Chateaus" with canopied Jacuzzis, outdoor hot tubs, and views onto Galeairy Lake. Go to one of the lodges (or interior sites, for that matter) in the park for real romantic options; Bear Trail Inn Resort is just silly. P.O. Box 310, Whitney, ON K0J 2M0 © 613/637-2662; fax 613/637-2615; www.couplesresort.ca. 48 units. Lodge and hillside rooms C$103–$154 (US$76.40–$114.20); bridal suites C$127–$181 (US$94.20–$134.20); chateaus and villas C$183–$319 (US$135.70–US$236.60); taxes excluded. DC, MC, V, debit. **Amenities:** Restaurant; outdoor pool; 2 outdoor tennis courts; badminton court; fitness room; sauna; shiatsu and acupuncture hut; water-sports facilities (canoeing, kayaking, windsurfing, sailing, tubing, paddleboats); horseback riding (extra); ATV rental; nature trails; mountain biking; cross-country skiing; snowshoeing; skating; games room; free room service; laundry room. *In room:* A/C, TV/VCR, fridge, fireplace, coffeemaker, hairdryer, and iron. 5 kilometers (3 miles) east of Algonquin Park's East Gate in Whitney, south of Highway 60 at the end of Galeairy Lake Road. No pets, no kids.

Riverview Cottages *(Value)*   On the road to Bear Trail Inn Resort, Riverview Cottages is probably the best place to stay in the Whitney area, and the best outside the park for park access. The two motels are cheaper, but they don't have the distance from the highway, the sturdy rooms, or the views of **Galeairy Lake** and the Madawaska dam. Riverview is a rambling collection of housekeeping cottages and a big log motel set back from the lake. There is a small beach by the water and a wide dock with canoes and kayaks tied to the side for day-paddles directly into Algonquin Park (for which Riverview Cottages provide free park passes). Each of the five basic cabins comes with its own fireplace, barbecue and fire pit, small veranda, separate kitchen area, and central living room. They're either one- or two-bedroom, and can accommodate between two and eight people. Most people rent them for a week or more, exploring Algonquin Park by day and cooking their meals here in the evenings. The brand-new-looking two-storey log motel on the other side of the road provides the other type of accommodation: two spare large rooms on the bottom with their own fireplaces and Jacuzzis, and three smaller rooms on top. All of the rooms but one have queen-sized beds, the last one has two twins. P.O. Box 29, Galeairy Lake Road, Whitney, ON K0J 2M0 ℂ 888/387-9440; fax 613/637-5258; www.riverview cottages.com. 10 units. 1-bedroom cottages C$130 (US$96.40); 2-bedroom cottages C$155 (US$114.95); downstairs motel rooms C$115 (US$85.30); upstairs motel rooms C$98 (US$72.70); taxes excluded. C$20 (US$14.85) per extra person. Kids under 6 free. MC, V. **Amenities:** Lake swimming, beach, badminton court, canoes, kayaks, paddleboats, mountain bikes; cross-country skis; snowshoes. *In room (motel rooms only):* Fans, TV, fridge, coffeemaker. 5 kilometers (3 miles) east of Algonquin Park in Whitney, south of Highway 60 on left side of Galeairy Lake Road. No pets.

WHERE TO DINE

Short of hunting for your own meat, you don't really have a lot of options here in Whitney. The **Wilno Tavern** 60 kilometers (37 miles) further east of Whitney in Wilno is a fun place to eat, and there are lots of choices west of the park. If you just want a fast, no-nonsense bite, then any of the suggestions below will do.

Algonquin Lunch Bar DINER   This is a classic truck-stop diner kind of a place, with a funky little lunch bar by the entrance and a big feeding room off to the side. It's not glamorous but it's dirt cheap, and the service is genuinely friendly. Plus you can purchase a hunting license with your milkshake—you can't do that at Arowhon Pines. Breakfast, lunch, and dinner are served either at the counter or over at the maroon tables. Classic truck-stop diners serve classic truck-stop fare: eggs and bacon for breakfast; sandwiches, soups, burgers, fish and chips, and poutine for lunch; roast beef and mashed potatoes for dinner. There are quality homemade pies for dessert, so make sure to leave room. P.O. Box 250, Whitney. ℂ 613/637-2670. Summer daily 6:30am–9pm; winter daily 7am–8pm. Breakfasts, sandwiches, burgers C$3–$4 (US$2.20–$3.00); dinners C$9–$11 (US$6.70–$8.15); tax not included. AE, MC, V. Located on the south side of Highway 60 behind the Shell station, 5 kilometers (3 miles) east of Algonquin Park's East Gate.

The Mad Musher CANADIAN   The restaurant, which is attached to a hostel-style guest house (see "Where to Stay," above), opened for business in early 2003. Entering The Mad Musher, you're faced with a labyrinth of rooms to choose from for your casual dining experience. I suggest a seat as far to the right of the restaurant as you can find: the tables by the window give you an awesome view of the Madawaska as it rushes by. The menu is casual, with some really tantalizing starters like calamari with tzatziki sauce or bacon-wrapped scallops; for entrees, you can choose from traditional dishes like steak, trout, salmon, and chicken. And—lo and behold—the Mad Musher carries venison stew. If you want a taste of venison this is the meal for you, served on a bed of brown and wild rice and made with a succulent wine-based sauce. P.O. Box 89, Whitney, ON K0J 2M0 © 613/637-2820; www.madmusher.com. Summer 8am–10pm; winter 9am–8pm. Breakfast, lunch, and dinner C$4.95–C$18.95 (US$3.70–US$14.10) North of Highway 60 in Whitney, 3 kilometers (1.9 miles) east of Algonquin Park's East Gate.

Parkland Restaurant AMERICAN   Attracting a mostly park clientele, the Parkland Restaurant cranks out inexpensive breakfasts, lunches, and dinners in generous portions. The decor is your basic Canadian-wilderness-prefab, complete with screened-in patio overlooking the **Madawaska River.** The best deals here are the ever-changing daily specials, like the C$5.50 (US$4.10) peameal bacon with fried onion and cheese heaped onto a kaiser bun. The fare gets heartier as dinner approaches; burgers, fish and chips, and tuna sandwiches are replaced with steaks and potatoes or chicken Kiev with vegetables. The Parkland Restaurant is one of the only licensed spots in Whitney. Come on a summer night and enjoy a beer and a game of pool on the table in the back. P.O. Box 306, Whitney. © 613/637-2820. Summer daily 8am–10pm; Winter daily 9am–9pm; closed November. Burgers and lunch specials C$5–$7 (US$3.70–$5.20); dinners C$10–$18 (US$7.40–$US13.40); tax not included. MC, V. Located on the north side of Highway 60 just down from the Algonquin East Gate Motel, 5 kilometers (3 miles) east of Algonquin Park's East Gate.

2 Dwight & Highway 60 West

24 km (15 miles) east of Huntsville on Highway 60; 18 km (11 miles) west of Algonquin Park's West Gate on Highway 60 at the junction of Highway 35 and Highway 60.

The majority of visitors to Algonquin Park enter via Highway 60 and the West Gate. The strip of Highway 60 from Huntsville to the park has been developed to meet the needs of those tourists. Motels, restaurants, camping supplies—it's all here, spread out across about 30 kilometers (18.6 miles). The greatest concentration of services is

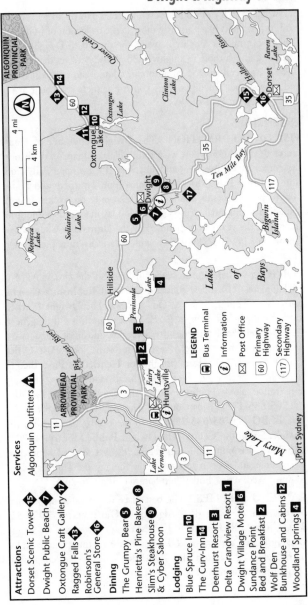

Dwight & Highway 60 West

Attractions
Dorset Scenic Tower 15
Dwight Public Beach 7
Oxtongue Craft Gallery 17
Ragged Falls 13
Robinson's
General Store 16

Services
Algonquin Outfitters 11

Dining
The Grumpy Bear 5
Henrietta's Pine Bakery 8
Slim's Steakhouse
& Cyber Saloon 9

Lodging
Blue Spruce Inn 10
The Curv-Inn 14
Deerhurst Resort 3
Delta Grandview Resort 1
Dwight Village Motel 6
Sundance Point
Bed and Breakfast 2
Wolf Den
Bunkhouse and Cabins 12
Woodland Springs 4

LEGEND
🚌 Bus Terminal
𝒊 Information
⊠ Post Office
60 Primary Highway
117 Secondary Highway

in Dwight, which you wouldn't even notice is a town since, from the road, it just looks like a slightly more dense collection of buildings. Dwight central lies roughly between the turnoff to Dwight Beach Road and the turnoff to Highway 35. Mostly it's residential, but there is a general store, a laundromat, a liquor store, a post office, and a few other amenities. Plus you can launch your boat at the public beach on Lake of Bays.

ESSENTIALS

VISITOR INFORMATION   The **Dwight Chamber of Commerce** (© 705/635-1644; www.huntsvillelakeofbays.on.ca) is near the corner of Highway 60 and Highway 35. It's open daily from June to Labor Day (Mon–Wed 10am–5pm; Thursday and Friday 10am–6pm; weekends 10am–3pm), then only on weekends until Canadian Thanksgiving (the second Monday in October). Inquiries the rest of the year can be handled by the **Huntsville Chamber of Commerce** (© 705/789-4771), which basically runs the Dwight office.

SERVICES   There are no banks in Dwight; the closest ATM is 16 kilometers (10 miles) south in Dorset at **Robinson's General Store** (see "Things to See & Do," below). The **Dwight Market,** located right by the Dwight Beach Road turnoff, is a little general store that sells basic groceries, fresh veggies, and meat (they have a little butcher shop inside). Next to it is the local **Post Office** (© 705/635-1771). Head straight for **Henrietta's Pine Bakery** (see below) for delicious fresh-baked breads and pastries. The only laundromat along Highway 60 is the **Dwight Coin Laundry** (© 705/635-17711) just south of Highway 60 on Highway 35. The **LCBO** (© 705/635-2891) is in the nearby plaza, called the **Dwight Shopping Centre.** The **Dwight Public Library** (© 705/635-3319) has public Internet access. It's next to the Chamber of Commerce, and is open year-round on Tuesday and Thursday, 4pm to 8pm; Wednesday, Friday, and Saturday 10am to 2pm.

CAMPING SUPPLIES   The best place to get camping supplies on this side of the park is **Algonquin Outfitters** (© 705/635-2243), located 8 kilometers (5 miles) east of Dwight at Oxtongue Lake, just north of Highway 60. They have everything you need; for more details check out the "Outfitters" section in chapter 3, "Exploring Algonquin Park."

THINGS TO SEE & DO

There isn't a whole lot to see and do in Dwight, especially as the park itself is only a few kilometers away. The **Dwight public beach** on Lake of Bays is a nice place for a swim and a picnic, as is the more dramatic **Ragged Falls** directly to the west of Algonquin Park itself (see "Picnicking & Swimming" in chapter 4, "Outdoor Pursuits in Algonquin Park"). **Dorset**, 16 kilometers (10 miles) south of Dwight on Highway 35, is a quaint little hamlet with a few bona fide attractions of its own, the best of which is the **Dorset Scenic Tower** (© 705/766-2211; www.dorset-tower.com). The old fire tower costs C$2 (US$1.50) to mount and looks out across Lake of Bays and the surrounding area—the views are especially stunning in the fall. Nearby is **Robinson's General Store** (© 705/766-2415), voted "Canada's Best Country Store" by *Today Magazine* way back in 1981. It still has charm and, more important, booty. There are 1,394 square meters (15,000 square feet) of hardware, produce, souvenirs, clothing, and home decorating items for old-fashioned shoppers.

WHERE TO STAY

There are some good places along the "Highway 60 strip" from which to base your travels into the park if you don't want to stay in one of the more expensive lodges or in one of the campgrounds. The **Blue Spruce Inn** (see below), **Timber Trail Algonquin** (© 800/463-2995), and **Bondi Village** (© 705/635-2261) on Lake of Bays all have cottages available for weekly rental. If you're just looking for somewhere to rest your head late at night, then any of the motels will be happy to take you in—provided they're not booked themselves, so call ahead if you're planning on visiting during high season. The **Dwight Chamber of Commerce** (© 705/ 635-1644) can provide a summer vacancy report.

Blue Spruce Inn   If you want to stay near Algonquin Park for a week or so, and you want your own little cabin but you don't want to bust the bank, then this is the place to come. The only problem is that a lot of other people have already figured this out, so you have to call way ahead for reservations. The layout is fairly simple: 14 cottages along Oxtongue Lake, with a separate motel complex off to the side. This is not the deep woods here—the space is open and fronts onto a paved road, sort of like a community center or a municipal park youth camp. But there are a few nice pine glades and the lake is just across the road. It's comfortable, homey, and unpretentious, and mostly it's close to all kinds of outdoor amenities, from the park itself to winter cross-country ski and snowmobile trails. If you plan on hanging around the grounds then there's a tennis court and a main lodge with games and billiards. The cottages are all totally self-sufficient, with multiple bedrooms and complete bathrooms (some have Jacuzzis) and kitchen facilities. They're also fully equipped for post-ski winter lounging, with deep couches, wood-burning fireplaces, and little corner TVs. Cottages are available only at weekly rates during the summer, for three to six keen individuals. The smaller motel units can be rented year-round on a daily basis; it's basic motel-decor here, though with the added kitchens and four-piece bathrooms you could stay motel-bound indefinitely. R.R.1 Dwight, ON P0A 1H0 ℂ **705/635-3230;** fax 705/635-9443; www.blespruceresort.com. 10 units, 14 cottages (60 capacity). Studios and suites (motel) C$87–$112 (US$64.50– $83.10), C$542–C$675 (US$402–$426.45) week; cottages 1–3 bedrooms C$105– $210 (US$77.90–$155.75), C$655–$1280 (US$485.80–$949.30) week. Extra person C$5 (US$3.70) in studios, C$10 (US$7.40) in cottages. Kids under 2 free. AE, MC, V, debit. **Amenities:** Lake swimming, beach, 2 tennis courts; games room; children's playground; cross-country ski trails; laundromat; housekeeping; canoe and kayak rental. *In room:* A/C (motel units only), TV/VCR, fridge, fireplace, microwave, coffeemaker, barbecue. South side of Highway 60, 7 kilometers (4.3 miles) from the west side of Algonquin Park.

The Curv-Inn *(Value)*   Okay, it's not the Ritz, but the Curv-Inn has a ramshackle charm that's all its own. Ambitiously billing itself as "the last stop before Algonquin Park," it's also the cheapest option out there for frugal couples who want their own room and a roof over their heads. It's a dictionary-definition motel—a dusty line of adjoining rooms on the highway next to a rickety restaurant with additional guest rooms on the second floor. But unlike many depressing motels, the vibe here is super-friendly. Smiling owner Dominick and his family whip up inexpensive breakfasts and burgers from the kitchen, and will even prepare customized Indian meals for C$6 to C$10 (US$4.45–US$7.40) with a little bit of advance notice. Behind the motel is an open grassy area on a river, with canoes and a floating dock for guests. It's possible to pitch a tent in this space, next to one of the fire pits, for C$10 (US$7.40) a night. There is also a separate A-frame cottage with a fully stocked kitchen. The motel rooms are very spare but will do in a pinch; the guest rooms over the restaurant are kind of a horror show and probably best avoided. The Curv-Inn has group rates for 10 to 20 people, and can also arrange full meal plans. R.R.1 Dwight, ON P0A 1H0 ℂ **800/730- 7988** or 705/635-1892; 11 units. Motel rooms C$49 (US$36.35); guest rooms

C$34.95 (US$25.90); A-frame cottage C$60 (US$44.50); campground C$10 (US$7.40); taxes excluded. Extra person C$10 (US$7.40) (not including campground). Kids under 12 free. AE, MC, V. **Amenities:** Breakfast/lunch room, river swimming; canoes. *In room:* TV w/ satellite. South side of Highway 60, 5 kilometers (3 miles) from the West Gate of Algonquin Park.

Dwight Village Motel   The Dwight Village Motel is a neat and tidy spot to bed down on the way in or out of the park. Overhauled a few years ago, the motel presents a charming front to the highway with its potted plants and dark wood siding. The rooms are clean and simple, all of them with two double beds and four-piece bathrooms. A reliable place to stay, it is understandably popular in July and August, so call ahead. P.O. Box 15, Highway 60, Dwight, ON P0A 1H0 *C* 705/635-2400; 10 units. Summer double C$99 (US$73.45); winter double C$59 (US$43.75); taxes excluded. Extra person C$5 (US$3.70), up to 4. MC, V, debit. **Amenities:** Non-smoking rooms; children's playground. *In room:* A/C, TV w/ satellite, fridge, microwave, coffeemaker. North side of Highway 60, just west of Dwight. No pets.

Wolf Den Bunkhouse and Cabins *Value*   Finally, Algonquin Park has its own backpacker-style hostel. Brand-new in 2001, the Wolf Den Bunkhouse is situated only 9 kilometers (5.6 miles) from the West Gate and has much of the rough-hewn charm of the park itself. It is the closest thing to camping without actually staying in a potentially leaky tent. Everyone pays C$20 (US$14.80) for a bed in either a bunkhouse or in the 2-, 4-, or 6-person cabins. The big log lodge in the center of the site contains all the shared washrooms, showers, and kitchen facilities; it also houses a big common area complete with deeply creased couches. The other social focus of Wolf Den is the large fire pit, where young Euros can swap tales of camping in the interior. Couples looking for privacy can call ahead to reserve one of the cabins. Linen can be rented for an extra C$5 (US$3.70). For swimming and fishing, the Oxtongue River is just across the highway. Appropriately enough, the Wolf Den also conducts wolf walks in partnership with the Algonquin Wolf Walk Program; 10% of all proceeds are donated to the Friends of Algonquin in aid of further wolf research within the park. Group Box 19, Compartment L2, R.R.1 Dwight, ON P0A 1H0 *C* 705/635-9336; no fax www. cottagelink.com/wolfden. 44 spots. C$20 (US$14.85) per night, per person; 2-person cabin C$50 (US$37.10); 6-person cabin C$120 (US$89). Open weekends in winter. MC, V. 9 kilometers (5.6 miles) from Algonquin Park's West Gate, south side of Highway 60. No kids or pets in bunkhouses.

WHERE TO DINE

There are a number of dining options along Highway 60—certainly more options than in the park itself, and the prices are less than at the fine-dining lodges (though the food isn't quite up to the standard of Arowhon and Bartlett).

Henrietta's Pine Bakery *Finds Value* BAKERY Fifteen years ago, fourth-generation master baker Heiz Hubert arrived from Germany with a folder of top-secret bread and pastry recipes. He set up shop on Highway 60, and since then the bakery's reputation has spread as far up as North Bay and as far east as Germany itself. Stop by the neat little pine hut for a delicious afternoon snack—though if you want to be sure of securing one of the specialty breads then come early (and help yourself to a free coffee), since they invariably sell out by 11am. Heiz spends each night baking focaccia, meat pies, sausage rolls, pizza buns, apple and butter tarts, muffins, cookies, hot-cross buns, and, of course, the breads themselves. Breads range from traditional whole wheat to German raisin, hemp, and olive (and much more besides). Dessert items all go for around C$1 (US$0.74), and the specialty breads for around C$3 (US$2.20). Everything else is somewhere in between. Henrietta's is closed in the winter. R.R.1 Dwight. © **705/635-2214;** fax 705/635-2953; Cash only. Mon–Sat 9am–6pm; Sun 10am–4pm. Open May to Canadian Thanksgiving. South side of Highway 60 in Dwight, just east of the Highway 35 turnoff to Dorset.

3 Huntsville

215 km (133 miles) north of Toronto, east of Highway 11. 42 km (26 miles) west of Algonquin Park at the western end of Highway 60.

With 18,000 people, Huntsville is the largest town in **Muskoka** county—a no-holds-barred Cottage Country Capital, geared to mass appreciation of the great outdoors. It sits on the Muskoka River, between Lake Vernon on one side and Fairy Lake on the other, with Mary Lake to the south and Peninsula Lake just off to the east. Like Algonquin Park, the area was first home to native peoples (in this case the Mississauga band), before they were displaced by settlers. The town got its name from the first white settler, Captain George Hunt, who rode in on a wave of European immigrants enticed by the Free Grants and Homestead Act of 1868. Unfortunately, the rocky Canadian Shield was a bit of a hindrance to agriculture; logging soon became the town's major interest. Then came the railroad, the steamboats, and with them a tourist cargo looking

Huntsville

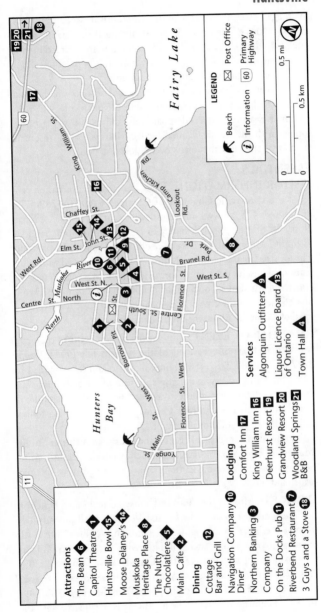

LEGEND

↘ Beach   ⊠ Post Office

ⓘ Information   60 Primary Highway

0   0.5 mi
0   0.5 km

Attractions

The Bean 6
Capitol Theatre 1
Huntsville Bowl 15
Moose Delaney's 14
Muskoka Heritage Place 8
The Nutty Chocolatiere 5
Main Cafe 2

Dining

Cottage Bar and Grill 12
Navigation Company Diner 10
Northern Banking Company 3
On the Docks Pub 11
Riverbend Restaurant 7
3 Guys and a Stove 18

Lodging

Comfort Inn 17
King William Inn 16
Deerhurst Resort 19
Grandview Resort 20
Woodland Springs B&B 21

Services

Algonquin Outfitters 9
Liquor Licence Board of Ontario 13
Town Hall 4

145

for rugged lakes and clean country air. Tourism is now the town's largest industry. The proximity to Algonquin Park certainly acts as one of the draws, but the Huntsville area is a tourist attraction in its own right every season of the year, with the population almost tripling on any given day during the summer.

Huntsville has more than 120 shops and services on the main street (actually called Main Street) and in the town core. The town epicenter is a pretty riverside boardwalk and an old swing bridge topped with the freshly painted Bridge Master's Cabin—a quaint touch that enhances the town's overall folksy appeal.

ESSENTIALS

VISITOR INFORMATION   There is a tourist information center at the **Huntsville Chamber of Commerce** (© **705/789-4771** or 888/696-4255; www.huntsvillelakeofbays.on.ca) at 8 West Street North off of Main, open Monday to Friday 9am to 5pm, Saturday 10am to 3pm, with summer satellite offices in Dwight and Baysville. The town website, at www.town.huntsville.on.ca, is packed with information and useful links. For information about Muskoka in general, either call **Muskoka Tourism** at © **800/267-9700,** or check out one of these websites: www.muskoka-tourism.on.ca, www.travelto muskoka.com, or www.wheremuskoka.com.

CALENDAR OF EVENTS   By far the biggest event of the town year is the **Huntsville Festival of the Arts** in July (© **800/663-2787** or 705/788-2787; www.huntsvillefestival.on.ca). Founded in 1993, the festival covers a shotgun spectrum of the arts, from classical and contemporary music to dance, theater, and literature. It brings in crowds from all over Canada and has been a big tourist boon to the town since its inception.

Another popular seasonal event is the **Muskoka Autumn Studio Tour** (www.muskoka.com/tour) in September, which features artists working in all kinds of media from stained glass to canvas, ceramic, stone, and more.

SERVICES   Most of the shops in Huntsville are located either on the Main Street strip or in the **Huntsville Place Mall** just north of town at the junction of Highway 60 and King William Street. All the major **banks** have branches in Huntsville, most of them impossible to miss on Main Street. The **Canada Post Office** (© **705/789-2221**) is at the corner of Main and Centre streets. For your pharmacy needs, there is a big **Shoppers Drug Mart** (© **705/789-4471**) at Highway 60. Huntsville has three major supermarkets: the

Independent Grocers (© 705/787-0500) and an A&P (© 705/789-9619) in the Huntsville Place Mall, and Huntsville Price Chopper (© 705/789-9172) right by the LCBO (© 705/789-2591) and the Beer Store (© 705/789-2741) north of the river, off to the left of Main Street.

There is free Internet access at the Town Hall, and terminals at the local library (© 705/789-5232) on Minerva Street. SureNet Communications Group (© 705/789-7873; www.surenet.net) at 40 Main Street has a small Internet cafe. For a photo lab and digital imaging center, go to Cavalcade Colour Lab (© 705/789-9603) at 34 King William Street.

OUTDOOR PURSUITS   Possibly the only outdoor draw in the area to rival camping in Algonquin Park is golfing in Huntsville. There are five local courses (and many more on the periphery) that court a range of visitors from families to tee-hardened professionals. The three best-known 18-hole courses are Deerhurst Highlands (© 705/789-2381), the Mark O'Meara–designed Delta ClubLink (© 705/789-0857), and the Bigwin Island Golf Club (© 705/635-2582). Deerhurst also has an 18-hole Lakeside course (© 705/789-7878). Other area notables include Huntsville Downs (© 705/789-4512), Diamond "in the Ruff" (© 705/385-2222), North Granite Ridge (© 705/385-0808), and Whispering Pines (© 705/789-4559). If you just want to practice your stroke, Martin's Farm (© 705/787-0505) has a driving range that stays open until dark. For course overviews, maps, and general golf details, Golf Muskoka (© 800/267-9700; www.golfmuskoka.com) maintains a telephone line and an informational website.

There's a lot of watersport enthusiasm in the summer. The town has jet ski and wake-board rentals for speedy youngsters, and canoes and kayaks can be rented from Algonquin Outfitters (© 705/787-0262) at 86 Main Street East. The Muskoka River between Lake Vernon and Fairy Lake runs right through the center of town and makes for a nice afternoon's paddle, especially since you can dock at any of the restaurants on the water when you're hungry.

Five kilometers (3 miles) north of Huntsville off Highway 11 is Arrowhead Provincial Park (© 705/789-5105), a mini-Algonquin with 388 drive-in campsites, 12 kilometers (7.4 miles) of hiking trails, a small summer interpretive program, and a long windy river and connecting lake for paddling. Like Algonquin, you need a C$8.50 (US$6.30) vehicle permit to enter the park. On the south end of **Arrowhead Lake** are four sandy **beaches,** which fill up on a hot summer day. **Hutcheson Beach** on **Lake Vernon** is another popular basting spot.

For **mountain bikers,** there are trails that run between Deerhurst Resort and town. **Hidden Valley** highlands area (© **800/398-9555** or 705/789-1773; www.skihiddenvalley.on.ca) has bike trails in the summer and fall, and **skiing** and **snowboarding** once the snow flies. **Cross-country skiers** and **snowmobilers** flock to the area during the winter to take advantage of the many kilometers of groomed trails at **Arrowhead** (27 kilometers [16.7 miles]), **Grandview** (15 kilometers [9.3 miles]), **Deerhurst** (15 kilometers [9.3 miles]), and elsewhere.

THINGS TO SEE & DO

There are plenty of things to do in Huntsville itself without leaving the town periphery. The **Lion's Lookout** has nice views of the town and surrounding area (especially in the fall) and can be reached in 15 minutes by walking south on Brunel Road, turning left on Look-out Road, and following it to the end. The **boardwalks** and docks along the river are a nice place to stroll; for historically minded walkers, **Heritage Huntsville** conducts guided tours of the old town on Tuesday and Wednesday mornings in the summer. These are run through the Town Hall (© **705/789-1751**) and cost C$5 (US$3.80) for a 1.5-hour tour. There is an excellent **Farmer's Market** ⚘ (© **705/789-8350**) Thursday mornings from 8:30am to 2pm in the Canadian Tire parking lot. There is also a Saturday market in the Mighty Dollar parking lot. They both run from the end of May to Thanksgiving and offer a large selection of crafts, fresh fish, and baked goods in addition to all that local produce. If you're looking to kick back with the morning paper or a book, **7 Main Cafe** (© **705/789-9592**) and **The Bean** (© **705/788-0590**) are both on Main Street, and both have comfortable seats for long-term lounging. Directly across the street from The Bean is **The Nutty Chocolatiere** (© **705/788-0986**), a huge ice-cream, chocolate, and candy store, inexplicably filled with nuns the last time I visited.

For less-sedentary activities, the **Yoga Room** (© **705/789-0367**) at 21 Chaffey Street offers drop-in evening classes throughout the week, winter and summer, and even organizes yoga retreats in Algonquin Park.

Echo Valley Observatory ⚘⚘ (Kids) (Finds) Located 15 kilometers (9.3 miles) east of Huntsville on a forested patch of high ground, the EVO houses a 40-centimeter (16-inch) telescope capable of revealing objects 10,000 times fainter than what we can make out with our own bug eyes. In the year since it opened the observatory has become very popular; reservations must be made 1 to 2 weeks in advance and booked through **Grandview Resort.** Grandview guests and members of the public meet after dark (about 10:30pm in the summer and 8:30pm in the winter) on the designated evening at Grandview reception, then take a 15-minute caravan ride to the observatory. A maximum of 20 sky-gazers alternately spot constellations on the outdoor deck through binoculars and take turns viewing incoming meteors through the telescope itself. The program lasts about an hour. Write to Echo Valley Observatory c/o Grandview Resort, 939 Highway 60, Huntsville ON P1H 1Z4 ⓒ 705/789-4417; www.naturetrails. on.ca. Adults C$20 (US$14.80), kids 12 and under C$15 (US$11.10), taxes excluded. Summer Wed–Sun; fall and winter Tues–Sat, after dark.

Huntsville Heritage Place (Kids)   Turn-of-the-century Muskoka is on display here, for kids and adults alike. The 0.36-square-kilometer (0.14 miles) site is really an extended pioneer village complete with a working steam train, sawmill, smithy, general store, two museums, and a dozen other historical buildings. Kids can feed the farm animals, walk on nature trails around the pond, and watch costumed narrators act out the vagaries of pioneer life. Admission includes unlimited rides on the *Portage Flyer* steam train, which chugs beside the river at noon, 1pm, 2pm, and 3pm during the summers, and 2pm and 3pm in the fall. 88 Brunel Road, Huntsville, ON P1H 1R1 ⓒ 705/ 789-7576; fax 705/789-6169; www.muskokaheritageplace.org. Adults C$17.50 (US$13), children 3–12yrs C$15.50 (US$11.50). May 15–Sept 30 daily, 10am–4pm; closed Saturday and Sunday May 15–June 29. Wheelchair accessible, no pets.

WHERE TO STAY

The Huntsville area is packed with places to stay, but they *all* fill up during the summer high season and on long weekends, so it pays to book ahead. The area's bed-and-breakfasts are probably the best-value accommodations. In addition to the two excellent ones listed below, **Val-Haven** (ⓒ 866/865-3866; www.valhavenbb.com) on Allensville Road comes highly recommended. Other B&Bs can be tracked down by the **Muskoka Bed and Breakfast Association** (ⓒ 705/645-9903; www.bbmuskoka.com). The website's "B&B Explorer" will pinpoint B&Bs by area, and a helpful operator at the above number will give you a full vacancy report. The **Huntsville Chamber of Commerce** (ⓒ 705/789-4771) also keeps an updated vacancy report for all accommodation in the area.

At the north end of King William Street are a few motels (the **Rainbow Inn** © 800/565-5514; www.rainbowinn.on.ca; also **King William Inn** below) and a **Comfort Inn** (© 705/789-8809). Other chains in the area include a **Travelodge** (© 800/578-7878 or 705/789-5504) at 225 Main Street West, and a **Holiday Inn** (© 800/465-4171 or 705/789-2301) resort and conference center outside of town on Peninsula Lake. It's resort central up here, with all kinds of options for urban fugitives looking to micro-manage their vacations. The two largest and best-known resorts, Deerhurst and Grandview, are detailed below.

EXPENSIVE

Deerhurst Resort ★★★ (Kids) At 3.2 square kilometers (320 hectares), Deerhurst is easily the biggest resort in Muskoka. It has two 18-hole golf courses (including the much-touted PGA-rated Highlands course), a massive network of hiking, riding, and cross-country skiing trails, and a gigantic sports complex with a kidney-shaped pool, courts, and fitness rooms (there are outdoor pools as well). The resort recently underwent a $30-million renovation—you'll feel the full effect once you walk through the grand Pavilion Hotel Lobby, which resembles a very posh, old English-style hunting lodge complete with massive chandelier and double-sided fireplace. The furnishings and atmosphere sum up the grandiose charm of the whole Muskoka experience, complete with a hand-painted antique map of the area. Enjoy the warmth with a drink in the Landing Lounge and you'll never want to get up out of your seat—this lobby is known for its oversized sofas and chunky wing-backed chairs. Deerhurst's 1,000 or so guests are very well catered to by the 700 or so staff, which undoubtedly contributed to the resort being voted "Best Resort in Canada" by the ever-readable *North American Inns, Bed & Breakfasts and Resorts Magazine.* Deerhurst offers every amenity in the book, from waterfront activity to nightly entertainment, first-class dining (the food at their flagship Eclipse restaurant is excellent), Aveda spa, supervised children's program, and frenetic booty-shaking discotheque. All of this happens in a luxurious setting overlooking Peninsula Lake, with nature trails winding off into the woods (though the grounds look a lot more like a golf course than a nature preserve). Guests have a variety of tasteful accommodation to choose from, at an equally wide range of prices—note that all accommodations include free access to Deerhurst's many activities, excluding golf and the spa. The most economical quarters are

Travelers rooms, which at C$99 (US$73.40) in the low season are quite a deal (there is nothing cheaper than C$149 (US$110.50) in mid-summer). At the top end are the luxury suites, with long views of either the lake or the golf course, depending on where your loyalties lie. These are very nice indeed, with multiple bedrooms, a central living room with fireplace, sunroom, kitchen, and dining area—basically, fully equipped apartments somewhere out on the green. They get less prohibitive in price the larger your group, especially since kids under 18 are free. Check the Deerhurst website for seasonal specials. 1235 Deerhurst Drive, Huntsville, ON P1H 2E8 Ⓒ 800/461-4393 or 705/789-6411; fax 705/789-2431; www.deerhurstresort.com. 425 units (475 bedrooms). Pavilion rooms and suites, C$139 (US$103.10) and up; Bayshore, Classic and Travelers rooms, C$99–C$329 (US$73.40–US$244); Deluxe and Luxury suites, C$199–C$859 (US$147.60–US$637.10). No charge kids under 18, two per family. AE, DISC, MC, V, debit. **Amenities:** Three restaurants; 2 bars; 2 18-hole golf courses; 2 indoor pools; 3 outdoor pools; 2 indoor tennis courts; 5 outdoor tennis courts; 3 squash courts; 1 racquetball court; fitness room; Aveda spa; 1 stage show; 2 children's clubs and activity programs; lake swimming; beach; extensive water-sports facilities (canoeing, kayaking, windsurfing, sailing, volleyball, paddleboats, fishing); horseback riding; nature trails; bicycling and bike rentals; concierge and activity desk; business center; executive business services; room service; babysitting; same-day dry cleaning/laundry. *In room:* A/C, TV/VCR/DVD, fax/modem line (some), Internet access (wireless and dial-up high speed in Pavilion Building and some Sports Villas), fridge, mini-bar, stereo (some), coffeemaker, hairdryer, and iron. 8 kilometers (5 miles) east of Highway 11, south of Highway 60 on Canal Road, follow the many signs.

Delta Grandview Resort ⭐⭐ *Kids*   Located across the valley from its main competitor, Grandview is a smaller, gentler Deerhurst that is nevertheless action-packed with things to do. The amenities list leans more toward the educational, with an excellent nature program and more than 15 kilometers (9.3 miles) of hiking trails extending out across 3.4 square kilometers (340 hectares) of land. Parts of this program—the guided hikes, the kayak clinics—are included with the price of accommodation, others—the boat and airplane trips (!), access to the **Echo Valley Observatory** (see Huntsville "Things to See & Do," above)—are on a pay-as-you go basis. The whole setting and setup of Grandview is more Muskoka-woodsy; this is a resort for people who at least want to be conscious of the surrounding environment, even if it is from the veranda of their deluxe luxury suite. The resort itself began as a farm; hints of it can still be seen in the original inn, now a bright and sunny dining room with old-fashioned decor (and a groaning buffet table). Guests can work up an appetite in any number of ways, on the golf course (there are two: a free 9-hole course and the flashy 18-hole Mark O'Meara Championship Course), in the rec center, on the bike and cross-country ski trails, or on the waterfront in their boat of choice. Grandview has two kinds of accommodation: you can stay either in one of the cozy hotel-style rooms, or in one of the luxury suites—some of which are actually time-share condos owned and decorated by seasonal vacationers but available to regular guests. These latter suites have sunken living rooms and two or three bedrooms, their hominess making them ideal for larger families looking for a week in the country. *Caveat*: The rates below are very approximate. Delta has an insane range of rates based on thousands of Byzantine permutations. Basically, the longer you stay the cheaper it gets, especially in winter. There are some excellent-value winter and summer packages available, so make sure to check out the website before giving up.   939 Highway 60, Huntsville, ON P1H 1Z4 ✆ **800/461-4454** or 705/789-4417; fax 888/315-1515; www.deltahotels.com. 143 units. Standard rooms C$99–$229 (US$73.40–US$169.80); Signature suites C$189–$369 (US$140.20–US$273.70]; Luxury suites, 2–3 bedrooms C$199–$470 (US$147.60– US$348.60), taxes excluded. Kids under 18 free. AE, DISC, MC, V. **Amenities:** Two restaurants; 2 golf courses; indoor pool; outdoor pool; indoor tennis courts; exercise room; bike obstacle course; spa; sauna; stage show; Kidzone and youth programs; lake swimming; beach; extensive watersports facilities (canoeing, windsurfing, sailing, paddle boats, kayaking, fishing); waterskiing and wake-boarding (extra); nature trails; mountain biking; concierge and activity desk; babysitting; same-day dry cleaning/laundry. *In room:* A/C, TV/VCR, fridge (suites), coffeemaker, hairdryer, and iron. 8 kilometers (5 miles) east of Highway 11, south of Highway 60, follow the signs.

MODERATE

The King William Inn   Located just north of Huntsville's main strip, this neat little motel does its best to maintain a regal face on an ugly stretch of highway. It does so in the quality of the rooms themselves: the standard rooms are all spacious and clean, with televisions and one sturdy, quilted double bed. The "deluxe" room is almost identical to the standard but for a larger television, darker wood-grained furniture, and larger queen-sized beds. Finally, there are two princely rooms with a single king-sized bed in each, separate Jacuzzis, and roaring electric fireplaces—palatial amenities for a motel. I wouldn't say this is a place to spend a week with the kids, but it will do as a home base for golfing and Algonquin Park explorations, and if you are four people in one of the standard rooms it is good value. 23 King William Street, Huntsville, ON P1H 1G4 ℭ 888/995-9169 or 705/789-9661; fax 705/789-7871; www.kingwilliaminn.com. 27 units. Summer: standard double C$105 (US$77.90); deluxe double C$125 (US$92.70); Jacuzzi rooms C$145 (US$107.50). Winter: standard double C$79 (US$58.60); deluxe double C$99 (US$73.40); Jacuzzi rooms C$125 (US$92.70). Taxes excluded. Extra person C$10 (US$7.40). Kids under 12 free. AE, DC, V. *In-room:* A/C, TV/VCR, fridge, coffeemaker, PC data jack, hairdryer. Pets only in standard rooms.

Woodland Springs 🌟🌟 *Value Finds*   George and Gaye Musselman are the hosts you've been looking for all your life. Their wonderful *way*-off-the-beaten-path cottage (best to call for reinforced directions) was built in 1908 and embodies the B&B ideal. It is ramshackle and warm, filled with comfortable couches and curious antiques (like a Mennonite family Bible with entries dating back to the 1800s). Olde Muskoka charm is everywhere. Guests can breakfast on a screened-in gazebo overlooking Peninsula Lake, relax on a hammock by the water, read on the porch, or just snuggle up in front of the fireplace. The three rooms (this really is a cottage-sized spread) are small but homey, with thick-quilted beds and creaky cedar-strip walls. They all share the two guest bathrooms, one of which has a deep claw-foot tub. The cutest quarters in the house is the Sunflower Room upstairs, with a three-quarter-sized four-poster bed, cherry beveled furniture, and an original eyebrow window peeking out at the lake. Comfort and charm aside, there is an even more compelling reason to stay with the Musselmans: Gaye's breakfasts. In addition to the usual waffle, eggs, and bacon fare, Gaye has developed some delicious original recipes that include the "Egg in a Nest" (a perfectly executed cheese soufflé with the yoke suspended in the center), the "Mennonite Maple Glazed Nugget" (a braised smoked ham and maple syrup confection), and "Baked Bananas" (sweet bananas in cider, maple syrup, and honey yogurt). This gourmet sensibility extends to the special weekends Woodland Springs organizes in advance for groups of six. The most popular of these is a C$225 (US$171) culinary weekend with hands-on cooking demonstrations from a certified chef du cuisine and a six-course meal. Other weekends include a "Wellness Weekend" for women, a "Quilter's Retreat," and a few others discussed on the website. 1231 Put-in-Bay Road, P.O. Box 5242, Huntsville ON, P1H 2K6 ℭ 877/427-1112 or 705/789-9543; www.penlake-woodlandsprings.com. 3 units. Double w/ shared bath C$95 (US$70.45), C$105 (US$77.90) and C$115

(US$85.30). Breakfast included. MC, V. **Amenities:** Lake swimming, canoe, kayak, boat cruises (extra charge), TV with satellite, all rooms non-smoking. 15 minutes northeast of Huntsville. Take Deerhurst/Canal Road south from Highway 60, bearing right over Canal Bridge (just past Steamers restaurant) on Muskoka Road 23. Follow road for 1 kilometer (0.6 mile), veering left at fork. Continue 1 kilometer (0.6 mile) more to Put-in-Bay Road sign straight ahead. (Note: dangerous intersection.) Follow gravel road 2 kilometers (1.2 miles) to Musselman sign on left, near end of road. Adults preferred, no pets.

WHERE TO DINE

The Huntsville area has dozens of restaurants and there are more on the way as the area's reputation as a tourist destination grows (check out **www.wheremuskoka.com** for a longer list). All budgets and all palates will find a match here. We'll start at the cheaper and greasier end of the spectrum: both **McDonald's** and **KFC** have outlets at the north end of town, and the orange **Pizza Pizza** sign is impossible to miss by the bridge. The **Northern Baking Company** (© 705/789-5616) on Main Street sells tasty sandwiches, snacks, and pastries to go, in addition to a wide range of fresh breads. Absent are the really high-end dining places, of which there are a few in the area: the **Norsemen** © 800/565-3856 or 705/635-3473; www.muskoka.com/norsemen) on Highway 60, **Steamers** (© 705/ 789-6411 ext. 4308) on the Deerhurst Road (owned by Deerhurst resort) and **Beau Ideal** (© 705/385-3772) 15 minutes south of Huntsville in Port Sydney. They are all reputed to be excellent, particularly the hidden treasure, Beau Ideal.

The Cottage Bar and Grill AMERICAN   "Fast, fun and mediocre" —not the most endearing tag line but definitely the most accurate. The Cottage was once *the* nightspot in Huntsville. When it went all family restaurant it must have lost its edge, though it still gets rollicking at a good pace summer evenings out there on the gigantic deck (complete with two bars). It's a big, busy place with a sprawling wood interior and people moving in and out of the sequestered booths. The menu is multi-culture-mutt—instantly gratifying foods plucked from all the great traditions: Mexican, Italian, Greek, Texan. Like On the Rocks and the Navigation Company Diner, the menu is the same all day, so you can mix it up by choosing burgers, salads, and quesadillas at dinner, or more sophisticated buffalo chicken pizzas and chili con carne at lunch. The vegetarian penne rigato is good; it comes with sautéed tomatoes, zucchini, artichokes, and lots of roasted garlic to enhance the social atmosphere. Rock on.

7 John Street, Huntsville ⓒ 705/789-6842. Reservations recommended week-ends. Open Sun–Thurs 11am–10pm, bar menu only 9pm–10pm; Fri and Sat 11am–11pm, bar menu only 10pm–11pm. Lunch C$3–C$10 (US$2.20–US$7.40); dinner entrees C$8–C$23 (US$5.90– US$17.05). AE, DC, MC, V, debit.

Navigation Company Diner MIXED GRILL   Known to the locals as the NavCo, this used to be the best food spot on Huntsville's waterfront. With a newly changed menu and ever-changing waitstaff, the NavCo is currently striving to make an impression. The long, narrow building was once where the old Muskoka steamers would depart with their cargo of freight and pas-sengers. Now passengers arrive by car, foot, and canoe, the latter tying up at one of the big docks just below the restaurant's brim-ming porch. Once inside, the big windows, comfortable booths, and rustic woodstove create a casual family atmosphere that's much in demand with locals and tourists alike; expect a wait on the week-ends, though the turnover is very fast (there are no reservations). The menu is mostly mixed grill, with oven-roasted back-ribs, steaks, jerk chicken, fajitas, and beer-battered fish and chips. The salads—spinach with mandarin orange and poppy seed dressing, fajita mix with shrimp—come in big bowls, perfect for hungry day-trippers. Make sure to try the delicious (and filling) house specialty, Mexican horns: soft flour shells stuffed with cheese, ground beef, and spices, baked and then served with sour cream. The NavCo also can be relied on to serve up a mean, traditional English-style fish and chips. All of these items are available for lunch and dinner. Arrive early if you want to get a seat on the porch. 180 Chalet Crescent, Huntsville ON P1H 1A6 ⓒ 705/789-7400. Open daily 11am–10pm. Appetizers C$4–C$9 (US$3–US$6.70); burgers C$7–C$9 (US$5.20–US$6.70); dinner entrees C$9–C$23 (US$6.70–US$17.05). AE, MC, V. Open May 24 to Canadian Thanksgiving (second Monday in October).

On the Docks Pub PUB FOOD   The only real pub you'll find in Huntsville is, literally, on the dock. This spot is held very close to the locals' hearts, and you too will be impressed to find imports on tap and a wide variety of bottled concoctions behind the bar. With great-looking pint-pulling staff, the pub is always the place to go to escape the younger crowd and experience a more mature and musi-cally inclined atmosphere. You can gaze down at the town from your protected perch and revel in the coziness of it all. With this in mind, the menu here is all comfort food—big portions to keep you rooted to your seat, of a quality higher than the Cottage across the river (and they don't serve fries with that, so don't ask!) The hearty ched-dar and ale soup with an order of garlic bread makes a good cheap meal. Cheddar is the key ingredient in a few more items: it's a pres-ence on the monster half-pound burger, heaped on the nachos, and promiscuous in the burritos. Quesadillas, sandwiches, salads, and chicken wings round out the lunch menu—though you can order any of them any time of day. Dinner entrees include curried chicken and shrimp, shepherd's pie, perogies, and a range of pastas, scarfed down quickly on Friday and Saturday nights to the accompaniment of a local band. 90 Main Street East, Unit 4, Huntsville ℂ 705/789-7910; www.muskoka.com/onthedocks. Open summers daily 11am–2am; winters 12pm–1am, dinner served until 11pm year round. Lunch C$5–C$9 (US$3.70–US$6.70); dinner entrees C$10–C$14 (US$7.40–US$10.40). AE, MC, V, debit.

Riverbend Restaurant ⭐ CANADIAN   Riverbend is ambitiously trying to "define Canadian cuisine," a project that has so far yielded some tasty results. The restaurant takes advantage of its picturesque location right on the Muskoka River by providing lots of breezy deck and screened-in porch space for diners, with a warm wood interior for the chillier winter months. The meat, seafood, and pasta menu is composed largely of all-Canadian ingredients: mussels from PEI, Niagara peaches, Lake Winnipeg pickerel, Milford Bay smoked trout. Many of these dishes also come with inventive Canadian garnishes or sauces. Combinations like the juicy roasted duck with pepper cider and the crispy (but not greasy) brie bundles in phyllo pastry and maple syrup work well; others—like the braised lamb shanks with beans, garlic sauce, beets, and blueberries—are a bit confusing to the palate. Regardless of what you order, the portions are rich and generous and full of interesting flavors. A knowledge-able and friendly waitstaff contribute to the welcoming ambiance—and there's a good chance they'll remember you from season to season. As far as lunch goes, you won't find a better-looking selec-tion anywhere in town: grilled portobello mushroom sandwiches, buffalo burgers, and thin-crust pizzas with a wide range of gourmet toppings to choose from. 8 Park Drive (off Bunel Road across from the high school), Huntsville ℂ 705/788-9484. Reservations recommended on weekends. Lunch served Mon–Sat 11:30am–2pm; dinner served Mon–Sat 5–10pm, Sun 5–9pm. Closed Mondays in winter. Appetizers C$5–C$10 (US$3.70–US$7.40); lunch C$7–C$10 (US$5.20–US$7.40); dinner entrees C$14–C$26 (US$10.40–US$19.30), tax not included. MC, V, debit.

3 Guys & a Stove ✿✿ LIFESTYLE CUISINE   The filming location for the cooking show *Who's Coming For Dinner*, 3 Guys & a Stove is owned and operated by local chef and television personality Jeff Suddaby. The food really is amazing—probably the best in the area. "Lifestyle cuisine" is how the menu is characterized—truly Canadian, it's an ingenious cultural mosaic of flavor and texture: spicy basmati rice with grilled lamb, roasted vegetables and feta cheese seasoned in a sweet and spicy pepper jelly, blackened tuna broiled with goat cheese and shiitake mushrooms, or chicken breast stuffed with ricotta, marjoram, and leeks with cranberry relish and grilled sour baby apples. The rest of the large menu is a unique and eclectic combination of soups, salads, flatbreads, pastas, rice dishes, grilled meats, and seafood, with what promises to be an excellent burger for scavengers at the low-cost end of the menu. The open-concept kitchen allows you to watch the chefs create the taste sensations as you come in the door, providing a little entertainment while you wait—and you probably will wait. Everything is cooked from scratch—food this good doesn't come instantly. The restaurant is always extremely busy, especially on Friday and Saturday nights when the demands on the kitchen and waitstaff are heavy. Reservations are accepted only for groups (though if you call ahead they'll put your name on the waiting list), so your best bet is to get there early. There is also an insanely popular breakfast skillet on Saturdays and Sundays. 3 Guys cooks with its own line of products, including a house roast of coffee, cran-maple syrup, and various vinaigrettes and preserves, and a cookbook is soon to hit the shelves. All of the retail products (cutely dubbed "Jeff") are available for sale at the restaurant, so you can take a bit of Jeff home with you at the end of your meal! Find out more about the show, the restaurant, and even the recipes at www.whoscomingfordinner.com. 143 Highway 60, Huntsville (just east of the King William St. intersection on the south side); ✆ **705/789-1815**. Lunch and dinner served Mon–Thurs 11am–10pm; Fri 11am–11pm, Sat 10am–11pm; and Sun 10am–10pm. All summer hours until 11pm. Weekend breakfast served 10am–2pm. Appetizers C$6.95–C$9.95 (US$5.15-7.40); burgers C$7.25–C$8.95 (US$5.40–US$6.65); pastas C$10.95–C$14.95 (US$8.10–US$11.10); main entrees C$14.95–C$29.95 (US$11.10–US$22.20), tax not included. MC, V, AMEX, DN

AFTER DARK

Summer weekends in Huntsville can get pretty rowdy. The resort staff–camp counselor–cottager–tourist combo is a potent brew that rushes through the area's few late-night watering holes. The most popular spot at the moment is **C.W.'s** (© 705/789-6411, ask to be transferred), Deerhurst's sprawling lakeside bar and dance club. In town itself there are a few places to check out. Right on the water, **On the Docks Pub** (© 705/789-7910) has live entertainment on Saturday and Sunday nights and is a friendly place to get a beer any night of the week. **Moose Delaney's Sports Grill** (© 705/787-1025) on Cann Street has pool tables; directly across the street is **Huntsville Bowl** (© 705/789-0788).

Both **Deerhurst** and **Grandview** resorts have live theater and Broadway-style family entertainment during the summer, and act as venues during the **Festival of the Arts** in July. **Theatre Muskoka** (© 705/765-0642) passes through Huntsville in late July. For celluloid loyalists, the **Capitol** movie theatre (© 705/789-2171) on Main Street has the latest Hollywood blockbusters on rotation.

8

A Nature Guide to Algonquin Park

Algonquin Park lies on the southern edge of the Canadian Shield, where it sweeps through central Ontario. The rugged topography of the park means it is home to a wide range of habitats. Some are up high (cliff faces, rocky ridges), some are down low (rivers and lakes, beaver meadows, spruce bogs), and still others fall in that wide space between (maple forests, conifer glades, roadsides). Different flora and fauna have figured out how to exploit each of these niches. The common raven likes to build its nest high up on rocky outcroppings, a bird's-eye view of forest dramas below. Otters stay to the riverbanks and lakeshores, and they are adept at fishing even the freezing waters of winter. Black spruce crowd the bogs, where carnivorous plants like the pitcher plant have learned to flourish in the nutrient-poor peat. The park is full of such specialists, each offering up an original survival tactic for those intent on understanding the secret life of the forest.

Any discussion of park wildlife would be incomplete without a mention of Algonquin's ultimate ecological bard, former Chief Park Naturalist Dan Strickland. Dan is the man. Much of what I have learned about the park's natural world comes from his lovingly written trail guides, *Raven* newsletters, and illustrated flora and fauna books.

1 The Park's Life Zones

The west side of Algonquin Park is a high dome of Canadian Shield rock 500 meters (1640 ft.) above sea level, sloping down to 200 meters (660 ft.) on the east side.

This difference in elevation has had a profound effect on park life zones. When the last glacier receded it left behind a rich load of glacial till. This remained in the west side, but on the lower east side the smaller pieces of soil were washed out by draining glacial waters (see "The Landscape," below), leaving uniformly sized sand grains in its place—coarser and less able to retain moisture. This east side dryness is compounded by the high west side, which intercepts the bulk of the rain sweeping in from Georgian Bay. What you get are two ecosystems: cold and wet on the west (only 85 frost-free days a year), and dry and warm on the east (105 frost-free days a year). The soil distribution has created a marked difference in forest type between the two sides. The west side is predominantly deciduous forest—sugar maple, birch, and beech, with spruce, cedar, and hemlock in the lowlands along lakeshores and between hills. The east side is predominantly conifer—white, red, and jack pine, with red oak up on the ridges.

But Algonquin Park has a second natural division. The park is located in the transition zone between northerly boreal forest and southerly Great Lakes deciduous forest. Spruce, hemlock, and tamarack are all northern trees, while the classic broad-leaf maples and birch are the dominant forest of southern Ontario. Crossover zones like this mean an abundance of wildlife, since you get some typically southern animals at their northernmost range, and other typically northern animals at their southernmost range. This leads to the improbable sight of northern moose grazing next to southern deer, of arctic ermines and fishers cavorting in the same woods as the less hearty southern raccoons. In fact, Algonquin Park is known as something of a birder's paradise because of the number of northern birds that can be found within its boundaries: the common loon, raven, boreal chickadee, gray jay, and spruce grouse, to name a few.

To make things even more complicated, park naturalists often refer to the park's five major habitats: hardwood forest, conifer forest, spruce bogs, beaver ponds, and lakes (winter actually qualifies as a sixth distinct habitat since the forest has a very different population once the snow falls). Each of these habitats has a different species composition governed by distinct ecosystem processes. The Visitor Centre breaks these down in a not-to-be-missed series of educational dioramas (see section 3, "The Visitor Centre," in chapter 3, "Exploring Algonquin Park").

2 The Landscape

The rounded exposed rock at the shoulders of Algonquin lakes, so representative of the park aesthetic, has a dramatic history 2 billion years in the making. This rock has been on a journey from the planet's surface down deep into the outer crust and back again—a slow-motion rollercoaster through the stratum.

The story, in non–geology professor parlance, goes like this: 14.5 billion years ago, the universe banged and made a huge mess out of nothing. There were explosions and collisions and super-novas—one supernova tossed some heavy material into a cloud of interstellar dust and before long you got the sun and some planets, including this one. Then, 4.5 billion years ago, the dense iron set-tled in the center, the lighter rocks straddled the mantle, and volca-noes fired molten lava all over the place. All that volcanic or igneous surface rock cooled off, and some of it still remains here at the sur-face as part of the mineral-rich **Canadian Shield**—3.5 billion years old in parts, though most of the rock around Algonquin Park— located at the southern edge of this Shield—isn't much older than a billion years.

Once those Shield rocks cooled off they started to erode; sand and silt were swept into the sea as sediment. The ages passed and the sediment piled up, eventually crushing the bottom layer under 20 kilometers (12.4 miles) of material—enormous pressure that hardened some of that sediment into sandstone and melted and recrystallized other parts into granite and gneiss. Then up rushed another tectonic plate from the south, driving full speed into our protagonist crust and buckling it up into a mountain range so high it would have made today's Rockies look like the indoor ski hill in West Edmonton Mall.

The big conceptual jolt comes when you realize that all the rocks you see are basically the exposed subterranean roots of that ancient mountain range. From 20 kilometers (12.4 miles) below they rose on an upwelling of crust while the eroding mountain range dropped to meet them. The last force to work the surface were the glaciers: four of them in the last million years, icy yo-yos bulldozing up and down from the north pole. The last glacier covered the whole area in a chunk of ice 3 kilometers (1.9 miles) thick. When it finally retreated 11,000 years ago, it dragged out the basins of present lakes and deposited boulders, rocks, and drifts of "glacial till"—the soil foundation for much of today's west-side forest.

Thus the basic contour of the land you see today was formed. The large number of lakes is a legacy of glacial meltwater and the run-off of gigantic **Lake Algonquin** to the west (of which Georgian Bay is the only remaining section). When the retreating glaciers opened up a low section of land at the top of Algonquin Park, Lake Algonquin spilled in and filled the valleys before draining east through the **Fossmill drainage outlet,** of which the water-sculpted **Barron Canyon** was a part (for more on the history of the Barron Canyon, see section 3, "Achray & Brent Day Hikes," in chapter 4, "Outdoor Pursuits in Algonquin Park"). There are still cold-water species of fish in the park that belong to that remote glacial age. The temperatures in Algonquin were lower then, and a hardy northern black spruce forest predominated. As temperatures rose these were replaced with conifers—jack pine, red pine, white pine—and eventually the southern hardwoods crowded into the rich glacial till soil on the park's west side.

3 The Flora

With its many habitats, Algonquin Park supports more than 1,000 species of plants and 34 species of native trees (though only 26 are really common). These range from tiny lichen to the park's largest organisms—the gigantic white pines, looking positively dashing along the waterways. As mentioned above, soil type has everything to do with tree distribution in the park's east and west sides, with softwoods in the former and hardwoods in the latter. The tree composition, in turn, determines the ground ecology—hardwood forests have a layer of thick leaves on the forest floor, and the broad leaf canopy allows very little sun to penetrate in high summer. Conifer forests, by contrast, are sunnier and more open. Distinct wildflower populations flourish in these different worlds, though there is considerable crossover. Of the wildflowers mentioned below, red trillium and Indian pipe are typically found in hardwood stands, and pink lady's slipper and wild lily of the valley are in with the conifers. There are many more wildflowers, of course—more than 200 species by some estimates—found all along the highway, in beaver ponds and bogs, and even blazing on the rivers. They appear in the park in two blooms. The first is in late April to late May, when sunlight bathes the floor of the deciduous forest and the spring beauties, trilliums, and trout lilies all shine. The second bloom comes in mid-summer, when flowers like orange hawkweed and magenta fireweed light up the roadsides and the pickerelweed blazes purple next to the gliding canoes.

TREES

American beech   American beech trees look like they've been wrapped tightly with elephant hide; the bark is smooth and gray, with faint horizontal contour bands rising up from the base. Each branch emerges in a seamless joint from the truck and feels unbreakable. In fact, beeches live to be very old—more than 400 years in some cases. This is a difficult feat, for the same admired skin of the beech is actually quite thin, making the tree vulnerable to injury and disease. What's more, black bears love nothing more than to pile onto the crest of a beech and fed on the beechnuts, dragging the new shoots down and generally pulverizing the whole treetop (leaving telltale claw marks all the way up the trunk).

American beech

Black spruce   The black spruce is a northern tree, found in dense forests closer to Hudson's Bay but confined mostly to wet bog areas here in the park. Its sad, scraggly appearance makes it easy to spot from the canoe—the branches are sometimes sparsely needled and hang shop-worn from the spindly trunks. But this seeming feebleness masquerades a hardiness few species can equal; where other trees would starve for nutrients, the black spruce flourishes, extracting a living from the inhospitable bog's partially decayed sedge. Their branches hang so low they dip into the moss and develop roots of their own, eventually breaking off and becoming new trees.

Eastern hemlock   Everyone loves a hemlock grove—cool, shady, with a fine carpet of needles and lots of space to maneuver. The trees themselves are so picture-perfect that they almost look fake: straight brown trunks, strong branches, short flat green needles with a plastic springiness. Hemlocks like moist soil conditions, hence their abundance around lakeshores. A hemlock sapling is very durable; it can live in very shady conditions and wait hundreds of years for an opening in the canopy before launching into vigorous growth.

Eastern hemlock

Jack pine   These disheveled trees look like they've been hammered by a lifetime of wind storms, but they also have a lot of character. The tree grows almost exclusively on the park's sandier east side, in soil with low fertility. They don't get very big—no more than 15 meters (50 ft.)—and they don't get very wide—trunks at full growth are about 25 centimeters (10 inches) around. The short needles grow in pairs; around them are clenched cones that can stay closed for 25 years before a forest fire sweeps through and releases the seeds—the grizzled old-timer making the ultimate sacrifice for a new generation of seedlings. With the park policy of fire suppression, fewer and fewer jack pines are regenerating.

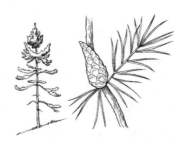

Jack pine

Red oak   Although red oak can be found all over southern Ontario, they are near their northern limit here in the park. They're found mostly in high, dry areas—the park's east side, or on south-facing ridge tops. The broad leaf of the red oak has sharp points and a distinctive elongated shape. The acorns—which take two summers to develop—are an important dietary supplement for bears, deer, and other wildlife. Although oaks blend into the forest in the summer, they stand out in the autumn as their rusty brown leaves are the last to fall.

Red pine   Although red pine look a little like white pine, up close their distinctive splotchy pink and black bark sets them apart, as do their needles (which come in clusters of two) and the balled-up look of their foliage. These trees like sandy soil, hence their abundance near beaches and on the park's east side. The need of their seeds for exposed mineral soil (and no shade) means that the red pine relies heavily on forest fires to propagate. The park's policy of fire suppression is not good news for the tree—new populations are having difficulty getting started. Giants like the 350-year-old red pine at **Dickson Lake** are likely to be the last of their kind.

Sugar maple   The leaf of the sugar maple should be recognizable to everyone—it is bang in the center of the Canadian flag, in a vibrant red that it actually comes close to achieving during the autumn color peak. Maples are also famous for their maple syrup, which North American kids on school trips sample gleefully in the early spring. It is the dominant tree of Algonquin's west side (indeed, it is one of the dominant trees all the way down to the American south), covering 70% of the forest. Its abundance is due to the fantastically hearty nature of the seedlings. They helicopter down to the forest floor by the millions and can force their roots right through the thick layers of duff and dead leaves. Others just can't compete!

Sugar maple

White birch   White birch stand out in the forest like vertical coils of magnesium—you can practically read by the glare. Most young campers will remember this eternal admonishment: "Don't strip the bark off live trees to start your campfire, find it on the forest floor." White birch are very common in the hardwood forests. They grow fast and require direct sunlight to flourish. In fact, a young birch sapling cannot grow in its mother's shade, so naturalists think that an abundance of birch means that the area is regularly scoured by canopy-clearing forest fires.

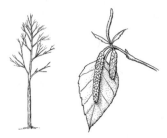

White birch

White pine   In the early 19th century, Algonquin Park was wall-to-wall white pine, giants that towered 40 meters (132 ft.) over the canopy. Except for in a couple spots (**Dividing Lake** and an area just off the **Crow River**), most of these trees were hacked, shipped, and turned into British man'o'wars before the turn of the century. Plenty of younger white pines remain, however, and many consider them symbols of Algonquin Park. They are beautiful trees: tall and straight, with feathery needles (in bundles of five) that diffuse the light. Although concentrated on the drier east side, white pine can be seen gripping the rocky shores of lakes all through the park—wherever competition from other trees is scarce and sunlight is abundant.

White pine

White spruce   White spruce are found all over the park, often in the company of balsams, pine, and birch. They like wet conditions, though they're valley trees more than river trees. They have a hand-some conical shape and can reach heights of up to 25 meters (82 ft.). The small needles project almost perpendicular to the branch and are clustered with green scaled cones, each with 130 or so protected seeds.

White spruce

WILDFLOWERS

Fireweed   Fireweed used to be seen only in recently burned areas. The slender seed pods (each plant can produce 45,000 over the course of a year) would parachute across the landscape, alight on the ashes, and almost immediately take root. Bright pink fireweed spikes could grow as high as 1.8 meters (6 feet), filling damaged areas with a wash of color in no time. Fires are rare nowadays, but the fireweed still manages to find plenty of suitable habitats: usually disturbed roadsides and sometimes open pastures. Here, from July well into September, this native species gives even the orange hawkweed a run for its money.

Fireweed

Indian pipe   These strange flowers are like bleached spirits on the forest floor. Their translucent white stalks and heads are faintly luminous—in fact, the plants have a total lack of chlorophyll, an indication that they don't depend on sunlight for sustenance. Their source of food comes from below, not from above. They are parasites, feeding on the humus litter of the forest floor and tapping into the roots of the big hardwood trees that shelter them.

Indian pipe

Orange hawkweed   In June and July, this wildflower fills the sides of Algonquin roadways with its bright orange bloom. It is both a common flower and an alien one. The plant arrived from Europe sometime in the late 19th century and immediately colonized fields and pastures. Irritated farmers called it the "devil's paintbrush," and since then a mythology has grown around its many powers (cures bad vision in hawks; cures insomnia and excessive sexual desire in humans).

Orange hawkweed

Pickerelweed   So-called because pickerel shelter and lay eggs in the plant beds. Pickerelweed is a very common sight along Algonquin Park's rivers and lakes. Usually part of a much larger colony of plants, it forms a network of underwater roots that fills the waterway. Purple blossoms rise above the water on thick green spikes, often accompanied by a single leaf. When the plant is finished flowering, the supporting spike wilts and dumps seeds into the water.

Pickerelweed

Pink lady's slipper   Also known as a moccasin flower, this sexy orchid is characterized by a single drooping veined pouch like a tongue. The plant is stemless; the supporting "stem" is actually the flower stalk—40 centimeters (16 inches) or so in height. Pink lady's slipper is found in conifer forests and around the edges of bogs. An ingenious series of mechanical adaptations are responsible for its method of pollination. Bees force their way through the top of the pouch and then tumble into the interior, unable to remount the steep sides. They have to leave the flower by another exit, one that channels the bee past the plant's stigma and anthers, thereby ensuring a dusting of pollen on its belly.

Pink lady's slipper

Pitcher plant   The pitcher plant is a bona fide meat-eater, a nice-looking flower that is actually a death trap for unsuspecting insects. The purple, red, or yellow-green flower nods about 40 centimeters (16 inches) or so above the furled leaves at its base. Attracted by the bright color, insects land on one of the leaves and slide down into the hollow funnel-shaped interior. At the bottom is a small pool of collected rainwater. The trapped insect is prevented from scrambling back up by the downward-sloping bristles. So it drowns instead, its body digested in the enzyme-rich liquid.

Pitcher plant

Red trillium   These solitary flowers bloom in May, and can be found all around the hardwood forest. They are Algonquin Park's most common trillium. Three diamond-shaped red petals (sometimes with a purple cast) emerge from the stalk several inches above the collar of dark green veined leaves. Their raunchy smell attracts carrion flies, who act as pollinators.

Red trillium

Wild lily of the valley   Found in carpets across the conifer forest floor, each wild lily of the valley is a cluster of white blossoms cupped from below by a raised green leaf. Their small green berries (bitter but not poisonous) turn red in the autumn.

Wild lily of the valley

Yellow pond lily   Anyone who has ever canoed in the park has seen the bright yellow flowers of the yellow pond lily, bobbing on the surface of the water among the broad strong rafts of lily pads. Each of these leaves is able to float on the water, and in so doing acts as a sort of oxygen pipeline for the main section of the plant at the bottom of the pond. Many Algonquin animals depend on the pond lily for sustenance: the moose, the beaver, and a host of tiny gnawing insects. Some depend on the pads for other things—like the lounging frog, which uses the lily as a hunting platform.

4 The Fauna

Algonquin Park rivals the great game reserves of Africa in the sheer number of animals that call the forest home: 45 mammal species, 138 bird (though only about 90 spend a lot of time here), 49 fish, 14 reptile, 16 amphibian, and God only knows how many insects. Your chances of seeing wildlife in the park are very good, and we're not just talking about squirrels, chipmunks, and frogs chirping from the campground pond. Moose are out in force in May, slurping on the salt deposits by the side of the road. Early morning in the forest both moose and deer are a little bolder, and beavers and otters stir on the water. The loons are a permanent fixture out on the lakes, as are the great blue herons and the distant circling broad-winged hawks. The big carnivores—bears and wolves—aren't seen very often; indeed, most people only ever hear the howls of the latter.

Birders get all hot and bothered about Algonquin Park because of the number of northern species. Actually, birds from all over seem to pass through the park, attracted by nesting sites as different as rocky cliffs and sloppy bogs. The best time for bird-watching is spring, from late May to early June, when nesting season starts for most of Algonquin's birds; out come the bright plumage and the flashy songs of males announcing their turf. Throughout the summer birdcalls ring out in the forest—if you're spending a lot of time in the park, a cassette of bird recordings is an excellent investment. A little recognition will make you seem like a star naturalist to your friends, though you may just annoy them ("Hark! Is that an olive-sided flycatcher I hear upon these gentle winds?").

MAMMALS

American beaver   More than 10,000 beavers call Algonquin Park home. They were not always so abundant; around the turn of the century their numbers were decimated by trappers. Algonquin Park was established in part to provide a sanctuary for these and other fur-bearing animals.

The American beaver is a seriously weird creature. First of all, it's actually a rodent, the biggest in North America. Everyone knows about this rodent's lodge-dam-tree-chewing lifestyle, but less appreciated are the bizarre physical adaptations the beaver has evolved to meet its specialized needs: webbed hind feet, flat rubbery tail used both as a rudder and as a warning alarm (slapped against the surface of the lake), see-through eyelids, lips that close *behind* their huge incisors (so they can keep on chewing underwater), two layers of fur, sealable ear valves, and castor glands that excrete a sweet perfume (to mark their territory). An adult beaver weighs 15 to 30 kilograms (33–66 lb.), chubbing up on a diet of bark, leaves, and twigs. The urge to build in beavers is all-powerful; put a beaver in a bath with the sound of running water and it will try to start a dam. There is no thoughtfulness to the process; it is pure instinct, evolved from the need to create a deep enough habitat to protect the beaver in the winter. A pond that freezes to the bottom will trap the beaver pair (beavers mate for life) in their lodge and starve them. So they raise the level of the water just enough to access the food pile accumulated in the summer and fall. Safe in their cozy lodge, no wolf, coyote, or fox can get at the couple. It's very romantic.

American beaver

American black bear   Though not nearly as big as their grizzly and polar bear cousins, male black bears (sometimes they are a more brownish or cinnamon color) that weigh more than 200 kilograms (440 lb.) have been found in the park, though the average size is usually between 70 and 140 kilograms (154 and 308 lb.). Bear size further fluctuates due to the animal's year-round living conditions: practically all of the weight they put on in the summer and fall they lose by the time they emerge from hibernation in the spring. Hibernation is an interesting process. From November to April, bears bunk down in their dens (usually beneath a stump, in a cave or the hollow of a tree) and stop eating and drinking altogether. Their heart rates drop from 40 to 10 beats a minute, their body temperatures decline, and their bodies live exclusively on their reserves of fat. Unlike many hibernating animals, a bear can be roused during hibernation and is capable of moving if disturbed. Cubs are born in late January, with two as the average litter size. The newborns nurse for the remainder of the winter, and stay with their mother throughout the next year and into the next hibernation period. Father bears don't share in the upbringing and aren't particularly affectionate if they come across one of their cubs: usually they try to eat them.

Wild bears live for 14 years or so, surviving on a fantastically varied diet. They will eat almost anything: carrion, garbage, deer fawns, insects, grubs, bees, berries, seeds, grass, and leaves. For a discussion of what to do if you encounter a bear, see "Bear Encounters" in chapter 2, "Planning Your Trip."

American black bear

American marten   Martens are about the size of a small house cat and indeed they look like a cross between a cat and a fox. The marten's glossy fur is golden or dark brown, with a patch of orange on the throat and chest and a light-colored face. Martens take to the treetops like otters take to the water. They fly across the canopy like trapeze artists, chasing chipmunks and squirrels. Other food sources for the marten are birds, mice, frogs, bugs, and berries in the summer. They range across the park, real ramblers with no fixed shelters except when with young, and then the females nest in a tree hollow or rock crevice.

Eastern Canadian wolf   Despite the occasional hype about wolves, they are not dangerous to humans and few park visitors ever see one. As it stands, they will likely be seen even less often since their numbers are diminishing (see "The Ecosystem" below for a larger discussion of Algonquin's declining wolf population).

Wolves hunt in packs of two to six, roaming 500 to 600 square kilometers (193–234 square miles) of territory. They prey mostly on deer and beaver—not moose (unless the moose are extremely old or sick), since the moose's huge size and flashing hooves make it too hard for the small eastern Canadian wolf to handle. Food for these carnivores is extremely scarce in the winter; most of the pups born in the spring don't make it through to the new year, and the wolf population in the park constantly seesaws between 300 in the early summer and 150 in the late winter.

Packs adhere to a rigid hierarchy, with an alpha male at the top and lesser males all the way down to the weakest animal. Females have their own hierarchy, though they are always subordinate to the males. With such a rigid social system, there is very little fighting among wolves—just the occasional ritualized threat. Indeed, "cooperation" seems to be one of the cornerstones of pack behavior (along with "tyranny"). When a female is lactating, she babysits all of the pups while the rest of the group goes out hunting.

Algonquin wolf

The Strange Case of the Algonquin Wolves

Until the 1960s, the wolves of Algonquin Park were thought to be gray wolves (*Canis lupus*), which roam over most of Canada and Alaska and are what most Canadians picture when they think about scary wolves coming to get them. Then, in 1970, two scientists from the Ontario government noticed that the wolves in Algonquin were actually quite a bit smaller than typical gray wolves, with a browner coloring and even some splashes of red behind the ears and neck. Was this a subspecies of the gray wolf, or was it another kind of wolf altogether?

In 1995, expert wolf taxonomist Ron Nowak identified the Algonquin wolf as a subspecies of the gray wolf, one of five such subspecies in North America. This settled speculation for a short while, but before long two geneticists from McMaster and Trent universities forwarded yet another theory. These wolves were not a small race of the gray wolf but a whole different species, one directly related to the endangered red wolf (*Canis rufus*) of the southeastern United States. At the moment, this seems like the most likely theory. The thinking goes that a few hundred years ago, the range of the red wolf was much greater than it is now, and may have extended from northern Mexico all the way up and into Canada. When the industrialized U.S. pushed west, most of these wolves were pushed out, and a small population in the north got separated from the bulk of the population down south. To make matters even more complicated, these northern red wolves began cross-breeding with both gray wolves and coyotes, creating a big hybridized lupine mess.

The name that has been suggested for these wolves—which include the wolves of Algonquin Park—is the **eastern Canadian wolf** (*Canis lycaon*). They are not an "island" population that exists only in the park, but part of a broad band of wolves that number in the thousands and extend from Quebec to Manitoba and down into Minnesota. Algonquin Park, however, is their largest protected habitat.

Eastern chipmunk   Everyone knows what a chipmunk looks like: small and cute as hell, with red-brown fur and white and black stripes down its back. They're very bold, and can be taught in a few minutes to scamper into the hands of campers and retrieve seeds and nuts. They're also hilariously greedy. A chipmunk will stuff his cheeks full to overflowing (when full, each cheek is as large as the animal's head), deposit his stash, and come back tirelessly for more. This industriousness extends to their lairs. Chipmunks dig a network of underground galleries, with some rooms used to store food, others to store excavation debris, and one more to act as a leaf-padded nesting room. Chipmunks don't eat just seeds and nuts; they supplement their diet with insects, berries, slugs, and even salamanders.

Eastern chipmunk

Fisher   With their broad furry foreheads and short round ears, fishers look a little like Ewoks. They are larger than martens, with blunter features and much darker fur. Fishers don't fish. The name is thought to be a corruption of the French word for *polecat*, which it resembles in appearance. Fishers are 100% land-lubber—in fact, their hunting circuits of 60 to 100 kilometers (37–62 miles) are much wider than those of its marten cousin. Though the fisher feeds on mice, hares, squirrels, and the occasional piece of carrion, its most unusual dietary supplement is the common porcupine. For a long time no one could figure out how the fishers managed to kill porcupines without getting speared. Their technique, it turns out, is pretty prosaic. They dart in and bite the animal repeatedly in the face, a process that can take upward of half an hour. Eventually the porcupine collapses and the fisher has his meal. Fishers take up to 3 days to eat a porcupine; when they're finished nothing remains but a few bones and the quill-covered skin.

Fisher

Moose   Moose are huge—the biggest animal in the park. A big bull moose is more than 2 meters (6.6 ft.) high at the shoulder, and weighs well over 500 kilograms (1100 lb.). The moose's size is matched only by its general awkwardness; with its spindly legs, great matted torso (complete with dangling flap of skin under the neck), humped shoulders, and enormous ears, the moose is the wild-eyed bell-tower hunchback of the animal kingdom. But these are suitable adaptations, and the end result is an animal that can move at close to 55 kilometers (34 miles) per hour through the undergrowth, legs lifting vertically from the snow or its swampy feeding ground. Moose forage primarily at dawn and dusk, feeding on young leaves in the spring and water lilies, rushes, and sedges in the summer. It is not uncommon to come across moose at such times, burying their heads in the bulrushes and generally ignoring your canoe (unless you get too close, and then they'll just loftily turn their backs and saunter away).

Rutting season for the moose begins in September. Adult bulls storm around the forest looking for bulls to challenge and females to seduce. One tactic bulls use for the latter is rolling around in their own urine—coating themselves in a sexy perfume for the swooning ladies.

Moose

(Fun Fact   **The Mystery of Moose & Deer Population Patterns**

A hundred years ago, when logging was first introduced in the park—and, indeed, before Algonquin Park even had a name—loggers noticed that there was a tiny deer population but a large number of moose. As logging continued through the 1920s, there was a dramatic change: the deer population increased to 100,000, and the moose population decreased considerably. By the 1960s, when logging became less attractive and fewer forest fires went unmanaged, the deer population began to plummet once again while the moose numbers increased.

In the 1990s, when once again moose quite considerably outnumbered deer within the park, studies were undertaken to examine a number of factors: habitat, weather, migration/evolution, logging, forest fires, and pests (such as ticks) can all affect the numbers of each species.

For years, the bizarre pattern baffled loggers and park naturalists alike, and only recently has the mystery been solved. What is the common factor in the deer and moose population numbers?

It was discovered that deer carry a parasite called *brain worm*, which doesn't affect them due to the evolution of the species. However, due to their shorter life span, moose have not evolved to combat this parasite and therefore die in great numbers from brain worm, while a high deer population is maintained.

Moose can also carry a parasite called *winter tick*, which burrows in and sucks on the blood of the host animal. This doesn't organically affect the mammal, but having the ticks causes a moose to scratch and rub off most of the hair in the affected area. Several ticks on one moose can cause severe hair loss—leading to hypothermia and even death in the late winter and early spring. In 1998/99 the park lost half of its moose population to winter tick.

Today, moose populations are up in the 4,000 range—and, once again, the deer population is at a lower mark. Because of maturer forests (less non-treed pastures) and several strings of bad winters, deer have been relatively scarce in the park. This is not to say that sighting a deer is unusual nowadays but it is no longer the guaranteed certainty it was 20 years ago. Much more of the park has regrown since early invasive square-cut logging in the 1800s and early 1900s. Since then, forestry management has developed an intelligent way for the two species to co-exist with little invasion from the logging that still goes on in the park.

Northern flying squirrel   Like little furry kites, these squirrels leap from tree to tree, often gliding more than 40 meters (132 ft.) on their downward descent. They are decent flyers, able to jog left or right in the air, and can even slow down pre-landing by arching back. Their bodies, or course, are perfectly adapted for this. They look like pale gray flashers in the air, with two large folds of skin connecting their extended wrists and ankles, and a long flat tail. Unfortunately you will probably only ever see them by flashlight, as they are completely nocturnal. They hunt mostly 2 hours after sunset and 2 hours before dawn, their big black eyes able to make out shapes in the dark. Northern flying squirrels eat mostly nuts, seeds, buds, insects, and bird eggs if they are lucky.

Northern flying squirrel

Raccoon   Algonquin Park is near the northern limit of the raccoon's habitat. While southern raccoons are active throughout the year, raccoons found in the park often hibernate for a few months as there is little in the way of food during the winter. Raccoons are unmistakable with their white faces, black masks, and striped tails. The rest of their sturdy bodies are covered in brownish salt-and-pepper fur. Although carnivores, the raccoon will eat almost anything—fruit, acorns, grubs, insects, worms, eggs, birds, rodents, snakes, turtles, frogs, fish, and garbage (as practically any home-owner, rural or urban, will tell you). These animals are very intelligent and curious. Whole families accompany the mother on her nighttime foraging excursions, sometimes moving single-file through the forest.

Raccoon

Red fox   Red foxes have a luxurious reddish-yellow coat, with black "stockings" on their feet and white-tipped tails and bellies. They weigh only 3 to 5 kilograms (6.6–11 lb.); most of what looks like body is actually bushy tail. They have short lives—sometimes only a year, though some have been known to live up to six. In accordance with so short a span, much happens in the annual life-cycle of a fox. Males and females bond in early winter, they mate in the new year, and a litter of five or so pups is born in the spring, only to disperse in late September (young foxes are ready to mate by their first winter). The father stays with his family in the meantime, using his acute hearing to help him catch hares, squirrels, chipmunks, and mice for the pups. Most of the hunting is done at night, and a good part of it relies on scavenging wolf kills.

Red squirrel   The energetic chirping of a red squirrel is a common enough sound in the northern woods. Intruders who get too close to a squirrel den get soundly chirped—foot stomping and hand gestures are occasionally thrown in for good measure. Their red fur can err on the side of gray and brown, though the white ring around the eyes is pretty consistent. Red squirrels prefer conifer forests; indeed, pine cones are a major part of their diet. In addition to berries and mushrooms, these animals are big meat eaters, and often tackle prey not much smaller than themselves (including mice, birds, and even small rabbits).

River otter   Part of the weasel family (which includes badgers, skunks, martens, fishers, and minks), otters are simply the coolest animals in the forest. Or anyway, they have the best time. Otters have an irresistible streamlined appearance with sleek brown fur, a long muscular tail, and nimble little webbed feet. They use their smooth shapes to toboggan down banks of snow and wet grass and shimmy through their water habitats in search of crayfish, fish, frogs, and small mammals. You can see otters cruising along a river current with their bellies to the sun, playing just for the fun of it. Otters survive the winter easily; they are as content in cold water as in warm, and can occasionally be seen poking up through an opening in the ice with the latest catch in their mouths. Three or four blind and toothless kits are born in the den among the tree roots (though sometimes otters appropriate beaver lodges), usually in March or April.

River otter

Snowshoe hare   It looks like a rabbit, but really it's a hare, the main distinction being that hares are born with fur intact and are hopping through the forest two hours out of the womb, while newborn rabbits mew blind in their nests for weeks. Snowshoe hares have beige-brown coats in the summer and all-white coats in the winter. They get their name from their large hind feet, which are so broad and coated with stiff hairs that the animal can scurry across the deep snow without breaking the crust. Hares eat plants and grasses in the summer, and twigs and bark in the winter. Most hares don't make it through the winter—foxes, wolves, and owls snap them up. But never fear; with such energetic mating more are always on the way.

Snowshoe hare

BIRDS

Barred owl   At night in the park, you can often hear the barred owl's distinct hoot: "Who cooks for you? Who cooks for you-allll..." with a drawn-out last note. While you are sleeping, the big brown barred owls are hunting.

They have evolved an amazing series of high-tech adaptations to help them in their quest for the perfect field mouse. The first is the dead quiet of their approach. The forward edge of each feather is serrated, which breaks the flow of air over the wing and acts as a silencer. Owls also have huge eyes, 100 times more sensitive than our own. But their coolest features are their ears. The openings on both sides of the head are asymmetrical—one is higher than the other, with a different-shaped opening. This means that both ears receive the same sound waves differently—the owl creates a "neural map" in her head, which allows her to pinpoint her prey in space.

Black-backed woodpecker   Mostly black with an orange patch at the top of its head, the black-backed woodpecker can usually be spotted around bogs, beaver ponds, and conifer forests. Like other woodpeckers, they excavate nests in trees with their powerful beaks. Unlike other woodpeckers, the black-backed woodpecker does not pound holes to find its diet of ants, larvae, and beetles. Instead it pulls whole flakes of bark off the dead tree, exposing its wriggling prey.

Black-backed woodpecker

Boreal chickadee   The boreal chickadee is another northern species, with a brown top and a pale underbelly. They're usually found only on the park's western side, where the Algonquin dome rises to its highest point (and conditions are coldest). It is thought that these birds mate for life, though it's not a very PC partnership, since the female builds the nest (though the male helps to excavate), and then has to beg the male for food when she's incubating.

Boreal chickadee

Broad-winged hawk   Algonquin Park's most common bird of prey is brown on top—though you will only ever see its pale blotched bottom from below. This bird is small and compact (about the size of a crow), with a dark fringe of feathers along the flat wings and wide tail bands. Broad-winged hawks like to hunt in the open meadows caused by former beaver dams. Their sharp binocular vision picks out tasty garter snakes in the grasses, though their diet can also consist of small rodents and insects.

Broad-winged hawk

Common loon   Algonquin Park is associated with the loon more than any other bird. Most lakes have at least one pair (loons mate for life), impossible to miss with their gorgeous summer plumage: jet-black heads, striped band around the neck, and checkered white and black coat. For many the loon's yodel—which ranges from plaintive and drawn out to insane and cackling—is the most memorable thing about the bird.

Though they aren't much as flyers and they're almost useless on land, loons are phenomenal swimmers able to hold their breath for 3 minutes or more. They eat mostly fish, which they pursue underwater at high speeds, using their big webbed feet to swivel left and right. Loons nest on shore, usually no more than a meter or so from the water's edge. Chicks (usually two) follow their parents around all summer, and fly south with them in November just before the snows fall. Sometimes a group of loons can be spotted in late August and early September as they gather to migrate for the colder months. This grouping is very rare and is called a "raft." A raft can be as large as 30 to 40 loons with offspring and is an amazing sight.

Common loon

Common raven   The high black silhouette of a raven is a very common sight in Algonquin Park. They are said to wheel and tumble in the sky for the pure pleasure of it, and indeed I have seen ravens slide on their back down icy slopes in the winter only to clamber up again for another run.

For all their playfulness, the raven is a resourceful predator—a songbird with the appetite of a hawk. Ravens feed mostly on carrion, winter and summer. They nest high up in rocky cliff faces and the tallest trees, a pair of ravens bonded for life. Ravens are not to be confused with crows, who are much smaller and "caw" instead of croak.

Common raven

Gray jay   Another northern specialty, the tiny gray jay actually stays in the park year-round, weathering the deep snows and lack of food supply. The secret of their survival is a maniacal chipmunk-like hoarding of food. Insects, fruit, and even pieces of meat are collected throughout the summer and stashed in thousands of treetops throughout the park. They drowse in their snow-covered nest (made of grass, twigs, and spider's silk; lined with feathers), venturing out to their stores when hungry. Gray jays are notorious for being very friendly, raiding picnic tables in order to bolster their winter supplies.

Gray jay

Great blue heron   Great blue herons are the sentinels of Algonquin waterways, standing stock-still where the river bends. They are easy to spot: very tall with blue-gray feathers, a few projecting quills on the lower underside of the neck. Their sharp bill is their hunting tool. They wait patiently for a passing fish or frog before spearing it with a lighting movement. When disturbed the great blue heron unfolds its large wings and takes off low across the water, ever so slowly gaining in height.

Great blue heron

Hooded merganser   With their huge afros, the funky hooded mergansers are impossible to confuse with other ducks. The female of the species is brown, the male is more vividly black and white—the crest itself is a white disk with a black leading edge and spine. They feed on small fish and insects. Like other mergansers, the males ditch the females soon after mating (but unlike other mergansers, other females of the species don't all dump their brood onto one poor mother, left to raise 50 chirping chicks).

Hooded merganser

Merlin   This agile, compact falcon is Algonquin Park's fastest bird —it can snatch a swallow out of the air at 80 kilometers (50 miles) per hour, not swooping but bee-lining in from behind. It has a brown body and a raptor's sharp, alert face. The merlin needs large open spaces to hunt, so big lakes like Opeongo tend to have a few nesting nearby. Overall there are not a lot of merlins in the park, though lately their populations have been rising—little noted by most park visitors, who pay far more attention to the hopeful prospect of returning peregrine falcons (nothing so far...).

Merlin

Osprey   Also known as the "fish hawk," the osprey is a very impressive hunter. It glides high above clear lakes, looking for tell-tale surface disturbances. When a fish is spotted, the osprey bombs in feet-first, jerking the fish out of the water and carrying it off to its big lakeside nest—conspicuous clusters of big sticks at the top of dead trees (like the nest at **Johnston Lake** on the park's east side). Ospreys mate for life; he feeds her when they are courting and when she incubates. They are lovely birds, with a sharp beak, strong talons, and white and gray plumage. Their wings have a distinct bend at the wrist, which allows them to be easily identified though there are rarely more than 30 nesting pairs in the whole of the park.

Osprey

Pileated Woodpecker This is the largest woodpecker in the park, as big as a crow with a crow's jet-black body. The head has an unmistakable look: shaped like an isosceles triangle, with a sculpted red crest and a punkish white zig-zag on each side of the neck and face. Pileated woodpeckers eat mostly carpenter ants (which they dig big rectangular holes to get at), though they will eat acorns and nuts.

Pileated woodpecker

Red-eyed vireo The red-eyed vireo is found in large numbers all over eastern North America, including Algonquin Park's hardwood forests. Here they are heard far more often than they are seen; they are tremendously assiduous singers, often piping out their repertoire of tunes (more than 40 songs on rotation) for hours on end. The short whistled phrases are separated by a pause—listen for an up-down fluted sound, so common as to be background noise on the trail. For a bird so audibly conspicuous, red-eyed vireos have a very modest appearance: small yellow-gray bodies with a pale underside.

Red-eyed vireo

Spruce grouse   Like an exotic chicken, the spruce grouse stands proud in the black spruce forests, its red top and dappled brown, black, and white plumage bristling at attention. These are the birds most sought after by birders in the know—they're hard to spot even here at their southernmost range. Once spotted, you could probably walk right over and pick them up, since they have a bad evolutionary habit of freezing when located. During the April mating season, the male kicks up a dramatic aerial fuss, opening his fan tail and flashing his moves.

Spruce grouse

Turkey vulture   The turkey vulture is a big bird, with a big range that covers most of the U.S. and southern Canada. Though the actual number of birds in the park is probably quite small, they are easy to spot in the sky with the distinct shallow V of their wing spread. Like all vultures they're pretty ugly, with small red heads, ghoulish mottled rings around the eyes, and disproportionately large bodies and wings (the underside two-toned brown and cream). Their masterful use of updrafts and thermals means they can glide for long periods without flapping their wings, saving their energy for those rank carrion finds that send vultures into tailspins of flesh-eating ecstasy.

Turkey vulture

REPTILES, FISH, & AMPHIBIANS

Brook trout   Brook trout average about 35 centimeters (14 inches) in length, and have dark green backs, red and white spotted sides, and white bellies. Although they grow faster than lake trout they do not live as long, so lake trout tend to be the larger fish. Also a cold-water species, the brook trout can be found in 230 Algonquin lakes, though only in a very particular range—the top water layer is too warm, and the bottom water layer lacks the necessary oxygen supply, so as a result the brook trout live in a transition body of water between these two layers, known as "trout water." They are equally demanding when it comes to their reproduction needs: their fall spawning beds must be gravel or sand, and spring water must well up from below the bed. Only then will the female deposit her eggs and the male fertilize them. Once this is done the female brook trout covers them over, leaving them to develop in peace for the next six months. Like their lake trout cousins, the brook trout feed on insects and minnows.

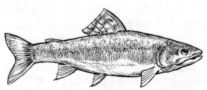

Brook trout

Lake trout   Cold-water fish like the lake trout are relatively rare in Ontario, but they flourish in Algonquin Park—they can be found in 150 or so park lakes. They are long and slender, with an even patterning of light spots along their full length and a sharply forked tail. Lake trout feed on minnows, crayfish, and insects—species present in the cold waters of spring, but that retreat into warmer water as the summer progresses, leaving the lake trout in their deep cold ghettos, forced to subsist on insect larvae and plant life. Lake trout spawn in the fall at night, returning to the same rocky spawning beds year after year.

Painted turtle   With its smooth black carapace and arched head, the painted turtle strikes an elegant pose sunning on a log or on a shoulder of exposed rock. The rest of the time these turtles spend in the water, feeding on small animals and greens. For reasons that are not properly understood, about 70% of adult turtles are female. They lay their eggs in the sand and then bury them before heading back to the pond, never to see them again. Painted turtles can often be seen on the Mizzy Lake Trail, many of them blotted with actual paint as a large group in the area is used for research purposes.

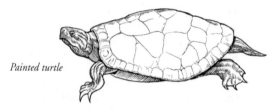

Painted turtle

Red-backed salamander   This is Algonquin Park's most common salamander, a narrow little fellow about 10 centimeters (4 inches) long with a red-brown streak on its back, often found under wet logs or a damp covering of leaves. This type of salamander has neither lungs nor gills; it breathes by absorbing oxygen through its skin, a process that requires the skin to be moist, hence its preference for dank hangouts. The red-backed salamander eats worms, slugs, insects, and most of the other tiny creepy inhabitants of forest floor.

Red-backed salamander

Wood turtle   One of the park's most important (and often over-looked) residents, the wood turtle is a fixture on North America's endangered species list. These shelled creatures normally are 14 to 20 centimetres (5.5–8 inches) long, with skin that is brown and free of markings; young turtles are gray or brown, and have exceptionally long tails. Wood turtles enjoy a habitat of clear streams, rivers, and woodland near forest, and thrive on berries, dandelions, worms, insects, and mollusks. Their dining techniques are unique and strange: as they rock from side to side, the vibrations of their front feet against the ground entice unsuspecting earthworms to the surface, where they are promptly eaten.

5 The Ecosystem

As with the rest of the world's wild places, most of the stress on Algonquin Park's ecosystem comes from humans. Visitors themselves constitute the first source of pressure. We flock to the park and leave polluted tokens of appreciation: piles of waste, human and manufactured. It's possible the land can survive this onslaught, but not so the animals. Nuisance bears, to name just one vulnerable species, are drawn by the garbage to campsites. Park officials do their best to trap, tag, and move them, but if the bears return they are killed. Prohibiting the use of bottles and cans in the interior helps, but the corollary of this is having enough wardens in the park to enforce these rules. At present there are not. Without an adequate number of active wardens, the health of the park is in some respects determined by the attentiveness or carelessness of the campers.

Logging is another activity that impacts the park ecosystem. The potential philosophical conflicts of trying to be both a caring steward of the natural environment on the one hand, and extracting resources from that same environment on the other are discussed in chapter 1; this is simply a brief overview of how logging affects the character of the Algonquin forest.

Trees can be harvested in 78% of Algonquin Park, though if you account for all the bodies of water and their surrounding buffer zones, the real figure is closer to 57%. Sophisticated silviculture techniques are used that favor specific tree selection over clear-cutting; several years after a cut signs of past logging are not immediately apparent. That said, what you do see is a calculated (and in that respect unnatural), middle-aged forest, punctuated by the occasional small clear-cut and gravel quarry. The park's policy of fire

suppression—designed to protect its valuable stands of timber—
means there are no new forests, and its policy of logging all trees in
the "recreation/utilization zone" by the time they reach a certain age
means there are no old forests. A middle-aged forest is a healthy forest, but it may not be one able to support all of Algonquin's traditional species. For example, conservationists fear that the park's
policy of fire suppression may be inhibiting big pine regeneration
(especially with regard to jack pine, which depend directly on fire to
open their cones and release the seeds).

The more than 2,000 kilometers (1,240 miles) of logging roads
in the park also have an impact on forest ecology. In addition to the
obvious fact that no big trees grow on these roads, animal habitats
become fragmented, and the roads themselves act both as habitats for
aggressive invasive species (which love disturbed areas and out-
compete the locals) and as corridors for their dispersal.

This invasion of non-native species is another ecological problem
facing the park. Although southern Ontario's notorious purple
loosestrife and zebra mussels have made few inroads into the park,
other species like the gypsy moth and the rusty crayfish have.
Northern pike have infested many of the lakes in Ontario and
have made it all the way into Booth and Kitty Lakes in Algonquin.
They're on the verge of reaching Lake Opeongo, which would be
bad news for the park's beloved trout population.

There is a growing public concern that the population of Algonquin Park's **wolves**—currently numbering about 150—may be in
decline due to the hunting and killing of wolves outside park
boundaries (in the 1960s there were 55 packs in the park, today
they number between 30 and 35). Although the habitat of this
distinctive wolf (see "The Strange Case of the Algonquin Wolves,"
above) extends from Manitoba to central Ontario to southern
Quebec, Algonquin Park remains its largest safe habitat. In May
2001, the wolves were designated a "Species at Risk" by the Federal
Committee on the Status of Endangered Wildlife in Canada, and
the **Canadian Parks and Wilderness Society** began campaigning
for a full year-round ban on hunting and trapping wolves outside
the park. That said, there is no direct proof that the wolf decline is
due to over-hunting on the part of humans. Park naturalists have
suggested it may just be a natural fluctuation of the population in
response to their changing habitat—30 years ago there were more
deer. Whatever the case, for many these wolves embody the wild

spirit of Algonquin. A disappearance from the park could harbinger a tragic disappearance from the planet.

Acid rain is another threat to the park, and one clearly out of park managers' hands. When airborne pollution chemicals mix with rain droplets they become little pellets of acid between 40 and 400 times more acidic than normal. Algonquin lakes are particularly vulnerable to this acid because of their low nutrient contents—there is very little material to act as an absorbing buffer. Fish take in the poisons and pass them on down the food chain, affecting all the animals that live in and around the lakes. Poisoned **loons** lay thin-shelled eggs that do not hatch properly. Although at present the loon population is constant at 40% lake occupancy, they may be one of the first species to disappear from the park if no action is taken to control industrial emissions. These emissions have a further effect on the park in the form of **global warming.** Algonquin Park straddles both northern and southern habitats. One potential consequence of continued global warming is the gradual disappearance of northern species from the park—the gray jays, the moose—as this transition zone continues to recede toward the pole.

Ecosystems are fragile things, where a change in one component can lead to a snowballing disruption of the whole system. There may be an Algonquin Park for a long time to come, but without its jack pines, wolves, moose, beavers, bears, loons, and trout, it may not be a wilderness we care to visit.

Index